IN MID-AIR

ALSO BY ADAM GOPNIK

IN
MID-AIR

Adam Gopnik

riverrun

First published in Great Britain in 2018 by riverrun

riverrun
An imprint of

Quercus Publishing Ltd
Carmelite House
50 Victoria Embankment
London EC4Y 0DZ

An Hachette UK company

A CIP catalogue record for this book is available
from the British Library.

Hardback 978 1 78648 922 7
Export Trade Paperback 978 1 78648 923 4
Ebook 978 1 78648 925 8

10 9 8 7 6 5 4 3 2 1

Typeset by CC Book Production
Printed and bound in Great Britain by Clays Ltd, Elcograf S.p.A.

CONTENTS

FICTIONAL MYSTERIES

FACTIONAL MEASURES

INTRODUCTION

This book collates many, in fact most, of the short essays I've written and read over the past decade for BBC Radio 4's 'A Point of View', recorded most often on Thursday mornings in New York, and broadcast on Friday nights and Sunday mornings throughout the UK. The title references the oddity of the arrangement. I felt caught in mid-air, or mid-Atlantic, every week, living in New York while referencing, and talking to London – as though I'd been suspended, eerily, somewhere in stationary orbit half way between the two.

The title also references a favourite book of mine, Max Beerbohm's collection of his radio pieces for the BBC, 'Mainly on the Air'. Beerbohm, of course, was speaking from London to London – if of an older London to a newer one – but, different though that intention is, I have always been an admirer, even an adulator, of his tone, and had a vibration of it somewhere in the back of my mind – a thought, doubtless, that would turn poor Max and his Edwardian idolaters over in his and their, grave graves.

To say I was overjoyed to be offered a spot within the APOV rotation, and even more pleased to be serially re-invited to try again, suggests the American estimation – in British eyes, perhaps, the overestimation – of the BBC as an institution. It's a reciprocal infatuation. Brits, I've found, idealize the *New Yorker*, my magazine home in America for the past thirty-plus years, in something like the same way – imagining it, I've often found, to be more directly continuous with the legendary magazine of the Ross–Liebling–Thurber era (with Dorothy Parker and Robert Benchley usually thrown in as make-weight, though neither did their best work for the magazine) than perhaps it is. I am accustomed to having breezy British reviewers of my books, not always hostile ones, detect a '*New Yorker*' tone or manner in them, though in truth if that tone exists at all it is now as a refugee dialect in the work of one or two nostalgists for a now mostly defunct style. We speak Thurber and White the way émigrés in Broadway cafeterias once spoke Yiddish.

But the British readers may be righter than the American writers know. We laugh hollowly at the idea of a persistent tone, given how much has changed – particularly as we labour on one more quick hitting thousand-word comment on gun massacres or the political crisis. Yet the DNA of the magazine is persistent, and many of the things that mark it out from all others – its lengthy pieces, its love of facticity, its now too rare but still instinctive leaning into humour – do remain constant and vibrate best from far away, if not high above.

And so, we Americans and Canadians – to arrive at my point, which won't survive too lengthy a build-up – do the same thing with the BBC, particularly as it persists on radio. We see it as a consistent whole, stretching back to Beerbohm and Stephen Potter and Joyce Grenfell and for that matter the Beatles playing live, a constant if ebbing sea of smart plays and wise commentary and Saturday morning songs – hyper-civilized, and very different from the semi-hysteria and commercial yobbery of American radio. There was a period in my younger life, living in Paris in the early Seventies, when the BBC was my whole connection to the English-speaking world, my entertainment, my island. I could never get enough of its excellences, from the coolly well-organized trad-jazz programmes to the bland sounding but decisive political commentary. I suspect that, in places far more remote than Paris, this sense of connection to a civilized tradition, supplied by the BBC, has long rung true.

And so, I have in my own delusional way, tried to maintain, or indulge, something like that imagined tone in these pieces. Neither too heavy nor too light, using a tone unafraid of whimsy – Nabokov says somewhere that anything of quality in writing has some aspect of the whimsical, self-consciously pleased to be pleasing – and making its political points with a sideways blow rather than a direct strike. To hear this tone articulated by a Canadian-American with unduly slow, syllabically laboured, rabbinical pronunciation – encouraged in this by my producers, who worried that my normal rushed tones would whiz right by their listeners as little more than a hiss of crushed consonants – was probably in itself all the entertainment I offered.

It is a standard trope for journalists to sneer at anything that seems like collected short journalism. But my favourite books, or some of them, consist exactly of collections of these kinds of short occasional essays, including those of Wolcott Gibbs, and E. B. White. I love, to make a reference more recherché even to British readers, to read the old collections of 'Fourth Leaders' from *The Times*, very short funny pieces, many of them, if my informants are right, written by Peter Fleming, Ian's superbly well-equipped older brother. I can't get enough of books of miscellaneous pieces of short humour and commentary; looking up at my bookshelves as I write, I see not only White and Gibbs and Beerbohm, but Alan Coren and Michael Frayn. For a long time, pieces like this populated the pages of the *New Yorker*, and I wrote ones very much like those included here – on Nobel Prizes and cash machines and the Museum of Modern Art's garden in the snow. But, as time went on, and the magazines exigencies became more urgently political – and, as

I suppose, the tone of such things too old-fashioned, however much they were loved by writers, and I think, by readers of the less strenuously insider kind; it's really other journalists who become impatient with them – there was less space for them, although on occasion one can still sneak one past the umpire. Quaint or modern, I like that stuff. To maintain a tone of rueful comedy in a small space while still scoring a point or two and keeping a shapely shape seems to me in its way as beautiful a pursuit as has ever ignited any haiku – which such pieces hope to resemble in their tininess of scale and largeness of echoing rebound.

I've organized the pieces on the page into three parts. 'Family Matters' gathers the many pieces I did on domestic comedy, from the 'Marthanomics' practiced by my wife to the sadness of kids leaving homes. 'Fictional Measures' includes all the ones about the arts, mostly, though not exclusively, about the art of writing – and brood not so much on 'aesthetics' as on 'meta-aesthetics', the way that seemingly peripheral things – authors' names to vanilla yoghurt – affect our feelings about an artistic whole. I seem, on re-reading them, to be interestingly – or is it merely monotonously? – obsessed with Shakespeare, who keeps coming back, and with Dr Johnson, who shows up often too. Both of these may seem like fusty preoccupations, but my own view is that Shakespeare really does remain eerily evergreen, no matter what damage is done by trying to make him 'relevant'. Nicholas Hytner in his recent memoir records, sadly but accurately I think, that the sound and action of even Restoration comedy, still potent when he was young, has by now passed out of general understanding, even among educated people. Mirabell and Millamant still made sense in 1960 in a way that they do now only – as they say in American progressive grade schools – 'with support'. But Shakespeare, and Hytner would agree, doesn't need any support at all. This is, I suspect, because though the allure of his work lies in the phrases and verbal magic, its solidity lies in its character making and story-telling. Memorable people doing memorable things is a good formula for permanence, even better than shapely sentences making significant shapes.

If both of those collations share the high-hearted tone advertised above, the third family of pieces, called 'Factional Measures', recognizes its own more dubious nature in its choice of title. 'Faction', i.e. political warfare, is never a good thing for writing. The primacy of party politics above all else is a literary sin. 'To party gave up what was meant for mankind,' Oliver Goldsmith said sharply of Edmund Burke, believing that a man who could define the sublime and the beautiful was wasting his time in parliamentary debates. Too many poignant second thoughts have to be surrendered to a ruling political passion. Old jokes may date; old squabbles certainly do.

Still, as these years of Sunday talking went around, I had to increase my own engagement with the political emergency that rose in both countries. Responding to it became part of everybody's responsibility as a citizen. As the world changed, I changed with it, and found myself having to take on more and more responsibility for making sense, particularly, of the madness that was descending upon American life. My aim, in these pieces, became to define, in ten-minute bursts, what ought to be meant by the liberal humanist tradition at a time when it was under an assault not known in Europe and America since the 1930s. The crisis that rose in America and is not resolved yet was not one of ideology but of integrity, and what mattered most was not the future direction of government, but the future of liberal democracy itself. The oscillation of power in a mature democracy is normal and necessary and we should expect a period of progressive change to be followed by one of retrenchment, even of reaction; to ask for anything else is to do the one thing that a democracy can't do, and that is to make strong opposition illegitimate. The moral genius of liberal democracy is exactly to say that dissent with the programme of politics in power is as essential as power itself. There is no more beautiful phrase in English than 'official opposition'. The evil lies in the attempt to banish that legitimacy, to make opposition seem unpatriotic.

I pray for a time when party can leave the party. Until then, only a fool can pretend that the emergency is less than it is, or has been. I tried to say this, and thank the BBC for sticking by me, when the true words I spoke were, as I know is the case, at moments extremely 'controversial'. It was hard to insist, and harder still for the higher-ups to insist on my behalf, that I was not taking a party position on the question, for instance, of Clinton vs. Trump, because it was not in any sense a party question. It was an existential question, pitting one politician who, whatever her faults, accepted the premises of liberal democracy against another who, whatever the pathos of his followers, emphatically did not.

Even before any of this became evident – when it was still possible to persuade oneself, however delusionally, that the worst could not take place – I wrote and submitted for the series (and then withdrew, and then rewrote and resubmitted and withdrew and resubmitted) a liberal humanist credo. I withdrew it, again and again, for fear, I think now, of seeming too portentous, less than because I doubted that a credo could fit within a ten-minute slot. (A credo is a statement of what one knows to be true – if it surpasses ten minutes, it has become a statement of what one wants to be true.) It was broadcast at last, with an irony so brutal that one can only shiver at it, two weeks after the election of an enemy of everything that liberal humanism stands for and suggests to the most powerful office in what had once been the most powerful liberal democracy. I would have to be as narcissistically deranged as Trump, to suggest that had I broadcast it earlier, anything would have altered. As it was, it had not only the zero effect that would-be pundits can predict for all their interventions but something closer to

8

a less-than-zero effect, a kind of anti-gravity persuasiveness. I offered it not only knowing it would do no good, but knowing that its not being able to do any good before meant that it would do less than no good now. Nonetheless, I still believe the words I offered in that dark moment, whose darkness has not yet lifted, to be true and the most significant, or at least sincere, that I have ever written.

I believe still what I said then, that liberalism (or liberal humanism, to give it its more proper name) is one of the great spiritual adventures of humankind, and that the proof that it is far more than some kind of weak and dated parliamentary centrism lies in its consequences: the emancipation of women, the spread of universal democracy, the extension of civil rights to homosexuals, the end of torture and censorship, a faith in free inquiry into man's origins, and with it the discovery of earth's true place in the universe and of human being's true history on earth. All of these great gifts are the consequences of those radicals of the real who made the liberal tradition. Far from being the limp non-alcoholic translation of religious ideas, its makers are spirited and passionate pilgrims against it. Hume and Voltaire, Mill and Harriet Taylor, Epicurus and Popper – the central humanist tradition is one not made in the ruins of metaphysics, but in conscious and joyful defiance of them, in which freedom from authority, and the need to make all our meanings for ourselves, is liberating, literally life-giving, inasmuch as it gives purpose and meaning to our lives, and to the wisdom about the world we pass on.

To which words I might add only an essayist's codicil: that if the liberal humanist tradition writ large involves those great and imposing philosophical figures, the liberal tradition lived, so to speak, small – and all real life is small living – has as one of its blossoms exactly the kind of comic essay that I had had to put aside in order to pontificate. It is proof of a cosmic Santa Claus that the real originator of liberal thought is not some philosophical parser of social contracts, but Montaigne, the originator of the miscellaneous essay that starts in puzzlement and ends in more. It was Montaigne's central insight that there are no central insights. Everything in life involves its opposite.

By giving life to this truth, Montaigne animates for the first time an inner human whose contradictions are identical with his conscience. He urges on us the essential lesson that variety is not the spice of life. It is its meat and drink. Comedy is its spice. Only by seeing the absurdity of our preoccupations can we see ourselves as absurd as we truly are. The effort to make small Sunday morning jokes is as true to the humanist commitment as that of making any number of Saturday night speeches. Comedy, even comedy made in a volcano's mouth, can never really be trivial. Laughter is the answering volcano people possess. It is our own form of intimate explosion.

So my thanks to everyone at BBC Radio 4 who made delivering these small explosive essays one of the purest pleasures of my professional life: particularly, to Richard Knight, Sheila O'Shea, Adele Armstrong, and, from on high, Gwyneth Williams, and so to everyone else at Radio 4. Moeko Fujii, my astonishing assistant/apprentice, expert in everything and yet exhausting about none of it, assembled the collection, organized its sections, and helped me cleanse its paragraphs.

I would dedicate this collection to Clive James, who preceded me in the APOV chair, and shaped its contours – even more because his life's work as an essayist, journalist, and commentator was all about getting stuff like this right, finding a public tongue that would be waggish without being coy, and high spirited, even high hearted, without being fatuous. Not to mention breaking down walls between high and low, without being cheap about either, doubting categories while insisting on values. In all our efforts to remind ourselves, to use a quote from Beerbohm, that sanity need not be philistine, Clive's voice will be one of the most enduring.

I would dedicate this book to him, save that would seem more than a little presumptuous, like dedicating a book of advice on child-rearing to your mother. She already knows how. She showed you. So, while still offering it to him clandestinely, I'd ask him to share the dedication proper with another friend and favourite writer, Anthony Lane, whom I often imagined as my ideal listener for these pieces – turning on the radio, as I saw it, on a Sunday morning in Cambridge between chores and choir, and hearing the slightly too-rabbinical voice of his too-earnest American friend, offering measured ambivalences on everything. As it happens, this never took place – I don't think he listened to a single one – but then we always write for imaginary listeners in imaginary countries, mediated by imaginary institutions. Somehow, within the imaginary ether we inhabit, a single voice may still be heard. That's what the air can offer.

Family Matters

Embarrassing Teens and the Teenage Truth

10 June 2012

Recently in America, nothing has been argued about more, or more vociferously, than child-rearing methods. As though such a thing existed. One might as well talk about wolf-watching methods. They do it to you; you don't do it to them. You may have heard, for instance, of the self-proclaimed 'Tiger Mom' – that Asian mother who boasted of pushing her kids brutally through school and towards success – though surely the memoir of the Tiger Cub will be the one to read.

The real truth about teenage or adolescent kids is simple, though, and I will announce it here. The one thing that is written into the human genome is that, exactly at the age of thirteen, your child – in a minute – and no matter how close or sympathetic the two of you have been before, will discover that you are now the most embarrassing, ridiculous and annoying person on the planet. This is a universal truth.

It will sometimes be expressed in a tone of pitying condescension, and sometimes in one of exasperated wrath; you can tell, depending on whether the modifier or the noun is stressed: 'Dad, you are *so* weird,' is almost affectionate, while 'Dad, you are so *weird*,' is close to hostile. The thirteenth birthday arrives, and the genome lights up like a Christmas tree when the mayor throws the switch. The parent who only a few years – a few months – before was a fount of wisdom and expertise and even companionship, becomes those three things: ridiculous, embarrassing and annoying.

The three fall in a neat exact order, and a highly specific sequence. You are first of all ridiculous because of your pretensions to be cool. You persist in the belief that you know good pop music from bad, or something about the relations of teenage boys and girls. And this in spite of the obvious truth that you are barely sentient, with one foot rooted in the dim, ancient past while with the other your toes are already tickling eternity. You are embarrassing because, in spite of being ridiculous, you are not content to keep your absurdity decently to yourself, but insist on parading it around in public, greeting the thirteen-year-old's friends and teachers as though you were a normal human being and not a kind of ward of the state, on the brink of being permanently committed. It is bad enough to be ridiculous, but do you also have to be so public about it? And you are annoying, because, in spite of being ridiculous, and in the face of the wild public embarrassment you obviously cause, you still actually think that you can give advice and counsel – strongly suggest, or even command, the thirteen-plus-year-old to do things.

No parent can hope to eliminate all three, but what every parent is capable of doing – and all that any parent is capable of doing – is to eliminate exactly one of the three as an accurate descriptor. 'I may be ridiculous and annoying,' you can say, honestly, 'but I am not embarrassing.' Or, 'I know I embarrass you, but you cannot accurately call me ridiculous.' One out of three is the game of life.

What I might call my special insight into this truth is that I have discovered, I believe, that this one-in-three rule is generational. That is, each descending generation can, and on the whole does, eliminate one of these three. At least in the kind of modern urban family where the first generation came to the new country, or rose from the mines and working classes (in my case, both), while the next became educated middle-class people, and then the next (my own) became worried, harried professionals, hovering over one or two hyper-favoured kids. Your grandparents, for instance, were, to your parents, wildly embarrassing and hugely annoying but they were never really ridiculous. Their lives ran consistently together from one end to the other. Even when they were young Jewish people, they were, so to speak, old Jewish people.

As, in another context, even when our grandparents were old working-class people they resembled what they had been like as *young* working-class people. Their beliefs and rituals and ways of life ran true; they were creatures of habit, but not of fashion; and we always grant to habit the near holy aura of ritual. It's the same reason that Millet's peasants, in his paintings, seem so dignified to us: if they changed their smocks and *chapeaux* every season they would be merely pathetic, but there, in the same costumes, they submit to the centuries and can hold their heads up – or rather bow them down, but you get the point.

Our grandparents, similarly, were always themselves, and made no attempt to become some other self, seen in a glossy magazine. They accepted the immutability of identity.

Our parents, in turn – though they often struck us as annoying beyond belief and ridiculous beyond measure – could not accurately be called embarrassing. Theirs was a middle generation of aspiration; first to education, which they achieved, and then to sophistication, which they thought that they had achieved. They were ridiculous because they were so constantly in flux: they changed their hairstyles and their clothes – look at those old photos. Ridiculously hirsute in the Sixties and then absurdly wide-lapelled in the Seventies. But you could not call them embarrassing – they were interesting people. They had had interesting lives, they were broadly cultured, they knew which way was up, whether they were looking at a Brancusi sculpture or a six-inch spliff. You might not want to share a spliff with them, but they were not embarrassing in front of your friends. They had the avidity of the ambitious.

Our generation – the third generation – are, as our kids assure us, by far the most ridiculous and the most embarrassing generation that has ever lived. We are ridiculous because, where our parents liked to share stories of their cooler youth with us, we actually think that our super-cool youth is still going on. We have no idea of how out of it we are, and yet persist in acting as though we're with it. We don't have the decency to withdraw back into our own generation; we advance into theirs. This is ridiculous beyond words, embarrassing beyond measure, and yet we are not, really, annoying. When our kids want something, we try to oblige, within reason. They play us the dirge-like music of Radiohead, or the glee-club chanting of Arcade Fire, and we listen for hours, piously. They insist on texting us rather than actually making a phone call, and we obligingly learn to text ourselves.

A couple of summers ago, my own now seventeen-year-old son, knowing that we were going to London on a summer visit, came into my office and asked, very sweetly, if it might be possible to go a few days early so that he could attend the Blur reunion concert in Hyde Park. Not only did I assent at once, but I actually insisted on going with him, wearing madras shorts and an old shirt and ducking beer bottles. You can hear me on the live recording, singing along to 'Tender': 'Come on, come on, come on . . .' Really, you can. I don't know why he finds it ridiculous when I insist on this.

I know what you are asking: What can come next? Once the cycle is exhausted generationally, what follows? I was puzzled by this too, until, sharing these thoughts with my son, he said, evenly and without a trace of rancour, 'You know, it's your not being annoying that's the most annoying thing about you. You're sort of . . . meta-annoying.'

The cycle, I saw, will not begin again. It will simply advance, like modern art, into new areas of self-conscious annoyance, more ironic ridiculousness, more self-aware embarrassment. The truth about kids therefore, whatever Philip Larkin may have said, is to stay in as long as you can; and have as many kids as possible. That way, there is bound to be a child, somewhere in the unfolding generations, who, dismayed by this meta-madness, will look back on you as the embodiment of simple, unaffected life, of the unridiculous, of peasant-like poise combined with sage-like reticence.

'That's your dad?' they will say, looking at your old iPhone photo among all the holograms. 'He's so . . . period.'

'Trust me. He was ridiculous,' your own child, now an ageing great-grandparent himself, will say.

'I don't know. He looks . . . kinda cool. Was he annoying?'

'No,' your now aged child will admit. 'He took me to this Blur concert, once.'

'You were lucky,' the kid will say.

And your child, through his grey beard, will nod – reluctantly, perhaps, but he will nod. He'll have to, because it's true. Life is made tolerable by such small-imagined mercies.

The Curse of a Ridiculous Name
6 July 2012

I have a funny name. I know it. Don't say it isn't, or try to make me feel better about it. I have a funny name. My children and social networkers tell me that. And you out there have even been tweeting about it: '@bbc.pov.Gopnik: what kind of name is that? Hashtag weirdnames.'

Gopnik. It has a strange sound, and an ugly look. It manages to be at once starkly plain and extremely uninteresting, boringly unadorned and yet oddly difficult to say. Despite the stark, Orcish simplicity of its syllables, it manages to be hard to pronounce. 'Golnik' or 'Gotnik' people say, swallowing or spitting out the middle consonant.

A first name is malleable. Your Chancellor of the Exchequer began life under the name of Gideon Osborne – a name that might only have helped him become one more short-tenured professor of dark arts at Hogwarts. But he plucked the safer and saner 'George' from among his other pre-names, and seized the country's trust with it. For a while, anyway.

Last names are more durable. My parents tried to elevate the name by giving all six of my brothers and sisters poetic Welsh or Hebrew names, such as Morgan and Blake. All good names, but with no middle names at all to help. 'Gopnik' rises immediately after each one, like a concrete cinderblock wall topped with barbed wire, to meet them bluntly as they try to escape.

It's not just a funny name. It has become, in the Russia from which it originally hails, an almost obscenely derogatory expression. A *gopnik* in Russian, and in Russia, is now a drunken hooligan, a small-time lout, a criminal without even the sinister glamour of courage. When Russian people hear my last name, they can barely conceal a snigger of distaste and disgusted laughter. Those thugs who clashed with Polish fans at Euro 2012? All *gopniks* – small 'G'. And I'm told that it derives from an acronym for public housing, rather than from our family's Jewish roots, but no difference.

My wife, even before the Russian-equals-*gopnik* business, tried gently to pry apart her potential children from my name. Her last name is Parker. Simple as that. And she would much prefer that her offspring go through life without the difficulty of their father's name. 'Let's just call them Parker,' she urged when we married. 'And then,' she added gently, as one talking to a small child, 'you can give them your name as a sort of secret middle name.' We ended by doing the worst thing you can do to a child in these times: we hyphenated.

The real trouble is this. Like every writer, I would like my writing to last, and most writers who have lasted not only have euphonious names, but names that somehow resonate with their genius. 'Jane Austen': how can you not write matchlessly wry and intelligent novels with a name like that? Who would not want to be named 'William Thackeray' or 'Evelyn Waugh'? The solid sense and then the elegant malice are written into the names – even the androgyny of 'Evelyn' adds to the slight air of something-not-quite-right that his prose implies. I envy even those writers blessed with Restoration Comedy names. 'Will Self': what better name for someone whose subject is impulse and the ego? Or the satirical 'Tom Sharpe' – or the subtly sexually ambiguous 'Stevie Smith'? In the Latin world, get a name like 'Gabriel García Márquez' or 'Mario Vargas Llosa', and you can practically make reservations for Stockholm, direct from the baptismal font.

Are there any big modern writers who have really funny names? Only Kipling, I think, and that is an accident of the participle. More to the point, are there good writers who are now forgotten, as I am pretty sure I shall be, because their names are so funny? Yes, I have to say with dread, there are: for instance, the twentieth-century American poet W. D. Snodgrass. Snodgrass was a truly great poet, the originator, if anyone was, of the style we now call 'confessional poetry', a hero to Robert Lowell and Sylvia Plath and the rest. But he had that funny Pickwickian name, and he knew it. He used to make fun of his own name: 'Snodgrass is walking through the universe!' one poem reads. (I, too, make fun of my surname, in the hopes of keeping off the name-demons.)

No use. For all his priority, I bet that you have heard something of Robert Lowell and Sylvia Plath and Anne Sexton but that, unless you are a specialist in American poetry, you have never heard of W. D. Snodgrass.

The subject has led me, gloomily, to search for the first reference to the power of names over writers' reputations. Oddly – astonishingly – I think we can find it quite precisely. It occurs in the best and most famous scene in all of English biography, that moment in Boswell's *Life of Johnson* when, in 1776, Boswell craftily arranges a dinner between the arch Tory Dr Johnson and the radical libertine John Wilkes. The two men, political opposites, come together over their love of learning and good food.

Wilkes is talking about the lost office of the city poet, and says: 'The last was Elkanah Settle. There is something in *names* which one cannot help feeling. Now *Elkanah Settle* sounds so *queer*, who can expect much from that name? We should have no hesitation to give it for John Dryden, in preference to Elkanah Settle, from the names only, without knowing their different merits.'

Wilkes's cruel but accurate remark is a big one, a herald of the coming Romantic era as much as any poem about a lake or a lilac. For while the classical sensibility that Dr Johnson represented involved an, at times, undue respect for the authority of sense, the coming Romantic sensibility that Wilkes heralded involved, above all, a hypersensitivity to the accidents of sensation. Things become whatever feelings they evoke; if a name evokes an aura, it becomes it. Academics even have a name for this: they call it 'phonetic symbolism'.

The irony, the final irony, is that my kind of essay writing (a lot of it anyway) depends on finding meanings in the minutiae of sensation, which is just where the tragedy of a name like mine resides.

The only writer I can think of in all of English literature to have out-written his name – to have been given a really weird and funny-sounding name and yet replace its phonetic symbolism with a new symbolism of its own being – is ... Shakespeare.

We are so used to that name by now that I think we forget how truly odd it is. A blunt description of an intrinsically funny action – shaking a spear. It is not even a dignified action, as 'Swordthrust' might be. He is merely 'Shake-spear'. In his own day, it was obviously the first thing people noticed about him. The very earliest reference we have to him as a playwright involves the critic Robert Greene sneering at his funny name. 'He supposes he is ... the only "Shake-scene" in [the] country.' And a later wit wrote a play in which a dim undergraduate keeps talking about 'sweet Mr Shakespeare, Mr Shakespeare', obviously for the comic effect of the repeated funny name. Indeed, the name 'Shakespeare' is exactly like the name of a clown in Shakespeare, whose funny name would set off pages of tiresome puns. 'Prithee, sirrah, and where do you shake that spear? Come, sir!' 'Oh, sire, in any wench's lap that doth tremble for it.' And so on. You know the kind of thing I mean.

Indeed, if he had died of the plague, as was as likely as not, after writing only two plays and some poems, I wonder if we would not now have to suppress a laugh when we heard his name in class. 'The minor poets of the Age of Jonson,' some don would intone – or 'the Age of Fletcher', or 'Lovelace', for surely someone else left in his shade would have risen in the space left clear by his absence – 'were Drayton and Davenant and the short-lived Stratfordian, Shakespeare.'

And then the students, desperately memorizing for the exam: 'Yeah, there's Beaumont and Manningham and then that other one – you know, the one who died young and wrote the Roman play with the twins and those weird bisexual sonnets, which I actually kinda like – you know, the guy with the funny name . . .'

But he kept on writing, about bees and kings, and other things, and so lost his name and became himself. It can be done, it seems, if one writes long enough and well enough.

But the bar, *that* bar, is too high. And the phonetic symbolism of my name is too absolute. The spectre of those *gopniks* in their crewcuts and parkas rise to overwhelm all hope. It is fixed. I shall remain, and now say goodbye, and then vanish, as a – and A. – Gopnik.

The Secret to a Happy Marriage

29 March 2013

Anyone who tells you their rules for a happy marriage doesn't have one. There's a truth universally acknowledged, or one that ought to be anyway. Just as the people who write books about good sex are never people you would want to sleep with, and the academics who write articles about the disappearance of civility always sound ferociously angry, the people who write about the way to sustain a good marriage are usually on their third.

Nonetheless (you knew there was a 'nonetheless' on its way), although I don't have rules, I do have an observation after many years of marriage (I've promised not to say exactly how many, though the name 'Jimmy Carter' might hold a clue).

This principle, or formula, came to me when I was thinking about something else entirely – usually a good sign, lateral thinking being generally saner than the logical kind. I was brooding on the marriage of Charles Darwin and Emma Wedgwood, his cousin, for a book I was writing that was in part about the Darwins. In 1838, when Darwin was first thinking of marriage, he made an irresistible series of notes on the subject – a scientific-seeming list of marriage pros and cons. Against the idea, he listed 'the expense and anxiety of children' and the odd truth that a married man could never 'go up in a balloon'. In favour of marriage, he included the acquisition of a 'constant companion and friend in old age' and, memorably and conclusively, decided that a wife would be 'better than a dog, anyhow'. And the Darwins went on to have something close to an ideal marriage. As he lay dying in 1882, the distinguished scientist, who had irrevocably altered the consciousness of the world, and knew it, said simply: 'My love, my precious love.'

What made it work? My theory is that happy marriages, from the Darwins on down, are made up of a steady, unchanging formula of lust, laughter and loyalty.

The Darwins had lust, certainly – ten children in seventeen years suggests as much, anyway – and they had laughter. Emma loved to tease Charles about his passion, already evident in youth, for obsessive theorizing. 'After our marriage,' she wrote to him early on, 'you will be forming theories about me, and if I am cross or out of temper you will only consider: "What does that prove?", which will be a very philosophical way of considering it.'

And loyalty? Well, despite Emma's Christian faith, she stood by him through all the evolutionary wars, and did for him the one thing only a loyal spouse can do: pretend he wasn't in when German journalists came calling. So, marriages are made of lust, laughter and loyalty – but the three have to be kept in constant passage, transitively, back and forth, so that as one subsides for a time, the others rise.

Lust, I suppose, needs no explanation. I will add only that when I told our children complacently once that if my wife had been five inches taller, she would have been out of my league, she replied – accurately – that she *was* out of my league, and always had been, and that if she had been five inches taller we would simply have been playing a different sport. Nor does laughter need much annotation. The greatest joy in life is to discover that the same absurdities of life seem absurd to you both, creating that lovely moment of breakage when the masquerade of courtship you have been enacting becomes suddenly a backstage embrace: We're onto each other, and to the world, and will forever be in cahoots.

The trick is that marriage is played upon a tilted field, and everything flows downhill towards loyalty.

We've all seen them: marriages from which lust fled decades ago, and laughter became hollow back in the 1990s, but which continue to run on loyalty alone. They persist on a primitive attachment, no better, and in many ways quite like, that of a couple living in rubbish bins in a Samuel Beckett play, held together by an incantation of repeated phrases in the face of the encroaching hopelessness. Loyalty alone can sustain a marriage, but not happily, and not for long.

And so people are inspired, again and again, to try and pass directly back from loyalty to lust – to relight or rekindle a marriage with the old passion. This produces the romantic getaway, the hotel room rented for the night on Valentine's Day, and all the rest of the pathetic arsenal of relighting a fire that went out ten summers ago.

It never works. If anything, more divorces are caused by attempts at erotic rejuvenation than by ongoing mutual bitterness. When your troubled friends head for the Caribbean, you know that it is all over. 'We tried everything, even Venice,' your friend says, and you sigh for them. You can't transcend loyalty and get back to lust in one short step.

This is because the three-part formula of lust, laughter and loyalty is one in which you can only return from one end of the equation to the other by passing through the middle term. It's like getting to the café car on a train: you can't avoid walking through the cars between. You have to pass through laughter to get back to lust, revisit funny to get to fabulous.

The real, deep, undisclosed problem therefore with maintaining a happy marriage is this: that although the things you both found funny early on will remain so, the larger sense of what is funny will divide over time. Any sane person, for instance, knows that the three funniest movies ever made are

This Is Spinal Tap, Monty Python and the Holy Grail, and one of the *Naked Gun* movies. My son knows this. I know this. Everyone knows this.

Yet my wife, to take an example completely at random, thinks that funny movies include things such as *Annie Hall* and *The Big Lebowski*. Very, very good movies, to be sure. The best. But not really *funny* movies. My wife, like many of her kind, thinks that funny movies are funnier when they have – you know – a *point*, and an emotional arc, elements of pathos and meaning. She thinks that funny should be funny-plus, instead of funny-funny. Fortunately, though it becomes harder as the years go by to agree on funny-at-length, everyone can agree on funny-in-brief.

And since the funniest single sketch ever recorded is Peter Cook and Dudley Moore's 1960s pub sketch – the one where Pete and Dud share tales about the famous movie stars they have had to beat away from their beds – it creates the perfect pre-aphrodisiac, the moment to begin to laugh again. This means that every marriage can be saved.

And so, I realize, with the blinding clarity with which Darwin reduced the mystery of life's passage simply to the struggle for existence, that all happy marriages can be reduced to the ongoing ability to continue to laugh together when Pete explains that he had to beat Betty Grable off with a broomstick.

Be lit by lust, enlightened by laughter, settle into loyalty, and if loyalty seems too mired, return to lust by way of laughter.

I have had this formula worked out – and repeated it, waggishly, to friends, producing for some reason an ever more one-sided smile on the face of my beautiful wife. Until, not long ago, I realized that there was a flaw in this idea. And that was that I had underestimated the reason that loyalty had such magnetic power, drawing all else towards it.

For I had been describing loyalty in marriage as though it were a neutral passive state – a kind of rest state, a final, fixed state at the end of the road of life. And then, against our better wishes, and our own inner version of our marriage vows, at our daughter's insistence we got a dog. And this is what changed my view.

'The expense and anxiety of children', indeed! Our daughter's small Havanese dog, Butterscotch, has instructed us on many things, but above all on the energy that being loyal really implies. Dogs teach us many things, but above all they teach us how frisky a state loyalty can be. Dogs, after all – particularly spayed city dogs that have been denied their lusts – have loyalty as an overriding emotion. Ours will wait for hours for one of its family, and then patiently sit right alongside while there is work to be done. Loyalty is what a dog provides. The ancient joke-name for a dog, Fido, is in truth the most perfect of all dog names: 'I am faithful'. 'I am loyal'. 'I remain'.

Dogs are there to remind us that loyalty is a jumpy, fizzy emotion. Loyalty leaps up at the door and barks with joy at your return – and then immediately goes to sleep at your side.

34

Simple fidelity is the youngest emotion we possess. So to my wife. She has been complaining for the past few years that I have not yet dedicated a book to her. I have always said that it is because I do not yet know how to express the extent of my feelings.

But now I do.

'To Martha,' I shall write at the beginning of my next book. 'Better than a dog, anyhow.'

She will, at least, understand the depth of passion, of lust and laughter and loyalty – of precious, long-married love – that those Darwinian words describe.

On Children Leaving Home
19 April 2013

I want to talk about children leaving home. Not running away
from home, though that happens, or kicked out from home.
But about the good moment, when the time is right, and off
they go. As it happens, my own eighteen-year-old son is getting
ready to pack his suitcase and head to college in the fall. When
I say 'pack his suitcase', I really mean it.

When he was born, one of his godfathers came over from
London and gave the infant boy a beautiful, antique, turn-of-
the-century trunk, covered with faded steamer stickers and
already filled with judicious presents for his leaving, such as
Trumper's Extract of Limes and a little black book embossed
with a gold title announcing that it was for the phone numbers
of blondes and brunettes.

'He'll keep putting things he needs in here, and when he

leaves home, he'll be ready,' said the godfather, whose gift showed him to be both a romantic and a realist. He probably saw the light shining in our eyes at the baby's presence, and knew that he might need a nudge to get out – or rather that we would, to let him.

Well, the day has arrived, almost, and I won't pretend I like it.

The thought of his leaving home is almost unendurable for me. It's partly because we have a kind of all-day radio sports phone-in relationship. The morning usually begins with an exasperated conversation about Chelsea's latest episode of over-spending and the evening usually ends with another about the difficulties of ice hockey's Montreal Canadiens, our two shared sporting obsessions.

And now, I know, that long, continual conversation is ending. Soon, I'll call him on the phone and start, 'Hey, do you see what Abramovich—' and he'll cut me short: 'Dad, I got to run . . . Let me call you back?' Two or three days later, he will.

I suspect he will return one Christmas soon with an icy, exquisite, intelligent young woman in black clothes, with a single odd piercing somewhere elegant – ear or nose or lip – who will, when I am almost out of earshot, issue a gentle warning: 'Listen, with the wedding toasts – could you make sure your father doesn't get, you know, all boozy and damp and weepy?' My son will nod at the warning.

I am blessed to still have his little sister at home, a thirteen-year-old who speaks a strange abbreviated Manhattan lingo.

'ILY', for instance, means 'I love you', which she utters at rapid machine-gun speed from her downturned head, while her thumbs are flashing over the keyboard of her phone, continuing text exchanges with five other thirteen-year-old girls. She is like a cross between Lieutenant Uhura on *Star Trek* and a Gatling gun, spitting out communications with the cosmos. But soon enough will come her message too: 'C U ILY'.

What I wonder about is why we love our children so asymmetrically, so entirely, knowing that the very best we can hope for is that they will feel about us as we feel about our own parents: that slightly aggrieved mixture of affection, pity, tolerance and forgiveness, with a final soupçon – if we live long enough – of sorrow for our falling away, stumbling and shattered, from the vigour that once was ours.

One theory, popular among the cold-blooded, is that we feel this way only because it's a peculiar feature of our new, smothering middle-class culture. Back in the day, they insist, parents yawned over their kids.

The poor had ten or eleven children and used them, the myth runs, more or less as the Norwegians used their sled dogs on the way to the South Pole, while the rich hardly saw their children from one year to the next, bumping into them occasionally at a Christmas party. Only the growth of middle-class manners made child love so obsessive.

Perhaps that's so. But then I think of that passage in the first of all Western classics, the Iliad, where Priam of Troy goes to Achilles for the body of his son, Hector:

'Honour the gods, Achilles; pity him.
Think of your father; I'm more pitiful,
I've suffered what no other mortal has.
I've kissed the hand of one who killed my children.'
He spoke, and stirred Achilles' grief to tears.
He gently pushed the old man's hand away.
They both remembered; Priam wept for Hector,
Sitting crouched before Achilles' feet.
Achilles mourned his father.

Homer's point, which moved the Greeks and still moves us, was that even in heroic society, the love of parents for their children as children was the strongest bonding emotion of all that humans knew, the one common emotion that could reconcile enemies in grief. Hector, the prince and hero of his people, was also – indeed, primarily – Priam's son.

The new and more scientific explanation for the asymmetry is that it is all in our inheritance. Our genes are just using us to make more of them. (That Dawkinsian idea of selfish genes always gives me an image of the galley slaves on a Roman ship, peering and panting out of their little window and then, with a silent nod to each other, deciding where to steer the ship while the captain frets helplessly above.) Our genes, we're told, force us to sacrifice for our children because they – the genes – want to make more of themselves, and our unequal love for our children is the only way to keep the children healthy enough for long enough to reproduce so that the selfish little buggers – the genes, I mean – can flourish.

The trouble with that explanation is that – as with all genetic explanations of anything involving human love – it restates truths we know already, only in slightly more robotic terms. An obvious truth – for instance, 'Women just love guys like Daniel Craig' – becomes 'Our genes compel women to be attracted to men with a full head of hair, broad shoulders and narrow waists, who are perceived as having high social status'. Oh. This does not illuminate our lust, it merely annotates it. It explains the origins but not the intensity of the effect.

Our love for anything cannot be explained by our possession of genes, any more than our love for football can be explained by our possession of feet. It is true that football would be impossible without feet, but the feeling it inspires long ago left feet behind, even Frank Lampard's. It is not that the big emotions we feel – love or lust or loyalty – are more mystical than their biological origins, but exactly that they are far more material, more over-loaded with precise dates and data, associations and allegiances, experiences and memories, days and times. The mechanism of life may be set in motion by our genes, as the mechanism of football is set in motion by our feet, but the feelings we acquire are unique to our own weird walk through time.

My own best guess about the asymmetry of parental love lies in a metaphor borrowed from the sciences: merely a metaphor, maybe, but one that – as metaphors can – touches the edge of actuality. One of the rules of mathematics and physics, as I, a complete non-mathematician, read often in science books, is that when infinity is introduced into a scientific equation it no longer makes sense. All the numbers go blooey when you have one number in the equation that doesn't have a beginning or an end.

Parental love, I think, is infinite. I mean this in the most prosaic possible way. Not infinitely good, or infinitely enno-bling, or infinitely beautiful. Just . . . infinite. Often, infinitely boring. Occasionally, infinitely exasperating. To other people, always infinitely dull – unless, of course, it involves their own children, when it becomes infinitely necessary. That's why parents talking about their children can be so tedious – other parents, I mean, not me or you – not because we doubt their love, or the child's charms, but because itemizing infinities is obviously the most boring thing imaginable.

We see this, with heartbreaking clarity, in those people we know, or read about, who continue to love, say, a meth-addicted child. And we think: 'Why don't you just give up?' And they look at us blankly, and we say: 'Oh, yeah. Right.'

The joke our genes and our years play on us is to leave us, as parents, forever with this weird column of figures scribbled on our souls, ones that make no sense, no matter how long you squint at them or how hard you try to make them work. The parental emotion is as simple as learning to count and as strange as discovering that the series of numbers, the counting, never ends. Our children seem, at least, to travel for light years. We think their suitcases contain the cosmos. Though our story is ending, their story, we choose to think – we can't think otherwise – will go on forever.

When we have children, we introduce infinities into all of our emotional equations. Nothing ever adds up quite the same again.

MONEY MATTERS

14 February 2014

'Money is pieces of paper with pictures of people on them,' a wise child once said, and she was right. 'Whose face should be on our money?', far from being a secondary, cosmetic question, turns out to be a big one. I knew, for instance, that the euro was in crisis the first time I ever saw a euro. It was the only insipid currency ever printed. There was nothing on each denomination except a bridge or arch, no pictures of people at all – and then not even an actual European celebrity bridge (the Rialto in Venice or the Pont Neuf in Paris), but a limp generic representation of a limp generic bridge. No one – not billy-goats or trolls or any of the other denizens of the actual European imagination – could live under such bridges.

The continent that gave the world the Inquisition and the telescope and the sonnets of Petrarch was reduced to the symbol of a melancholy arch presiding over a melancholy land that lay nowhere and had no folk. Not Goethe or Leonardo or Johan Cruyff – not even such consensus Europeans as Tintin and the Captain – were allowed to show their faces on the euro. (I suppose Hergé's questionable politics made even that impossible.) The absence of common heroes showed, more eloquently than any number of charts or graphs, that the eurozone had been linked together by fiat more than common feeling. I was also pretty sure that the euro would survive anyway, since if there is one thing you learn about French high functionaries it's that what they insist on having happen, happens, and reality be damned.

And so the imagery, the iconography, of money is more than just decor. It displays the true convictions of the commonwealth that intends to support its value. We put presidents on our money here in the US because, despite their obvious deficiencies, we make a papacy of the presidency, and treat it as a semi-divine state. You over there, I know, have been debating who to put next on your money, on the flip side to the Queen. I liked seeing Charles Darwin on the ten pound note, and although I certainly approve of the final choice of Jane Austen, I still think that you will discover dangers to having an ironist on your money. (I grew up in Canada, where we keep the Queen's picture on our money too, and there is, I will say, something odd about a genial lady ageing on the currency, with lines and liver spots.)

It's natural that money comes to represent our common life. In so many ways, it *is* our common life. In the best sense, it's a confidence game. The idea of money began, after all, when some early man or woman first realized that instead of lugging around the portable property that had value – seashells or gold nuggets or the like – you could simply carry tokens that stood for that property. Then the other early men and women had to learn to trust that the portable property was really back there, in the cave. It was left to modern man and woman to see that you could have the tokens without even having the portable property they once stood for. Now the tokens are so many removes from the property that what money stands for is really the full faith and confidence of the governments that print it: essentially, pounds and dollars and euros are IOUs from the army and navy, promising that our accumulated common goods won't be looted by Vikings or Vandals.

Now, for the first time, we have a sudden boom in micro-currencies, issued by notional nations or even neighbour-hoods, and we also have for the first time what are sometimes called crypto-currencies, Bitcoin being the most famous, and so the government–money nexus seems in serious doubt. As I grasp the concept of these micro-currencies and crypto-cur-rencies, it is essentially that the value of money need no longer be guaranteed by the nation state. A roving network of internet users can rely instead entirely on each other to ensure the value of the tokens. In the new virtual world, you can use an agreed crypto-currency to buy and sell while avoiding the government altogether – a particularly good idea if you happen yourself to be, so to speak, a Vandal or a Viking.

The future of micro-currencies seems to me more or less unlimited, since the central economic insight I've gained over the years is not that governments are more or less like households, but that households are all more or less like small states – which, like actual governments, tend to pitch two essentially irrational economic theories against one other.

I live in a household, for instance, that has its own economic policy – or rather, two of them. One was invented by my wife, Martha, and the other is my own. 'Marthanomics', as it's known, is strictly speaking a subdivision of the underlying field of 'Marthamatics', the theory by which two and two might make four but might as well make six, since how much bigger is six than four really? In this way, if something costs half as much again as you thought it would, it costs the same as you thought it would.

Marthanomics extends this principle. The writer Calvin Trillin used to say of his late wife, the wonderful Alice, that she believed that any extravagant purchase considered even for a moment should be considered money saved for spending later. Marthanomics simplifies this principle with the efficiency of genius: *all* money spent is money saved. Either the thing you are spending on will be so much more expensive tomorrow that it would be criminal not to buy it today, or else the thing you are buying will be worth so much more tomorrow that it would be a sin against thrift not to buy it now. 'I saw our vase at Bloomingdale's,' she will say of some extravagant thing that we could not afford when we got it, 'and you know what? The price has doubled. It's good we bought it when we did. We saved so much.' The act of spending and the act of making are seen, in Marthanomics, as essentially the same act, seen at two different moments in time.

This logic is irrefutable. And our home is filled with beautiful things. In fact, I wonder if that isn't what Keynes really had in mind with his famous economic crack about our all being dead in the long run anyway – that although we should consult futurity and the welfare of our children, we should not consult them *too* much, since if we continue to defer good things indefinitely, no one will ever have them at all.

Martha points out (she is pointing it out now, reading over my shoulder and holding my hands away from the keyboard as she does) that Marthanomics has grown up strictly in opposition to what she calls the 'Adam Avoidance' approach to the domestic budget. The first principle there is that any bill left in its envelope long enough should be considered as paid. This is matched by the insight that invoicing employers for work done is a bit vulgar, not to mention insulting, and should also be avoided if at all possible. Indeed, the overriding principle of my system is that all economic issues should be avoided if at all possible. If I were Chancellor of the Exchequer, I would simply leave all the documents locked up in my red box for months, and, when Budget Day came, I would get up in Parliament and try and change the subject.

I'm sure that your household has economic theories as odd and original, and that they, too, ought to be commemorated by their own coin. I predict that in the future every household will have its own micro-currency. The people down the street who buy only in quantity (thousands of rolls of toilet paper at a time) will have giant bills, while the ones who defer their taxes for too long can have a picture of Oscar Wilde on theirs, in memory of his great forgotten remark, when confronted by the taxman demanding that he pay tax on the house where, after all, he slept: 'Ah! But I sleep so poorly.' My family's micro-currency will have pictures of The Beatles and The Kinks, at their full glory, and vaguely psychedelic spirals and whorls all over it. And so it will go, house by house and family by family, making our micro-currencies like morning poems. For what is money, after all, but a game we have decided to play, a study in mutual confidence? What's money but a medium for the exchange of value?

DYING WITH DIGNITY

12 October 2014

Last year I recall talking about some of life's milestones. My nineteen-year-old son was leaving home for college, and now he has left, and it has been even harder than I thought it might be – although the good news is that when he does return, it's like a scene from a 1940s movie about a soldier's homecoming.

'Luke's home! Luke's home!' his mother and his sister cry, as the door opens, and our New York apartment seems instantly transformed into a grainy black-and-white clip, with a scratchy soundtrack and lurching strings. This tear-filled moment, I hasten to add, happens about every fourth day. He chose a college twenty minutes away by commuter train, close enough for him to come home to get a proper hipster haircut and be back by dinner to his dorm room, guitar and girlfriend.

So in some of these crucial transitions of life, modern people do better than earlier people have mostly done. We do much better with the start of life than people ever have before – infant and mother mortality both show this. And I would insist that, with all our follies, we still do much better with children than people mostly have in the past – hovering over-attentively around them being a small sin compared to beating them and sending them out into the fields and mines and factories.

The middle of life, frankly, we seem to do about as badly or as well as the last centuries did – the pains and difficulties of getting extricated from an unhappy marriage today seeming about the same as the pains and difficulties of not being able to get extricated from an unhappy marriage in the long centuries before.

But with the end of life we do very badly – I won't say worse, because it was never good, but with more indignity and casual cruelty than once attended on the rituals of dying. My own parents, I'm glad to say are, at eighty, almost indecently healthy, but this year we lost my father-in-law at ninety-five. My mother-in-law is only a year or so younger, a wonderful woman – a fine film director and a great beauty, her only fault (or chief virtue, depending on which side you stood) being how intensely she disliked me, though only for the first twenty years or so of my marriage. In any case, this extraordinary woman now has dementia, the cruellest of illnesses, which takes a person away from her memories and then takes her away from herself.

Well, any sentence that says that something is 'the cruellest of illnesses' is false, since they are all cruel. When we come to the end, the wrench of the pain lies in the reduction of a self to an object. With my father-in-law, the worst was to see this hyper-elegant man with his love of small exquisite things – a Canadian Anglophile with a yearning, mostly unrequited, for thin rolled-up umbrellas and polished-leather card cases – become a yellowing body hooked up to an oxygen machine.

The great deaths of eighteenth- and nineteenth-century literature and biography may be immensely sad, but they show the elderly at least enthroned in an old familiar bed. 'That will do . . . all a pillow can do,' said Dr Johnson at the end to his carers, and at least he was allowed still to be himself, moralizing to a cushion. Trying to define what it is that is so obviously and painfully missing from the way we die now, we all land on that one word 'dignity' and struggle to articulate what it means and how and why it's missing. Our first instinct, I think, is to feel that democratic equality is the right pathway to that lost dignity, that each of us should be placed on an equal footing with everyone else and our need for human respect rooted in our common humanity.

But I wonder. Anyone who thinks that equality creates dignity should consider the condition of an economy class cabin when the overhead lockers are being filled. We are all equal there, and none of us – not the woman who is standing on the shoulders of her husband to stuff her bursting bag into a tiny space, nor the nicely dressed middle-aged man beside her, trying to force his roller alongside – none of us is exactly . . . distinguished. We are all equal in the sight of the overhead bin, but none of us has any dignity there. No, dignity, I think, is an exceptional demand, one that depends on at least an illusion or masquerade of an anti-egalitarian, indeed pre-modern – indeed an essentially feudal – sense of deference.

Dignity is deference, and deference is irrational. Dignity is not found struggling with the luggage, but it is exactly there in the deference we give to the pilot as he heads towards the cockpit.

Most of us provide this deference to each other for bare seconds at a time, in a kind of musical-chairs game of deference that we play in life, so that everyone is provided a bit of social dignity in turn. It's to give our dinner party guests dignity that, when they arrive, we take drink orders and pass around hors d'oeuvres anxiously. We say, 'Now, you're not allergic to cashews, are you?' or 'I've been worrying all day that you are not a fan of paella,' as though we were lifelong servitors, family servants in our own family. We lend dignity to the social circumstance by momentarily invoking the old order of servility.

Now, some people do still breathe their last in their own beds, and though I would hardly call this perfect – it is still dying – it does seem to have some saving touch of the humane about it. A chef friend of mine, after his ninety-something father passed away on his upstairs bed, was able to go downstairs and make omelettes for the family – an odd but reassuring ritual. But the elaborate deference necessary to the idea of dignity is what makes providing dignity to the dying in hospitals and hospices so hard. The carers there, I don't doubt for a minute, want to do their best. But dignity, being irrational, has to be handmade, so to speak, by too-busy doctors, and then by overworked and underpaid nurses and orderlies. To always keep in mind the dignity of what must look to them like an undifferentiated and ever-changing row of poor forked animals in open-backed gowns, is immensely hard. They are instructed to treat their patients with dignity, to respect their patients' dignity, but they inevitably end up handing out dignity like pills on the meal tray.

They have learned by rote a set of instructions – Things To Say To The Family – that are indeed the right things to say: 'Your relative is gravely ill'; 'We want to do everything we can to make him comfortable'; 'We want you to participate in his "pain management".' In our current dispensation of dignity, everyone gets his or her share. But real dignity involves getting at least the illusion of receiving a little more than your share.

'Reason not the need,' King Lear says, and we shouldn't. Unreasonable needs are the essence of ageing intact. I sometimes thought, during the long nights of vigil when my father-in-law was passing away, that if I were king of the hospitals and hospices, I might change the dress code, making the attendants and doctors wear open-backed gowns at least once a week and giving the patients white coats and name plates and the apparatus of office. I might make certain that a portrait of each of the patients at the height of their now-faded powers – getting an award, celebrating an anniversary, or simply intimidating a neighbour – was there at the end of the bed along with their charts. I might offer Sam Weller-like valets and old-fashioned serving ladies for each patient, since what the doctors can do often seems marginal and what the valets and serving women could do for the patients' morale seems very real.

For most of us, the worry about getting older is not really about the passing years and their minor symptoms. In fact some of these clouds actually have their silver linings: *For every woman who is laid low by the menopause, there is one like me who feels liberated by the idea of never having to deal with cramps or a tampon again.* What is worrying is the thought of what might happen to us if we cross to the dark side, to the Tithonus side, of old age. Past the senior railcard, to a world of incapacity, indignity and incontinence. For what dying people really want is simple. It is life. My father-in-law didn't want to die with dignity; he didn't want to die. His last thoughts were of escape back to his own apartment, and of a novel he had written at ninety and had never had published. What did I really think of it? he demanded with his last breaths. He didn't want to be read to. He wanted to be read.

Watching the people we love die bit by bit is the hardest thing life demands until we recall that watching the people we love die bit by bit is in a certain sense what life simply is. It just usually takes more time for the bits to go by.

During my father-in-law's last days, when we kept vigil by his bedside, that nineteen-year-old boy had the good idea of taking the train into town and bringing his guitar to the hospital to play for his grandfather and the other patients. He suggested it to the nurses during his vigil, and they liked the idea – first turning it over in their minds to see where it was wrong, and why it ought not to be allowed and what was uncomfortable about it, only to see that it was actually a nice idea. But by the time he got to the hospital with his guitar, his grandfather was gone. Someday I'll hear what he planned to play.

CHARLIE HEBDO
11 January 2015

When I woke up in New York on Wednesday morning and heard about the horror in Paris earlier that same day – the cold-blooded murder of the staff of *Charlie Hebdo* magazine – I thought first of Wolinski, and then I thought of my friends Nisha and Saley.

Wolinski, of course, was one of those murdered in that massacre of elderly cartoonists, and several others, by two brutal terrorists. Well, to call them 'terrorists' is, of all strange things under the sun, to pay them a compliment. For they were not, like most terrorists, assailants of strangers whom they could not fully register as human: these were cold-blooded killers of people whose faces they were forced to see as they killed them, men so far gone in evil that they were willing to murder a roomful of helpless and unarmed old men.

We should, I know, not dwell on the mere tabloid details of this horror, and its dramatic conclusion, but seek to place it in context or proportion or . . . something. I find that hard. We underrate, or don't talk sufficiently of, the sheer deliberate cruelty, the sadism of terrorism. In what was what, I hope, the worst video any of us will see, we saw these same killers cold-bloodedly murdering a fallen policeman as he pleaded for his life, and making a casual joke as they did. These men enjoy killing helpless people. If there is a worse thing to be said about anyone, I would not know what it is.

But, no – Wolinski. I was going to talk about Georges Wolinski. I met him just once in passing, at a dinner in Paris. So I can't say I knew him at all, but I admired him greatly, even though the wild, coarse style of caricature he practised was not the one I like the most. An Asterix man, a Goscinny and Uderzo man, I would be lying if I presented myself as some kind of all-out fan of *Charlie Hebdo* and its contents. My tastes in humour are for the subtle and sentimental, and I never much like the overcharged and overstated, which their work as caricaturists certainly was.

But though I am probably a bit of a coward when it comes to comedy – I probably like it sweeter than I should – I am at least an instinctive pluralist: I really like there to be things in the world, and on the news-stand, that I don't like. *Charlie Hebdo* was not to my taste but I was always glad to see it persisting. It spoke of an older, rawer, French tradition that I could appreciate even if I didn't much care for it. France is an uptight country that needs the relaxation of the truly, weirdly unfastened – Rabelais could only be French, exactly because the refined needs the raw. But Wolinski – he was . . . cool. Big in presence, funny, warm, caustic and very Jewish. He came, I learned after, from a Polish-Jewish father and a Tunisian-Jewish mother, and came, exactly as much of my mother's family did, to Paris from Tunisia with the end of World War Two. To think of this grand, sensual old man, and then to think that the last thing in life he would see was a hooded look of hatred and the pointed metal nose of a machine gun, is to guarantee yourself a lost night's sleep, and not just one night either.

And then I thought of Nisha and Saley. They are Muslim friends in Paris. Nisha helped to look after our children when they were small and growing up there, and we became life-long friends. Their kids Facebook our kids and we always try to see them when we are in France – I saw him just last fall, when I was in Paris. Warmer, dearer people – more loving and conscientious parents – you will never meet. And they are not Muslim in name only: they are far more religious in the prac-tice of their tradition than I have ever been in mine. I know how complex their feelings can be about their place in France. Although they are now permanent Parisians, they told us once that they feel invisible in their country, and I still recall their delight, so many years ago now, in 1998, when France's won-derful multicoloured and many-cultured team won the World

58

Cup, and they drove to the Champs Élysées to celebrate the arrival – a false dawn, alas – of a truly one France made from many kinds.

Wolinski and Nisha, Jews and Muslims in France . . . The trap-lines of Islamophobia and Judaeophobia are different, of course. Hatred of Jews tends to concentrate on their undue eagerness to assimilate to the cosmopolitan life around them, which still cannot disguise their fundamentally alien nature: 'They are spies upon us!' is the cry. Hatred of Muslims tends to concentrate on their unwillingness to assimilate to the life and values around them in any way at all: 'They are saboteurs in our midst!' is the cry. But both have in common a refusal to look at people – the Wolinskis and the Nishas and the Saleys – and instead concentrate on, well, on violent caricatures, sprung out of the comic books where they belong, into angry minds where they don't, where they are no longer hypothetical absurdities but living targets.

To reject completely any notion of collective guilt is to bear down all the harder on the idea of individual responsibility. The notion that what some have called France's 'stark secularism' – or its level of unemployment, or its history of exclusion, that imposed invisibility – is in any way to blame or even a root cause for this, depends on being ignorant of the actual history of France.

But unemployed people don't typically – or indeed, ever – look eighty-year-old men in the eye and then blow their brains away. Excluded or invisible people always suffer from their sense of not quite belonging – as the Jewish immigrants of Wolinski's generation to France did, too. They write books, they protest, sometimes they even emigrate. They do not mock dying policemen and then complete their murder. To make the secular model, or anything except fanaticism itself, responsible for the horrors we have seen would be absurd, if it were not so obscene.

Fanaticism is the enemy, not faith. It always is. But only a fool would deny that faith has been the seedbed of fanaticism in mankind's long and sorry struggle for the light. That's why, when the non-religious commit acts of shocking cruelty and intolerance, as they often have and will again, it is normal for us to say that they have made a religion of their politics, or that they are in the grip of a blinding and inhumane dogma.

France has that 'stark secularism' not to defang faith, but exactly to keep faith from turning towards fanaticism – and it does this by compelling the faithful to look each other in the face and recognize that they must live together or die. Secularism is not a way of disarming religion. The basic social contract of the Enlightenment is that tolerance is there above all to guarantee the free exercise of faith. No one can try to forcibly convert a Muslim – or a Jewish, or a Catholic – child in France, or to prevent their worship. This comes at the low cost of accepting the right of all faiths to persist, including the faith of those who think that we should never have faith in anything.

This is a very new thing in the history of the West. Five hundred years ago it would have been unimaginable for French Catholics to accept this coexistence with Islam. A mere hundred years ago, as we know, Jews were hounded and imprisoned, and worse was yet to come. Ours is the great era of tolerance, and we have no reason to apologize for it.

Sometimes tragedy provokes individual eloquence. Hassen Chalghoumi, the Muslim imam of Drancy, a Paris suburb, rushed to the scene of the killings and said: 'I feel an immense sadness but above all anger. We can argue over liberty, but when we're in disagreement we respond to art with art, to wit with wit. We never respond to a drawing with blood. No! Never. These victims are martyrs, and I shall pray for them with all my heart.' Courage, said C. S. Lewis, that great Christian philosopher, is not simply one of the virtues, but the form of every virtue at the testing point. France is at a testing point this weekend, of truthfulness, decency and solidarity, and also of what they call the ability to 'desolidarize' – to put the people we know before the abstract categories we imagine. Come to think of it, making people, with all their flaws, fully visible while leaving ideal types alone, is exactly what the caricaturist has always done for us. It's their special form of bravery.

FAMILY REUNIONS
3 June 2015

June is the month of weddings, which trail family reunions along behind them like bridal trains or garlands. My own family had our own ten-year reunion, just last week by the rocky shore of Maine on the northeastern edge of America. None of us lives there, but it seemed a decent gathering point to get to from all the places where the centrifugal force of modern life had flung us.

It was a reunion only of the immediate family, but my immediate family could look, to outsiders, well, whatever the opposite of 'immediate' is. 'Hyperbolically attenuated', I suppose. I am, you see, one of six siblings. We mostly married young, and some by now have married twice; we often had children early, and those children, following in this weird Jewish hillbilly tradition, have by now had children, too . . . so that, these days, the immediate family consists of thirty-five people, ranging in age from six months to eighty years, and in vocations from college professors – which is rather the family trade – to carpenters and scene painters and even one private investigator, albeit a Canadian private eye, a more subdued and delicate apostle of the hard-boiled craft. We have an Asian wing, with our Kim Soo, and a Celtic one, with the smallest baby Teslyn.

Mine is a crazy family, but then they all are. One instance? Well, my grandparents met after my parents were already married – and my mother's mother so liked my father's father that they had an affair, and then divorced their spouses and married each other. So I had one set of grandparents, mother's mother and father's father, a cartoon version of my own parents.

My family still tends to collapse in on itself in this bizarre way. They – we! – troop down to breakfast as what my wife mutteringly refers to as 'the milling mob', in jogging pants and outsized T-shirts, to sit in small groups with coffee and renew ancient arguments, some lifetime-long, about books and records and ice hockey and the like. After milling, we, tend to clump – my wife's word, again – sitting in small groups, trying and failing to make outdoor plans for the day, and then going off to read or sit by the pool and tease and talk more. We're highly analytic in the small, micro instance, and anti-analytic in the macro ones. I mean by that that everyone talks and jokes about what we've eaten and seen and read, but how we all got here, and what we all are missing in life, or long for, is not a subject.

Jokes and teases are the currency; confessions and ancient quarrels rarely appear – or, if you ask my wife, the confessions and ancient quarrels have by now been so sublimated into the jokes and teases that no one any longer recognizes their true origin.

Still, when I watch the Irish or Southern gothic family movies, yielding up their full Meryl Streep of family recrimination and family grievances about Grandma's money and Grandpa's drinking, I am startled and grateful at the general good humour of my own. My wife's own family, infinitely neater, and more polite, who come to breakfast shiny in robes and dressing gowns, bury old sadness beneath the sweetness, until the sadness – old marital discord, hidden adulteries, heartbreak or disappointments – comes out sourly, or, worse, never does except in whispers. Whispering is not a *strong* activity in my family. When I read, on a recent London trip, John Cleese's memoir of his upbringing in Weston-super-Mare with his *very* English family – where no one ever said anything to anyone about anything at all that had ever happened that might have made them feel any emotion of any kind whatever – I feel grateful.

But the inescapable material of any family reunion, British or American, Jewish or Celtic, is always the same: each offers a hair-raising, or hair-losing, seminar on the effects of time on the human body and soul, and especially on the difference between ageing and growing. To put it bluntly, everyone at the reunion under thirty-five is still *growing*, physically and mentally. Everyone over thirty-five is merely *ageing*, physically and mentally, too.

The under-thirties' growth delights us: look at how lean and hungry Adrian looks now that he's thirty, while Andres at twenty-eight has grown a hugely impressive braided beard that makes him look half like a dwarf-warrior from Tolkien and half like Van Gogh's postman. Our own teenagers, Luke and Olivia – at the last reunion, ten years ago, sweet-faced small ones – are revealed to us as archetypal New York City teens. 'The Vampire Twins', they're instantly nicknamed by their cousins, or, else called, simply, 'Edward and Bella', in tribute to their pale skin, omnipresent sunglasses, black clothes and calm air of apparently slightly sinister, knowing cool – while we, their parents, of course, can still see only sweet-faced small ones.

The over-forties' ageing distresses us; or would, if we were not alarmed to be complicit in it. Bald spots grow, old beards whiten and waistlines expand . . . Fortunately, the really scary edge of ageing seems to get pushed back ten years every time we get together. Ten years ago, the forty-somethings seemed worrying old; now they look bright as pennies, and it is only the over-sixties who have to worry about no longer being young. The way that this frontier of ageing somehow recedes at each family reunion is a scientific wonder. (My wife insists that she is ageing backwards, like Benjamin Button.) I don't know how it happens, but it does. It's a great relief. It must have something to do with the fourth dimension.

The dividing line between those growing and those ageing is made still clearer by some tellingly contradictory behavior: those who are actually growing try to persuade everyone that they are just ageing; while those who have actually aged try to insist that they have merely grown. 'Oh, I've given up smoking weed,' an under-thirty may yawn over the afternoon. 'I've just, sort of . . . outgrown it, I guess,' though the ageing listener wants to say, and doesn't: 'No! You've learned something: inebriation isn't worth the time it takes.' Those who are ageing, on the other hand, try to persuade each other that they're really just growing. 'I've given up tennis,' (or skiing or handball), one of us may say urgently. 'It just doesn't, I don't know, interest me any more. I don't have the time for it, given everything else in my life right now.' The truth – that you have gotten too old to play it – is as unsayable as it is self-evident.

It was a good week, though, ending with a movie-worthy trip to a little honky-tonk amusement park on the pier at the nearby beach. I don't know if you have them still in Britain, but here amusement parks on ocean piers are zones of timelessness. The rides never change (in fact, they seemed to have rusted in place), and the people running the rides don't change (they seem to have rusted in place too), and all of us rejuvenate through the elixir of fear and panic and laughter about them. The amusement park is an equal opportunity infantalizer: it renews our childish pleasures even while exploiting them cynically – the knowledge that 'the carnies' are hoping to get you to pay three dollars for a single shot at an undersized target gives an acid sub-taste to all the spun sugar and fried dough they sell.

In the long struggle with time, the family is the only clock we have, to follow our own passage within it, and occasionally to stop it . . . And then all together we watch the nightly fireworks. You see them before you hear them, even close up. I had forgotten that, even close up, sound moving so much more slowly than light, there is still a small but discernible gap between the lights exploding and the boom of the gunpowder that set them off. The showers of bright sparkles and stars comes first, the child-traumatizing explosion just after.

The small children in our group are excited by the illuminations and then almost instantly scared of the noise, as we were once, too. Exaltation reveals itself as mere mechanism in an instant – but with the giveaway gunpowder boom, just a little bit dragged behind. I recall how my then two-year-old daughter would react, seeing the light with wonder and then cringing in increasing fear from the bangs, until we had to retreat into the parking lot – my now cool vampiric teenager in black leggings was then clinging to my chest, sobbing until the salvos of noise had passed.

Freud had it wrong in this much: families find themselves in the tiny space between the light we see and the roar we hear. In family life, if we are lucky at all, the brightness comes first, the bitterness some time after. We try to keep the memory of the fireworks while forgetting the fire that makes them work. Fortunate families like mine try to pry open and extend, somehow, the little interval of time between the bright light and the big boom, until it gives the illusion of being large enough to live in. Reunited, together in numbers, families extend that instant for at least the length of a wedding.

Sometimes, if we're lucky, it can even last a week.

THE INDISPENSABLE MAN

21 June 2015

Until a few weeks ago, I thought I was an indispensable man.

No, I didn't think that because of anything my wife or children said, and certainly not because of anything my employers suggested. My publisher seems content to keep my books in a state of what they assure me is voguish invisibility. No, my indispensability depended on a narrower field of triumph. I was indispensable to Saturday morning breakfast, as the only one in the family who could make Swedish waffles – produce them, bacon-garnished, with reliable aplomb. Since my two children were small, whenever I was home on Saturday mornings, I would make them those Swedish waffles – working from a store-bought mix, but adding in the extra egg and milk, melting butter in the microwave, keeping the maple syrup cold, the way their Canadian genes compel them to like it.

I put on a very good show – watching the heart-shaped waffle iron until it beeped, slapping the spatula down warily on its shining aluminium front, calling the children to the table and then producing the waffles.

Then, just a couple of weeks ago, I came home from a nightmarish lecture trip to Texas, where I had been stalled at an airport in San Antonio for two nights, and on Saturday morning bravely put on my 1960s-sitcom-dad face and called out: 'Anyone in the mood for waffles?'

Silence. Real silence. And there is no silence as silent as the silence produced by a fifteen-year-old American girl, with not even the tapping of her fingers on her smartphone. My daughter's was not merely an empty silence, but a pointed silence, warping the space around her in a very Einsteinian way. You could almost see it taking on shape and danger.

'It's OK, Dad,' she said at last. 'Mom and I will make them later.'

'Mom doesn't know how to make waffles,' I cried. 'She's never made waffles in her life.'

'She does now,' Olivia answered calmly. And then she quietly added these killer words: 'While you were away, we read the instructions on the side of the box.'

They read the instructions on the side of the box. It seemed like treason, like betrayal. To be fair to myself, I had not been hiding the instructions on the side of the box from them, as ancient pagan priests were said to hide the flimsy gimmicks of their impressive-looking fire-and-smoke ceremonies from their acolytes.

I just had been blithely confident that the instructions on the side of the box were the least of it. You could read them for years, and you still wouldn't know how to really make Swedish waffles. In fact, I know now – having scanned that treacherous box many times since – the instructions on the side of the box do tell you, in remarkable detail, everything you need to know to make Swedish waffles. The eggs, the butter, the milk, the stirring, the warning that they are thinner than you might expect. It really is all there. I had just read them so long ago that I had forgotten how complete they were.

'You can't learn something like that from the side of the box,' I protested anyway. 'They may show you the general method,' I said. 'But the general method is only part of it. It's all in the details.'

My wife chimed in, with what I think was meant to be kindness. 'Actually they came out very well. Not better than yours. But exactly the same.'

Othello's occupation was gone. They had not so much discerned a secret that I was keeping from them, as demonstrated to me a truth that I had not wanted to recognize – the elaborate show of my waffle expertise was resting on a cardboard foundation of fact.

The sudden destruction of my indispensability in the eyes of my family gave me, I'm bound to say, a new vision of just how rarely anyone on earth is indispensable to any activity at all. If this can happen even unto waffle makers, woe unto the rest of the world. This came home to me in the next few days with even greater force, after a sort of book-slide occurred in my study, and Alan Clark's diaries once again more or less fell onto my desk.

Clark's diaries had quite a vogue in the UK when they first appeared in the mid-Nineties. The son of the great art historian Kenneth Clark, Alan Clark was a right-wing Thatcherite of considerable wit, a blunt prose style, and appalling views on most issues. His diaries do make good reading – simply because any writing which dispenses with the normal human taboos against displaying the malice we all sometimes feel about our neighbours and colleagues, makes for good reading. But the assumed and competitive indispensability of his fellows in the Conservative Party is one of his themes. Though Mrs Thatcher is securely in power as he begins his diary, there is still already endless plotting among the men in her court as to who would be her successor, with each one congratulating himself that it must be him, given his own indispensable role in the Thatcherite dispensation. Who is more indispensable to the movement, Lord Young or Nigel Lawson? we are asked to consider, over much old claret.

Then, as Michael Heseltine conspires and Geoffrey Howe rebels, the crisis mounts: they have to keep this fellow in the cabinet, and how can she govern without that one?

They're . . . indispensable. And then, as the 1990 crisis mounts further towards its matricidal climax, the indispensable focus alters: how can we ever win another election, move forward, without our one indispensable woman as the leader?

Well, as you may recall, the indispensable men proved to be eminently disposable – so much so that these days no one even recalls their names. And the indispensable woman, though still memorable, did prove to be replaceable, inasmuch as her replacement, John Major – who no one in the length or breadth of Clark's diaries regards as indispensable – won the next election about as easily as she might have. He succumbed only to the next incoming club of indispensable men when they emerged as New Labour in the Nineties.

For the sure truth is that no one in politics is even remotely indispensable. Again and again, the indispensable man or woman passes from the scene, and what happens next is more or less the same thing as was happening before. Nobody ever seemed more indispensable than Franklin Delano Roosevelt, but a mediocre Missouri haberdasher did just fine when he had to, and more or less along exactly the same lines that FDR would have pursued.

What is true of politics is true of smaller places. I have worked at several institutions with indispensable men and women, and in each case, when the person the institution simply couldn't do without was done away with, things went on for good or ill, more or less as they had done before.

The star columnist who resigns in a fit, the prima ballerina who walks out on the brutal choreographer – there's a gasp, and then a gap, and then amnesia. Even the great stars of sports teams turn out to be less vital than they might seem. The statistical analyst Bill James once showed that the greatest star in US baseball won for his team at most four additional games over 162-game seasons.

What we really have in place of indispensable people are good institutions – strong teams, fine dance companies, reliable instructions on the sides of every box: parliaments that know how to legislate; presidents who, however violently they differ, know how to transfer power; civil servants who really do know how to serve the civitas through many kinds and administrations of momentarily indispensable people. The great conservative philosopher Michael Oakeshott used to say that governing and politics were, like baking, not something you could read from a recipe, a set of instructions. And he was not entirely wrong: a constitution, no matter how many rights it guarantees or freedoms it enumerates, is meaningless without a healthy practice of politics. But he was surely not completely right. There is more wisdom in recipes than those of us who pretend to kitchen expertise like to admit. I recall the late lawyer and writer John Mortimer's moving witness to how, in a corrupt Nigerian courtroom, lawyers and advocates working from a British model – and in wigs, no less – did bring about justice even in extremis. Instructions printed on the side of the box matter.

We speak often of how the family is the model small institution. But I wonder if we don't have hold of the wrong end of the spatula in that comparison, so to speak. It is not that countries resemble families in their dependency on a fixed patriarchal authority. It is that strong countries, like healthy families, are self-healing organisms that have so dispersed their authority and sense of common purpose that they get along just fine when the patriarch passes, or is stranded in a Texas airport. In life as we live it, there are no magic waffles and no indispensable men. There are really only family occasions, and reliable recipes.

My Encounter with Shingles

23 July 2017

Not long ago, I got diagnosed with the unpleasant and undignified illness known as 'shingles'. Shingles is, as I imagine you know, a form of childhood chicken pox, come back to life on the inside of your body, fiendishly settling on the nerves – often, as happened in my case, the ones on, or rather within, your face. It manages to be extremely painful and, as I say, completely without distinction – one of those illnesses that manage to combine triviality, indignity and discomfort all at once.

It is trivial inasmuch as no one dies of it (though in very rare cases it can settle on the optic nerve and provoke blindness), and undignified inasmuch as you get no credit from outsiders for suffering with it. Even its name is dumb, and makes the sufferer seem, well, silly. Shingles: the name is said to derive from the roofing-like skin rash that announces it, though I can hardly see the resemblance. It seems likelier to me that it was chosen in a jeering way by some bad-tempered diagnostician from a random list of undignified disease names. Having it is like having gout or neuralgia or lumbago or some other disease associated with the grumpy querulous older-man character in those bad 1960s movies about the rollicking eighteenth century – you know, the *Lock Up Your Daughters!* kind. 'Careful, now – the Squire's gouty toe is acting up.' Or, 'That damned lumbago! It always comes back in humid weather.' It's that kind of thing: 'Now, Father, don't go getting upset. You know how your shingles acts up at times like these.' 'If it wasn't for those damn shingles I'd give you a proper whaling, sir.' And so on.

The trick of it is ... that it hurts. Doesn't hurt in the dig-nified way that things ought to hurt, like a broken arm or a wounded leg. More like a low annoying tingle that won't go away – like having a toothache under the skin throughout your body. What to do for it? My doctor recommended taking ibu-profen – and then explained how taking just a little too much of it would destroy my liver. Doctors in New York, frightened of over-prescribing opioids, have been taught to relieve pain, I think, by alarming patients with the consequences of what the pain reliever might do to them: you are so worried about the side effects that for a moment you forget the agony.

Then I made a simple discovery: rum works. It was aston-ishing, in fact, to see how quickly a glass of dark rum – a 'jot' I suppose I should call it – over ice cubes worked to achieve maximum medicinal effect. Normally, I am not much of a liquor and spirits man – the rum was in the house for last year's Christmas eggnog – being instead a drinker of the kind whom Trump supporters sneer at for sipping Chardonnay at elite parties. (I actually don't like Chardonnay much, though for some reason the white wine grape has been given the full guilt of elite liberalism.)

I not only felt better. I suddenly felt serenely at one in the company of ghosts . . . Advertising executives – soldiers – sailors! – all those lost men who had peered into a glass of brown liquid and breathed a deep sigh of satisfaction, something the effete wine drinker never gets. *We* swirl and frown and sniff and worry, where they smell and sip; no wine drinker has ever taken a deep draught of his glass and said, 'Ah! What happened to the pain?'

I couldn't shave because of the rash, so I even had the right two-day growth to go with the rum. But the pain rose right again around midnight, and I had had enough experience to know that drinking alcohol late at night would keep me up for the rest of it. What to do then? Now, I had just come off of eight weeks with a musical comedy in New Haven – which was probably the stress that had caused the shingles. For complicated reasons, we changed leading men three times in three weeks, and though this is standard for musical theatre – Larry Gelbart once said that all he wished for Hitler was to be out of town with a musical – it was still . . . stressful.

A friend in the company had given me, partly as a joke, and partly as an act of kindness, a joint of what I believed was marijuana. I knew it was a joint because I recognized it from my high school days. 'This will help you get through the night,' he had said, but I hadn't smoked it – my own nights being more easily got through by fantasizing about being comforted by the leading lady. But I had brought it back, in some alarm, from the theatre, and there it was.

My curiosity was piqued because not long before that, my twenty-something son and I had been in Colorado together on a holiday and we had wandered into – I suppose you could put inverted commas around that 'wandered' – one of the cannabis dispensaries that ornament that state. It was one of the few times in my life when a basic principle of anthropology, oft cited but rarely bone-true, came alive. I suddenly sensed the arbitrariness of cultural lines and values. Here was something, cannabis, that, in my world, was musty, illegal and sordid – and here it was made open, shiny and appealing. The intoxicants had no meaning apart from the way we chose to organize them. One of the most interesting people I have ever met is the great Chicago sociologist Howie Becker. It was Becker's insight, back in the 1940s when he studied jazz musicians, that smoking weed was like any other kind of human activity – it had to be taught as a social ritual, and the social ritual was as much part of the effect as the drug itself. It takes a village to smoke a reefer. In high school, the Beckerian social scene demanded that we all try cannabis – but it left me feeling fuzzier than elated, and it had been decades and decades since I'd had any.

Late at night, I lit the New Haven cigarette and suddenly I got it. Ease, relaxation, a kind of pacific, unearned silliness very different from the sharper edged ecstatic goad of alcohol. I was getting the right feeling because I was at last in the right scene – the silent company of late night shingles sufferers.

The trouble came the next morning, when my seventeen-year-old daughter smelled the aroma in my study.

'Dad!' she said, first sniffing ominously, then widely alarmed. 'Tell me the truth. Have you been smoking marijuana?'

'It's for the shingles, baby,' I said apologetically.

'Dad, explain it as you will, that's a gateway drug,' she told me firmly, years of progressive school drug education warnings – all of which I of course have paid for – instantly slipping from her lips. 'There's a notable relationship between smoking cannabis and lowered performance in mental tasks.' She is a hyper-bright ambitious teenager who, in the way of contemporary American life, cannot let a moment of lowered performance slip between her and a desirable university.

'I'm just experimenting,' I said weakly.

She snorted. 'Dad, I'm not a cop, and I won't play one. I'll just say that today's experiment becomes tomorrow's lifestyle,' she added darkly, and left my room.

The trouble, of course, is that a middle-aged intellectual with no obvious source for cannabis, and a prohibitionist teenage daughter watching him like a hawk, has difficulty getting more. What to do now? I couldn't very well march into Washington Square and say, 'Hey – I'm buying.' Apart from the reality that my features are not entirely unknown to the public – well, that part of it that watches educational television very late at night – there was the reality that it was clearly a barter arrangement. If my – what to call him? – my *connection* said twenty-five dollars, could I really offer ten?

I put out a cagey all-points bulletin to my friends, and one of them, the chairman of a literary department I teach at from time to time, said, 'Are you on Whatsapp?' Over the self-obliterating texts – the last man in the world I would imagine doing anything but sniffing at a glass of '86 Margaux or vintage port – he put me in touch with an impeccable medical-minded bicycle delivery service. The cannabis came – but raw and unrolled, and so I had to go on YouTube to search for videos showing you how to turn raw cannabis into a smokable joint. You would be amazed to find out how many videos there are on YouTube gently instructing you on how to do this. Howie Becker would be proud. We are all the reefer village now.

So, for a week I sat with my four-day growth of beard and oscillated between sipping Barbados rum on the rocks and, later, pulling gratefully on a joint. (The joint got smaller. It was, I realized, a roach!)

'Dad is playing the shingles card again.' My daughter sighed. Here is the truth. I have never been so happy in my life.

Bearded, drunk, stoned – for the first time in my life, ambition and planning were not at the engine room of the everyday. The ship was just floating, drifting, and I was drifting with it. The discomfort rose as the night went on – an eerie, burning tickle – and then I had some rum. It rose worse as midnight approached and I lit up. Life seemed very simple.

Aghast, you are waiting for any moral to be attached to this tale of unshaven debauchery, and there are two I would like to draw. First, intoxicants of all kinds are part of the human condition, and over-use of intoxicants a permanent response to human pain. Wise drug policy accepts their existence and does what it can to teach through social work and nonpunitive help, with the understanding that addictive personalities exist and that addiction will happen. Prohibition and the police are the worst policy imaginable.

The deeper undeniable existential truth, as the shingles subside – as I have explained to my daughter, at crucial moments they rise again, necessitating another medicinal round – is that I realized how much my own hyper-disciplined, overly ambitious, driven life had taken from me. There is much to be said for lotus–land, a sound argument to be made to stop and drift, a reason for the islands. The long history of humanity is a struggle between the urge to work and strive and build . . . and the urge to just give up. And there is far more to be said on the side of just giving up than the people who want you working all the time would like for you to know. They told the slaves building the pyramids to stop sniffing the blue lotos flowers and build, build for the greater glory of Egypt. And the slaves said, 'Why?' For the moment, I am with the lotos-eaters. There is something to be said for nothing; an argument to be made for an end to argument, a first principle of pleasure to be not-too-passionately pursued. Oblivion is not a bad destination to allow your boat to drift towards. The day will come when my daughter will learn this, too.

Meanwhile if on the New York streets you see a middle-aged man with a castaway's beard and an inexplicable smile on his face, you will know that the shingles are back – and that I am playing their card. Just don't approach me empty handed.

Raising the Bar
13 August 2017

My son Luke, who is in his very early twenties, is working as a bartender in Baltimore this summer. I am delighted with this professional adventure, though my wife, his mother, is not, or not completely. When we were on holiday at the literary festival in Capri, I mentioned, as a form of solidarity with the bartender in a bar at the hotel we were staying at, that our son was a bartender, too.

'No, he isn't,' my wife interjected. 'He's a philosophy student and a musician, working as a bartender.' I thought this was unkind to the Caprese bartender – who was doubtless a philosopher and a musician too, working for the summer as a bartender. It's true that our son's major in college had been in music and philosophy, not bartending, but there he was, working as a bartender. I'm confident that if philosophy and music continue to call on him as much in the future as they have in the past, he will answer their call – as he has, I should add at once, avidly answered the call of the girl he followed south to Baltimore, explaining why it is in that mixed-up town that he is tending bar.

He is not actually, his ambitious younger sister reminds me, a fully fledged bartender – he is a bar*back*, which, to translate it into the terms of my academic family, makes him a sort of assistant professor of bartending, waiting for tenure to become a full barman. He fetches basil for the basil mojitos and ice for the gin and tonics, made with artisanal gin and local tonic. He tells me that he was never before aware that there are so many kinds of ice.

I am delighted by this on his account, because my sense of life is that we are largely made and forged by the jobs we hold in our early twenties. I had my own adventures as, among other things, a spectacularly bad library clerk, a catch-as-catch-can lunchtime museum lecturer, and as a 'grooming' editor at a then mostly gay men's magazine, along with several other jobs equally undistinguished and far from what I had officially prepared for. They left a mark on me and I don't mean merely that I learned, as my son has of ice, that there are many kinds of moisturizer. They taught me one essential lesson in life, which is that it often helps to get the job first and then figure out how to do it afterwards. Such jobs teach us far more than the jobs we are trained to do. They make us flexible and vigilant, and those things, as Auden says somewhere, are the adjectives of happiness.

Parenting, of course, is the ultimate, the highest example, of the job we get first and then figure out how to do afterwards. The baby arrives full-born and full-flown and then we start the process of learning how to parent it. And so I won't lie, and pretend that I do not worry about my son's spending the rest of his *life* as a bartender in Baltimore. The truth is that, like every parent, I want my kids to be in equal parts happy in the work they do and also doing work that seems to them – and yes, to me, too – meaningful, productive. In this way, parenting is an adventure that never ends or really alters. The demands it makes on our minds remain remarkably consistent even as the landscape of decision changes.

I should add at once to this part of the story that my sister, Alison, a child psychologist, strongly frowns at the use of 'parent' as a verb, insisting that it is a neologism and a false friend – we don't husband or wife, she says, we love and marry, and so with children: we can't parent them, we can only be there as they grow up. Her favourite metaphor is that we must garden them watchfully rather than attempt to carpenter them purposefully. The garden grows; and the made child suffers.

I buy this, and buy it mostly – with the one additional proviso, perhaps shaped by my own work and subjects, that raising children really is artful more than artisanal: more like writing or painting even than gardening, and nothing at all like following a

86

rule book. By that I mean that it involves the constant, vigilant reconciliation of opposing forces into a satisfactory whole – and the mistake we make is to try and turn it from a work of art-making into a set of laws.

Where people get it wrong, I think, is in accepting that raising children is an art, but then not accepting fully what art is. Art is not a skill or a set of rules, it's simply an acceptance of the ineradicable doubleness of human forces. Matisse, to name a master here, drew with *faux-naïf* simplicity and coloured with ravishing sophistication: if he had been all simplicity or all sophistication he would not have been Matisse. Art – it is, by the way, one of the things I make thematic in my new book – is always different from the artisanal, inasmuch as a work of craft, like a pet, is made for one purpose, while a work of art, like a growing child, must be readied for many. Craft objects are meant to play only one role in the world; if they sometimes play more, it is because of a discerning eye that emancipates them from their original purpose. 'That weather vane is beautiful enough for a museum,' we say. Art objects are meant to play many roles: if they play fewer, it is because of a limited eye that imprisons them from possibility.

So, with raising children – too much praise? Too little? For what behaviour? – it's all about getting a set of contradictory principles into the right kind of tension and accepting that their lives, like ours, are ineradicably double. You have to be hands-off, smiling, and full of instant perspective; you have to be engaged, unsparing in honesty, and devoted to the moment. Do we praise our kids and thus risk making them complacent and unable to be ambitious? Or feeling too fulfilled and unready for the necessary role that striving, trying, is pretty much what life demands? Woody Allen's famous line that life is 85 per cent showing up means just that: striving to do a job is mostly doing it. It is astonishing how many obstacles we put in the way of just showing up – and one of them is thinking that we don't need to, since we're terrific already.

Do we tell them they're uniquely wonderful (which is always true, at one level or another) or tell them that they are about the same degree of uniquely wonderful as everyone else (which is always true too)? Do we push them to do things they don't want to – or do we accept that they will find their own snaking path to happiness (which, to the degree that we ever found happiness, was exactly what we had to do)? Push or pause? Praise or not? Tell them to go forth and grab at the glittering prizes? Or share the truth that most of the prizes that glitter most turn out to be gilded and hardly worth having? Teach them Sonny Rollins's lesson before he goes on stage: Don't think you're not on trial for your life every time you pick up your horn, because you are – or Bruce Springsteen's before he does: that tonight is the most important night of your life, and that, hey, it's only rock 'n' roll.

The answer, of course, is both at once, all of the above, it all depends. Raising children is an art, not a science or a craft, and like all art it involves accepting tensions and contractions in characters and circumstances, made poignant or powerful, and shown to best effect to the world. They are the artists of their own lives but we can, we must, teach them the art of living: to accept that the contradictions and countercurrents that run through all existence, like those that run through great art, are the vital thing that makes it matter. Tend bar and do it philosophically! Make mojitos musically! Be both at once, and neither entirely, and a little bit of everything all the time. Scott Fitzgerald wrote once – it is one of my favourite quotations, and I am fond of quotations – that self-aware, but not self-conscious, inner tension is the source of all charm. It's true. And, one might add, the source of all good writing, too.

My wife merely wants him home from Baltimore. I miss him, too, and hope that, on his homecoming, he will mix a fine drink for his father, having spent his summer learning how.

Fictional Mysteries

On Bees and Being

3 June 2012

Over the past few weeks in America, arguments about gender and sex and identity have been buzzing all around us. Gay marriage is now not just a liberal principle but a liberal piety – and one knows a piety from a principle because even those who oppose it have to pretend to honour its core point.

No one is any longer allowed to say that they do not think that homosexuals should be allowed to decide to live together, even if Mitt Romney believes that they should not be allowed to rent tuxedos and pay for a caterer when they do.

An odd light, as our grandfathers would have written, got thrown on the issue the other day when my seventeen-year-old son was working his way through the text of Shakespeare's *Henry V*, with an eye to a student production.

Our children – I should explain – go to a wonderful but

slightly pixilated progressive school in New York, whose core pieties rest both on the necessities of ethnic and sexual diversity in all things and on the practices of the Elizabethan theatre. The kids are taught that all prejudice of any kind is always wrong; but that bed tricks and iambic pentameter are inherently virtuous.

Their ambitious theatre programme produces not merely *A Midsummer Night's Dream* and *The Tempest* but a full-dress four-hour production of Ben Jonson's *Volpone*. There are always four performances – two on Friday, one each for Saturday, and Sunday – and so four hours of Ben Jonson means, for a parent whose own core piety is to never, ever miss a child's performance, a total of sixteen hours struggling with the London slang of 1600. I suppose we also know a piety from a principle because we are prepared to pay a very high price to maintain it. In any case, there was *Henry V* on the table, and we arrived at Canterbury's famous speech on how the well regulated kingdom is like a beehive. You know the one:

> *They have a king and officers of sorts,*
> *Where some, like magistrates, correct at home,*
> *Others, like merchants, venture trade abroad,*
> *Others, like soldiers, armèd in their stings,*
> *Make boot upon the summer's velvet buds,*
> *Which pillage they with merry march bring home*
> *To the tent-royal of their emperor;*
> *Who, busied in his majesty, surveys*
> *The singing masons building roofs of gold . . .*

And so on.

The beauty of the verse could not conceal to the kids a weird absence. How could Shakespeare know that much about the division of bee-labour, the drones and the workers and the rest, and not know that the big bee in the centre was – a girl bee? Why make the top bee a king, and emperor? The standard academic piety, which I offered immediately, is to say that Shakespeare, living in a strict patriarchal society, made his beehive one too – but this sounded too stupid to be credible, especially since the, well, 'honey-tongued' Shakespeare presumably knew that one of the smartest pieties of any era was always to flatter the boss. When the top bee in his own hive was a queen, why not say so?

I decided to take advice, and emailed the great Shakespeare scholar Stephen Greenblatt asking for illumination – and he wrote back to say that he didn't know the answer, but so far as he knew lots of seventeenth-century poets make the same error. Greenblatt suggested checking with Virgil's *Georgics*, and sure enough, there, too, the queen bee is transgendered, dressed up as a king bee – this despite some lovely stuff about how the bee-moms take care of the bee-kids. A little more digging in the library and online – Google houses our own singing masons, building roofs of information under which we crouch, and steal some nectar – and I found out the bee sex confusion goes back at least to Aristotle, and was only solved in the late seventeenth century, when Swammerdam found that the king was, so to speak, cross-dressing and really had ovaries.

Swammerdam! One of those great Northern European names, like Erasmus of Rotterdam, that carries its credibility within its consonants. Soon I was deep, if briefly, in Swammerdamania. This guy was a seventeenth-century Dutch biologist who discovered that all the stages of insect life were part of one thing, and that the big bee had ovaries. A master microscopist, he worked every day from six in the morning till noon, hatless in the brightest sun he could find to illuminate his work.

And yet the story didn't end there. A reference in an eighteenth-century work on Swammerdam led, surprisingly, still farther back – and I then discovered that an English bee-keeper, exactly contemporary with Shakespeare, named Charles Butler, first affirmed, and in 1609, that the big bee was a girl, and wrote a book about beekeeping called nothing less than *Feminine Monarchy* to celebrate it. (It came of course, a little late for him to win brownie points with the Queen for doing it.)

Butler was an interesting and practical-minded character. A clergyman, and master at the Holy Ghost School in Basingstoke, he wrote a theological defence of marriage between first cousins, and then engaged his daughter to his nephew. Only other bee-keepers seem to pay a lot of attention to Butler. But it was clear that, far from being banished by patriarchal authority, the idea that the big bee was a babe was actually right out there, if you had asked someone like Butler who actually hung around with bees. The idea was not censored or disallowed, just pushed to the periphery of practical knowledge rather than being part of the core of official piety.

I see that I am becoming as long-winded on the bee question as Canterbury, and I shall move rapidly towards my own point. It is this: it is one of the core pieties of contemporary pedantry that thought proceeds in fortresses as ordered and locked as a beehive once seemed to be. We retreat into our world-view or framework or mentality and leave it only at peril or under pressure.

But in truth, the beehive of the human mind may have order at its core, but it has lots of loose and buzzy action around its entrances and exits, and it is that action that is the sign of life. Shakespeare thought that big bees were boys; but if he had bumped into Butler on one of his trips home to Stratford and the countryside, and had heard the schoolmaster say, 'Liked that Henry play, Will, and the nice beehive bit. By the way, the big bee is actually a girl,' Shakespeare wouldn't have been shocked, or had his world-view overthrown. He would have just said, 'Huh, really? You think? OK. If I ever do another bee poem, I'll adjust.'

The sticky honey of uncertainty, the buzz around the bee-hive's entrance – these are the signs of minds at work. When our children ask us, 'What's consciousness?' or 'What's life?' or simply, 'Why are some people born that way?' – all questions which in truth we don't have an answer for yet – we don't say, as perhaps we should, 'No one knows! Go find out.' We shrug and say, 'It's, um, sort of like . . .' one way or the other. What we do not know, we sketch rapidly in the air, and then shrug.

One moral of the tale of the bees is, of course, always to trust the Butlers rather than the Aristotles of the world. Trust the man who sees the bees instead of the old Greek philosopher who just had opinions about them. But it is also, surely, that the fortress theory of knowledge is always false. No age thinks monolithically, and no great mind begins in absolute clarity. Charles Darwin himself, skipping ahead centuries, had no idea how inheritance happened, but he didn't say, 'I have no idea how this happens!' Instead, he said, 'Well, it may be kind of like a blend of stuff in the parents or maybe it's like a blend plus stuff the parents have done. Anyway, as I was saying, natural selection works like this . . .'

Darwin made a fortress out of fog, and was content to do his work within it. Our mental life is more like the London of Holmes and Watson: we wander in the fog, making our way through it. Occasionally a clue or two helps solve the mystery within the fog, and then we walk back home happily in the pea soup. The fog is our habitat; the fog is our home.

As I brooded these long and buzzing thoughts, my wife, queen bee of our home, thought more fertilely. She knew that the real issue was not 'Who was the bee?' but 'Who would play the King?' She had a terrible intimation that these pious schoolmasters would do as they had done before with Prospero and Mercutio – that is, cast a girl in the key role of King Harry.

Our seventeen-year-old would once again be merely one of the singing masons, or civil citizens or even a poor mechanic porter. I wonder now if Shakespeare, when he wrote of hives and pointed towards kingdoms, was not, like Butler, really writing about the hive most near at hand. In other words, about the theatre, where everyone plays a part, and, drone or queen, you can't complain about the role you're given. There may be many mixed minds in an age but there are no small parts in well-conducted hives.

BEATLES TIME

15 June 2012

Over there this summer you are celebrating, as all of us over here know, a decades-old anniversary of uncanny auspiciousness: the jubilee of an institution that has lasted far longer than many thought possible, transcending its native place in Britain to become a source of constant, almost unbroken reassurance to the entire world. I'm referring of course to the truth that in a very few weeks we will celebrate the fiftieth anniversary of the first concert, and first photograph, of the four Beatles. I'm looking at the picture now. It shows the Beatles, as they would remain, together: John, Paul, George and now at last Ringo, in place at the drums, taken in that afternoon before one of their first public appearances on 22 August 1962.

And now I am looking at another photograph that shows the four in the very last photograph that would ever be taken of them – from 22 August 1969, exactly seven years later to the day, and, from the looks of the light, perhaps the hour. There is something eerie, fated, cosmic about The Beatles – those seven quick years of fame and then decades of aftershock. They appear in public as a unit on 22 August and disappear as a unit, Mary Poppins-like, exactly seven years later. Or take their beautiful song 'Eleanor Rigby'. Though Paul McCartney can recall in minute detail how he made the name up in 1966, it turns out that in St Peter's, Woolton's parish church cemetery, just a few yards from where Paul first met John on 6 July 1957, there is a gravestone, humble but clearly marked, for one Eleanor Rigby. Paul must have made an unconscious mental photograph on that fateful day and kept it with him through the decade. Even things that they did in a pettish rush become emblematic: they took a surly walk across Abbey Road because they were too exhausted to go where they had meant to go for the album cover, and now every American tourist in London walks the same crossing, and invests their bad-tempered stride with charm and purposeful-ness and point. The Beatles remain. It is no accident that the Queen's Jubilee, that other one, ended with Macca singing four Beatles songs. It wasn't just nice; it was only fitting (though it's a shame Ringo wasn't there to do the drumming).

There's a popular video my kids like called 'Stuff People Never Say'. Well, they don't say 'stuff', and one of the things the video insists that people never say now is 'I don't like The Beatles'.

Everyone liked them then, and everyone likes them now. My own children fight with me about The Rolling Stones and are baffled by the Spinal Tappishness of Led Zeppelin (why do they scream in American voices?). But The Beatles are for them as uncontroversial as the moon. Just there, shining on.

This is strange. Had the same thing been true for our generation – that the pop music that superintended our lives dated from before World War One – it would have been more than strange: bizarre. Why have they lasted? The reason we usually give is that they reflected their time, were a mirror of a decade, the Sixties, that we still long for. But the longer that I have listened to them, and the more that their time recedes into history, the more vital they sound. I wonder, even, if truly historic pop figures don't always have a backwards relation to their time. Charlie Chaplin, one of the few artists to have a comparable allure, was at work after World War One, the era of the automobile and the machine gun, one of the most disruptive moments in human history. But Chaplin's work, rooted in Victorian theatre and the Dickensian novel, evokes the values of the time before. The city in *City Lights* and *The Kid* is the London of 1890, not the New York of 1920. His art, energetic on the surface, was elegiac beneath.

I think this is true of The Beatles, too. The Beatles were not provocateurs, though often mystics, and their great subject was childhood gone by, and what to make of the austere, rationed, but in many ways ordered and secure English world that they had grown up in, and that was now passing before their eyes, in part because of the doors they had opened. Their most enduring work, the single 'Strawberry Fields'/'Penny Lane', tells on one side of the dream memory of a Liverpool garden where a lonely alienated boy could find solace, and on the other side of a Liverpool street where a bright, sociable boy could see the world. Remembered sounds – of brass bands and Twenties rinky-tink – ornament their music, and children's books, the *Alice* books particularly, fill their lyrics. Sexual intercourse may have begun, as Philip Larkin says, with their first LP, but their subsequent ones rarely had too much intercourse with sex. Their greatest hit singles, 'She Loves You' and 'Hey Jude', are songs of avuncular counsel, wise advice given by one friend to another who has got in over his head in a love affair. Peter Sellers did a hilarious piece as a middle-aged Irishman in a pub, using the words of 'She Loves You' as natural dialogue passed over the pub table. 'You know it's up to you. Apologize to her.' It worked, not because it was so incongruous, but because it sounded so congruous, so sensible.

The Beatles' music endures above all because we sense in it the power of the collaboration of opposites. John had reach. He instinctively understood that what separates an artist from an entertainer is that an artist seeks to astonish, even shock, his audience. Paul had grasp, above all, of the materials of music, and knew intuitively that astonishing art that fails to entertain is mere avant-gardism. We see the difference when they were wrenched apart: Paul still had a hundred wonderful melodies and only sporadic artistic ambition, while John still had lots of artistic ambition but only a sporadic handful of melodies. But in those seven years, when John's reach met Paul's grasp, we all climbed Everest. (Not an arbitrary choice by the way: 'Everest' was to be the title of their last album, and the place they had meant to go before they ended up going outside to Abbey Road instead.)

The fatefulness of their climb haunts many million others. I had moved with the girl who was to become my wife to New York City in the late fall of 1980, and it was with joy that we saw a birthday greeting from Yoko to John and Sean fill the sky just after we got there. That John was back at work in the studio, after five years away, as we soon learned he was, seemed a good omen for us. We were together in our tiny new home late at night when he was killed, just across the park. We might have heard the shots.

I don't think I've ever quite recovered from that night. My essential faith in the benevolence of the universe was shattered. Some compact that, at twenty, I thought the world had made with me – that things turned out well, that you ended up in New York with a girl you were in love with and The Beatles across the park – seemed betrayed. Or rather, I learned in a rush that night the adult truth, which is that the world makes no compacts with you at all, and that the most you can hope is to negotiate a short-term treaty with it, an armistice, which the world, like a half-mad monarch, will then break, just as it likes.

The Beatles' gift was for harmony, and their vision was above all of harmony. And harmony, voices blending together in song, is still our strongest symbol of a good place yet to come. In the world of symbol and myth that music can't help but create, melody lies behind us, and calls us, as John's beautiful song 'Julia' does, to our memory of a better past, or what we want to think was one. Harmony as symbolic form always lies ahead, as the realized-here herald of a better world where all opposites will sing together as one. That's why even Bach and Handel ended their greatest works with a chorale – to cheer us on to a world we might get to by hearing a chorus that sounds like it's already got there.

Art makes us alive and aware, and sometimes afraid, but it rarely makes us glad. Fifty years on, The Beatles live because they still give us that most amazing of feelings: the apprehension of a happiness that we can hold, like a hand.

What to Do with a Bad Review
22 June 2012

Every morning when I turn to the *Guardian* or *Daily Telegraph* website, I seem to encounter one writer or another offering his or her view of what the modern crisis is like, and how to make it less like a crisis. We authors, ma'am – to use the phrase that Disraeli would use with Queen Victoria, who had written a sort of book once – we authors do like to talk gravely about the future of mankind and the novel and the power of the word. But in truth, there are only two subjects that we authors, in my experience, actually talk about in private with any real zing from the heart. One is the size of our – or their – advances. The other, what to do about your – OK, our – bad review.

And, since those bad reviews stand in the way of those bigger sales, the two questions really collapse into one: What do you do when people who shouldn't be allowed to offer their opinion of cheap cheese say that they don't like your book, and do so in print? 'Ignore it,' I hear you cry, as one body, and that indeed is what the writer's spouse and partner and children (if they know) and agent (if he cares) and editors all say, too. Ignore it. Claim the moral high ground. So you've got a stinker in the *New York Times* – or the London one, for that matter. Who cares? No one reads them anyway, and anyone who does read them could see at a glance that jealousy and envy and sheer stupid malice have done their usual work.

And it's all true, or true enough. Jealousy and envy are big forces in life. It's an odd thing that in every Disney or Pixar cartoon, the plucky hero or heroine is bedevilled by an enemy whose sole motive, often as not, is envy – Ursula in *The Little Mermaid* or Hades in *Hercules*. But we fail to warn our children about envy's power until they're out in the world.

So the writer tries. He – we – claim the moral high ground. We walk around for a day or two, looking down pityingly on the poor benighted reviewer, a small smile of amusement at his expense playing around the corners of our mouths. But the trouble with claiming the moral high ground is that a writer who has just claimed the moral high ground doesn't look any different from a writer who is just standing there doing nothing. To the untutored eye, an impervious author looks just the same as an infuriated one.

The only other traditional response is the letter to the

offending publication, written late at night. The late-night letter to the reviewer, or the place the review appeared, is by far the most impassioned literary genre that exists, but no one except the writer, or very occasionally the writer's spouse, gets to read or hear it.

The late-night letter is always composed in three drafts. The first, or 2 a.m. draft, is written in a tone of light-hearted, stinging, supercilious irony: 'Much though I enjoyed Mr X's lively cabaret turn, of which my book was the ostensible subject, I did think that I might correct a few of the more egregious errors he made in the course of his caperings . . .' The next, 3 a.m. version revises itself into a tone of sneering, corrective truth-telling: 'The egregious errors that fill Mr X's review of my book are too many to enumerate, but perhaps your readers might like to know the three most, er, egregious . . .' And the last, or 4 a.m. version is downright enraged: 'The difference between criticism and character assassination having long ago vanished from your pages . . .' And so on.

The problem is that this last is the only version that the spouse gets to hear, since it is the one whose composition makes even the thought of sleep at last impossible, and that one, he or she knows, as soon as they've heard it, is really, *really* not worth sending. Had they heard the earlier, wittier ones, their view might be different, but you would never wake her, or him, up to recite the earlier versions. She'd kill you if you did – at least my wife would. Sleep is her idea of a good review of the day just passed.

Occasionally, the spouse is away, though, and that letter gets sent. Now, here is the truly interesting thing: the public, even the writer's closest friends, always secretly side with the reviewer against the letter-writing author. The author writing that letter may be a man or woman of exquisite taste and immense erudition, of literary skill and real moral authority. The reviewer may be, very often is, a cheap hack who specializes in spewing out snark for glossy magazines. But the world will chortle and back-slap the book reviewer, at least in spirit, and snigger and point at the poor author who has responded.

Why should this be? It is, I think, that no one really looks to book reviews, or theatre reviews or art reviews or movie reviews, or any reviews, really, for a fair or accurate appraisal of a work of art. We see them as a gladiatorial contest, or even a kind of bullfight – the reviewer in his suit of lights goading the poor authorial bull – and we feel as indignant at the author stopping the contest to protest the unfairness of the thing, as we would if the bull stopped the fight in order to write an indignant letter to a Spanish newspaper.

This was the sad state where things stood until the other evening, when I had a long talk with a friend of mine, another author, who had stumbled on an entirely new and ingenious way of levelling the playing field. He had tried the Big Ignore, and he had brooded on the Bad Letter, and he said he now has a new approach.

He now waits exactly four months – less would be too obvious, more too many – until his enemy, Mr or Ms X, writes something else, anything else. He then writes a warm letter, or email, of congratulation to him or her. Not anything too ornate or obsequious. Just: 'Hey X, Really liked your piece on David Foster Wallace and the ambiguities of irony. Fine job on an important subject, Hope you're well, Y.' I am in awe of the number of beautiful things this simple act accomplishes. First, it shows to the one person who most needs to be shown it that the author has indeed claimed the moral high ground after the nasty review. The magnanimity, the serenity, the imperturbable good humour of Y, the author, is forced into the face of the one person on earth who most needs to be shown it.

Next, and this is the subtle thing, maybe Mr X, the reviewer, though grateful for the appreciation (he's an author, too, after all), can't help but suspect, just a little, in some paranoid corner of his heart (it has many paranoid corners: he's an author), that he is being 'got at' in some way. Is Y, he wonders, just for a panicky half-second, actually mocking him? No, it can't be that . . . His piece on David Foster Wallace, was, after all, so great a piece that everyone would have to recognize it, even those he had wounded.

But for a fine, thrilling moment, the purpose of that first supercilious and unsent letter – to make the reviewer feel, not hated, but condescended to, dismissed – has been achieved. And finally, my friend tells me, the warm four-month-later letter invariably produces an apology for the bad review. 'Hey, I hope you didn't take what I wrote in the wrong way . . .'

Now, why should this be so? It is because while all bad reviews, to a first approximation, are accurate, as authors secretly know, all bad reviews are also, to a first approximation, *un*true, and the reviewer knows that, too. A writer is not some student who performs well or ill on an exam. A writer – any real writer anyway – is a person on the page, whole, and the books he or she writes are the whole of him or her. Our response to them is personal, and you can't really review a person: you can only respond to one.

I believe that from now on, every artist and every author should embrace my friend's tactic and make it strategic. Bombard your bad reviewers with advice, admiration and counsel, encumber them with your affection, afflict them with your overbounding warmth. Guilt and remorse will pour from them as surely as if they were ripe grapes that had been stomped on by a willing peasant.

Let the word go out from this day forth from author to reviewer: write that bad review, and I will recommend you to my friends, crash cocktail parties given for someone else to make a toast in your honour, until at last you develop a haunted look in your eyes, fearing my embrace. Write that bad review, and you shall have me for your lifelong friend. Ask yourself: is it worth it?

TURKISH NOTIONS

24 March 2013

Lately I've been thinking a lot about the Turk. That sounds, I know, like a very nineteenth-century remark. 'Have you been thinking about the Turk?' one bearded British statesman might have asked another in the 1860s, with an eye to the Sublime Porte and Russian designs on it, and all the rest.

No, the Turk I have in mind is both older and newer than that: I mean the famous eighteenth-century chess-playing automaton, recently and brilliantly reconstructed in California. And the reason I have been thinking about it is that – well, there are several reasons, one folded into the next, beginning with the Candidates Tournament for the World Chess Championship, being held in London this week, and enclosing, at the end, my own eighteen-year-old son's departure for college. If you haven't heard of it before, I should explain what the Turk is, or was. There's a very good book by Tom Standage all about it.

'The Turk' first appeared in Vienna in 1770 as a chess-playing machine – a mechanical figure of a bearded man dressed in Turkish clothing, seated above a cabinet with a chessboard on top. The operator, a man named Johann Maelzel, would assemble a paying audience, open the doors of the lower cabinet and show an impressively whirring clockwork mechanism that filled the inner compartments beneath the seated figure. Then he would close the cabinet, and invite a challenger to play chess. The automaton – the robot, as we would say now – would gaze at the opponent's move, ponder, then raise its mechanical arm and make a stiff but certain move of its own. Before it was destroyed by fire in New York in the 1850s, it played games with everyone from Benjamin Franklin to, by legend at least, Napoleon Bonaparte. Artificial intelligence, the eighteenth century thought, had arrived, wearing a fez and ticking away like Captain Hook's crocodile.

I should rush to say that, of course, the thing was a fraud, or rather, a trick – a clever magician's illusion. A sliding sled on well-lubricated castors had been fitted inside the lower cabinet and the only real ingenuity was that this let a hidden chess player glide easily, and silently, into a prone position inside. There was just a lot more room to hide in the cabinet than all that clockwork machinery suggested.

Now, the Turk fascinates me for several reasons. First,

because it displays an odd, haunting hole in human reasoning. Common sense should have told the people who watched and challenged it that for the Turk to have really been a chess-playing machine, it would have had to have been the latest in a long sequence of such machines. For there to be a mechanical Turk who played chess, there would have had to have been, ten years before, a mechanical Greek who played draughts. It's true that the late eighteenth century was a great age of automatons, machines that could make programmed looms weave and mechanical birds sing – although always the same song, or tapestry, over and over. But the deeper truth that chess-playing was an entirely different kind of creative activity seemed as obscure to them as it seems obvious to us now.

But in large part, I think people were fooled because they were looking, as we always seem to do, for the beautiful and elegant solution to a problem, even when the cynical and ugly one is right. The great-grandfather of computer science, Charles Babbage, saw the Turk, and though he realized that it was probably a magic trick, he also asked himself what exactly would be required to produce a beautiful solution. What kind of machine would you need to build if you could build a machine to play chess? And his 'difference engine' – the first computer – rose in part from his desire to believe that there was a beautiful solution to the problem, even if the one before him was not it.

We always want, not just the right solution to a mystery; we want a beautiful solution. And when we meet a mysterious thing, we are always inclined to believe that it must therefore conceal an inner beauty. When we see an impregnable tower, we are immediately sure that there must be a princess inside. Doubtless there are many things that seem obscure to us – the origins of the universe, the nature of consciousness, the possibility of time travel – that will seem obvious in the future. But the solutions to their obscurity, too, will undoubtedly be clunky and ugly and more ingenious than sublime. The solution to the problem of consciousness will involve, so to speak, sliding sleds and hidden chess players. But there is another aspect of the thing that haunts me, too. Though some sought a beautiful solution when a cynical one was called for, plenty of people – Edgar Allan Poe, for instance – realized that the Turk had to be, must be, a cabinet with a chess player inside.

What seems to have stumped these people was not the ugliness of the solution, but the singularity of the implied chess player. Where would you find a midget chess genius that could fit? they wondered. Or could the operator be using fiendishly well-trained children? Even if you accepted the idea of an adult player, who could it be, this hidden inscrutable master?

It turns out that the chess players who operated the Turk from inside were just chess players, an ever-changing sequence of strong but not star players, who needed the work badly enough to be willing to spend a week or a month inside its smoky innards. Maelzel picked up chess players on the run, wherever he happened to be, as Chuck Berry used to hire back-up bands on the road. So the inventor's real genius was not to build a chess-playing machine. It was to be the first to notice that, in the modern world, there is more mastery available than you might think; that exceptional talent is usually available, and will often work cheap.

And there lies what I think of now as the asymmetry of mastery – the mystery of mastery, a truth that is for some reason extremely hard for us to grasp. We overrate masters and underrate mastery. That simplest solution was the hardest, partly because they underestimated the space inside the cabinet, but also because they overestimated just how good the chess player had to be. We always overestimate the space between the uniquely good and the very good. That inept footballer we whistle at in despair is a better football player than we have ever seen or ever will meet. The few people who do grasp that though there are only a few absolute masters, there are many, many masters right below them, looking for work, tend, like Maelzel, to profit greatly from it. The greatest managers in any sport are those who know you can stand down the talent, and find more to fill the bench. It is the manager who is willing to bench Beckham, rather than he who worships his bend, who tends to have the most sporting success. And what of the handful of true, undisputed top masters? What makes the unique virtuoso unique is, in truth, rarely virtuosity as we have defined it, but instead some strange idiosyncratic vibration of his or her own.

Bob Dylan started off as a bad performer, and then spent ten thousand hours practising. But he did not become a better performer. He became Bob Dylan. And it should be said that those who possess ultimate mastery, the great born masters, as Bobby Fischer and Michael Jackson conspire to remind us, have hollow lives of surpassing unhappiness, as if the needed space for a soul was replaced by whirring clockwork.

Perhaps our children sense this truth as they struggle to master things. My own son, who was once a decent chess player, now plays guitar, and very well indeed. Not long ago he went to a party with me where a jazz combo had been dressed by the party-givers in ridiculous 1920s-style clothing. He pointed to a guitarist up there in his ludicrous spats and Gatsby hat, forced for money to clock ticky-tacky chords, and said, 'Dad, that man is a much better guitar player than anyone I have ever played with.'

That is the sad mystery of mastery, the one that we struggle to explain to our kids. It is very hard to do a difficult thing, it is very important to learn to do a difficult thing, and once you have learned to do it, you will always discover that there is someone else who does it better. The only consolation is that, often as not, those who do it best of all, are, one way or another, quite hollow inside. This seems like sage, if sober, wisdom to expect our children to master.

Science, Magic and Madness

12 April 2013

When you write for a living, over time you learn that certain subjects will get set responses. You're resigned to getting the responses before you write the story. If you write something about Shakespeare, you will get many letters and emails from what we call the cracked (and I think you call the barking), explaining that Shakespeare didn't write the plays that everyone who was alive when he was said he had.

If you write something about the scandal of American prisons, you will be sent letters, many heartbreaking, from those wrongly imprisoned – and you will also get many letters from those who you're pretty sure couldn't possibly be more rightfully imprisoned. Sorting out what to say to each kind is a big job. (My wife has a simple rule: Be nice to the ones who are going to be getting out.)

The oddest response, though, is if you write making an obvious point about a historical period or historical figure, you will get lots of letters and emails insisting that the obvious thing about the guy or his time is completely wrong. If you write about Botticelli as a painter of the Italian Renaissance, you'll be told sapiently that there was never really a renaissance in Italy for him to paint in. If you write about Abraham Lincoln and emancipation, you'll be bombarded, on a Fort Sumter scale, with people telling you that the American Civil War wasn't really fought over slavery. The Spanish Inquisition was a benevolent, fact-checking organization, Edmund Burke was no conservative . . . On and on it goes.

Now, these letters and emails come more often from the half-bright, some of them professional academics, than from the fully bonkers or barking. You can tell the half-bright from the barking because the barking don't know how little they know, while the half-bright know enough to think that they know a lot, but don't know enough to know what part of what they know is actually worth knowing.

Not long ago, for instance, I wrote an essay about the great Galileo, and the beginnings of modern science. I explained, or tried to, that what made Galileo's work science, properly so-called, wasn't that he was always right about the universe (he was very often wrong) but that he believed in searching for ways of finding out what was right by figuring out what would happen in the world if he wasn't.

One story of that search is famous. When he wanted to find out if Aristotle was wrong to say that a small body would fall at a different speed from a large body, he didn't look the answer up in an old book about falling objects. Instead, he threw cannonballs of two different sizes off the Tower of Pisa, and, checking to make sure that no one was down there, watched what happened. They hit the ground at the same time.

That story may be a legend – though it was first told by someone who knew him well – but it's a legend that points towards a truth. We know for certain that he attempted lots of adventures in looking that were just as decisive. He looked at stars and planets and the way cannonballs fell on moving ships – and changed the mind of man as he did. We call it the 'experimental method', and if science had an essence, that would be it.

In 1632 Galileo wrote a great book, his *Dialogue Concerning the Two World Systems*. It's one of the best books ever written because it's essentially a record of a temperament, of a kind of impatience and irritability that leads men to drop things from towers and see what happens when they fall. He invented a dumb character for the book named Simplicio and two smart ones to argue with him. The joke is that Simplicio is the most erudite of the three – the dumb guy who thinks he's the smart guy (the original half-bright guy), who's read a lot but just repeats whatever Aristotle says. He's erudite and ignorant. Galileo wasn't naive about experiments. He always emphasizes the importance of looking for yourself. But he also wants to convince you that sometimes it's important not to look for yourself, not just to trust your own eyes, and that you have to work to understand the real meaning of what you're seeing.

But on every page of that wonderful book, he's trying to imagine a decisive test – dropping a cannonball from a ship's mast, or digging a hole in the ground and watching the moon – to help you argue your way around the universe. There's a lovely moment – it could be the motto of the scientific revolution – when Salviati, one of his alter egos, says, 'Therefore, Simplicio, come either with arguments and demonstrations and bring us no more Texts and Authorities, for our disputes are about the Sensible World, and not one of Paper.'

In that essay I wrote about Galileo, I compared him to John Dee, the famous English magician, alchemist and astrologer, who was one of his contemporaries, who was also a consultant to Queen Elizabeth I, and who read everything there was to read in his time and knew everything there was to know in the esoterica of his time – but didn't know what was worth knowing. He knew a lot about Copernicus, for instance, but he also spent half his life trying to talk to angels and have demons intervene to help him turn lead into gold.

Well, it turns out that John Dee the magician and astrologer has his admirers – indeed his webpages and his fan clubs and his chatboard, just like Harry or Liam or Justin – and they took up the cause of the old alchemist with me. 'How dare you knock John?' his fans, some of them half bright, some of them just a little, well, barking, insisted. Wasn't he a formidably erudite man, particularly on just those subjects – stars and orbits and falling objects – that Galileo cared about too? Why shut him out of the scientific creed?

Well, that was the point I was making. And it seems to me worth making again – and then again, and then again. It just can't be made too often. The scientific revolution wasn't an extension in erudition. It involved instead what we might call a second-order attitude to erudition – and if that sounds fancy, it just means the human practice of calling bull on an idea which you think is full of it, and being unafraid to do so. Dee was a learned man – too learned a man, in fact, in whose head all kinds of stuff lodged, some obviously silly and some in retrospect sane, but impacted together like trash in a dump heap. Above all, his work is filled with supernatural explanations – with angels and demons and astrological spells.

Galileo emphatically did not believe in magic. Galileo has no time for supernatural explanations of any kind; indeed, when he goes wrong, as he did when he rejected the idea that the moon causes the tides, it's because he resists the right explanation because it just sounds too strange or magical. John Dee believes in some things that now belong to science, but in a hundred others that don't. And not once in his life did he ever seem to ask the essential question: Is this idea bull or is it for real? The smartest people of his time knew the score. Ben Jonson wrote his play, *The Alchemist*, about someone just like Dee. And he called his alchemist Subtle, exactly to make the point that you could be very subtle and very silly all at the same time. History has taught us that science didn't just happen in a burst. Alchemy and astrology evolved slowly and over time into chemistry and astronomy. Galileo even made a buck in his youth by casting horoscopes for rich people.

There were no bright lines. Indeed, sometimes science slipped back into astrology and alchemy and superstition and the occult. It's well known that Isaac Newton spent a lifetime searching for the Philosopher's Stone. But science never slipped all the way back. This new habit of throwing things off towers to see how fast they really fell, this experimental method, made sure that it couldn't. Truth no longer depended on the prestige, or the intelligence, or even the integrity of any one person. That's why Galileo had the last laugh on the Inquisitors.

Well, why does any of this matter, except to historians and the barking, or half bright?

It matters because every time we make science more esoteric than it really is, we make modern life, which depends on science, more complicated than it needs to be. The glory of modern science is that, while only a very few can understand its particular theories, anyone can understand its peculiar approach: it is simply the perpetual assertion of experience over authority, and of debate over dogma. When we insist, as all the wisest child psychologists do now, that every child is like a small scientist, we don't mean that she has esoteric knowledge of a broad range of subjects, or talks to angels, or makes lead into gold. We mean that she makes a theory about how her blocks are going to fall down and then tests it by knocking them over. And her range of knowledge in that way grows by leaps and bounds. Science is really just that child's groping, with wings on. No, not with wings on, rather up on stilts – awkward-looking earthbound instruments that get you high enough to see the world.

There's supposed to be a sign up on the Tower of Pisa: 'PLEASE DON'T THROW THINGS FROM THIS TOWER'. That sign is the best memorial that Galileo could ever have. Of course, I'm not sure that it's actually there. I'll have to go and look.

CUBISM

21 November 2013

I am about to attempt something ridiculous, perhaps absurd, even ludicrous: I am going to try and describe the look, and, I hope, suggest some of the meaning, of a century-old style of avant-garde art making, and I am going to do it on the radio. The style I shall try and describe has none of the obvious crutches of appealing subject-matter that sneaky art-describers can usually rely on – no pensive blue guitar players or ballet girls. I once met an elderly woman who still boasted of having been praised decades ago as the best-dressed woman on radio; I am about to join her absurd ranks, as a close formal analyst of art who cannot show you what it is he is analysing.

The odds of failure are very high, of course, maybe even off the charts; my one hope in attempting it is that the style that I shall describe is so shaped by practices that seemed, in their time, to be themselves absurd, ludicrous and ridiculous – and were relished by the artists who made the pictures for being just so – that my own low absurdity may meet their higher absurdity, and make something of it. The artists I am about to praise, and analyse, in a certain sense *wanted* to be the best-dressed women on the radio – the style they made had in it a certain perverse, gravity-defying mischief, with welcome elements of slapstick and comic absurdity – and so, perhaps, the essential comedy of the manner will come to my rescue.

The style I speak of is the one we call 'Cubism', and it was made by two men, the Norman Georges Braque and the Catalan Pablo Picasso, in Paris and various resorts in Spain and the South of France, just a century ago; it first emerged around 1908, under the influence of the late paintings of the (late) Paul Cézanne, and came to its height, and its head, in the summer of 1913, when the coloured, decorative, graphic style that art historians call 'Synthetic Cubism' began to replace the brown, muddled, chiaroscuro style that they call 'Analytic Cubism'.

That's quite an art-historical mouthful, and I crush it into a single sentence because I want to get past that stuff as quickly as we can. Neither of those names, 'Analytic' or 'Synthetic Cubism', for instance, really means much; but they do point to a break in the style, and a decisive one – and by pointing to a decisive break in a style that was at that time only about four years old, they remind us of a truth about Cubism, easily overlooked: it arose at a time of immense cultural acceleration.

I don't just mean that there was a lot going on. I mean that it was running at a very high speed. Most of the time, culture creeps forward by decades, as adults do; at rare moments it races by in months and years, like an adolescent. Anyone who came of age in the 1960s, and lived for its music, will recall how the hooded-eyed, electric Bob Dylan of 1966 was not just more mature than his younger self; he was a completely different creature from that sincere civil rights ruffian with an acoustic guitar of just three years before. (Though when we talk about Cubism, very much the collaboration of opposites, Picasso and Braque, we are closer to Lennon and McCartney, with Picasso the tough-edged anti-sentimentalist, and Braque the more delicate melodist of form.)

But I see that I am doing what every critic does when we approach Cubism; and that is to talk around the subject rather than through, or really about, it. I promised to describe as much as analyse, and now I shall – or try to, anyway. The 1913 picture I'll talk about is one that lives at the Tate in London – one of the rare classic Cubist pictures that made its way across the Channel despite a largely suspicious reception in Britain, so that conceivably you can go and look and check, sceptically, for yourself. The collage is called *Bottle of Vieux Marc, Glass, Guitar and Newspaper*. What do we see? Well, first of all, and rather startlingly, we see the masthead of *Le Figaro*, a paper still published in Paris – the actual thing, a little, but only a little, browned by time, pasted directly onto the picture surface. Yet it sits within a flat, rendered world, which indicates rather than realizes objects: a bottle, a glass and a guitar. We realize at once that, though we have a clear sense of a mundane totality – we're at a café table, it might be morning, since it's a morning paper, but more likely evening, as there's that Vieux Marc, and there's a guitar somewhere in the vicinity – still, all of that has been stenographically suggested by the most parsimonious of signs. What we're looking at is not suggested impressionistically, but rendered diagrammatically. We see through a faceted, prismatic glass, brightly. We're in a world of signs, pictograms, distilled down from appearances to their conceptual essence. The guitar placed in the centre of this collage is far from fully realized – but it's not a sketch of a guitar, really, more a list of one, rendered as a catalogue of familiar elements: a guitar, the picture gaily proposes, is a sound hole and a womanly edge and a fretboard of parallel lines, and if you get these things right, in what ever jaunty order you place them, you have got your guitar.

That kind of conceptual rendering is normal to children's art, and to what Picasso and Braque would have thought of as African 'tribal' art. I used to play a children's game where you had three geometric objects, and you had to dress them up with an erasable crayon to spell out a famous scene from a text. Three moustaches and you had the whole of a Dumas novel; a high Russian collar, and you were with Tolstoy. That's the kind of representation that's going on here: suave, rapid-fire, economical, and wittily minimal. At the same time, the picture isn't *all* like that. Some of the things we see, like the glass on the right, are illusions, suggesting the actual play of light on objects; this guy can *draw*. Other things, like that *Figaro* headline, are the real things, as they exist in the world, imported whole to the middle of an, in many ways, mysterious picture. We might imagine this as picture-making in motion; you walk around the objects, taking notes as you go.

What would we really think, I wonder, if we were truly amateur lookers, uncorrupted by art history? Would the picture baffle us? Many were, then. But what's interesting is that most of the 1913 audience, at least to judge by the popular cartoons and cabaret jokes that it provoked, thought, first of all, that Cubism was fun. This picture, they seemed to think, might be a kind of rebus, a riddle, one of those pictures that asks you to figure out from all of its parts what its message is. A word here, half a smile there, and a guitar part over here – it's a puzzle, meant as one.

The pictures were not, in truth, neatly programmatic. But we do get much closer to the spirit in which this picture was made if we think of them as a joke in this sense, as riddles and rebuses, than if we think of them as a profound philosophical reflection on the nature of space and time. Many commentators have insisted that Cubism's view of reality itself is somehow in tune with the new, exactly contemporary physics of Einstein, where time and space are also entangled together. This is true, in a way, but it is one of those truths that exist in the hazy cloud cover of the zeitgeist more than in the particular granular world of actual intention or practice.

Cubism is both metaphysics and mischief, entangled together. Both count, but the mischief is, I think, closest to its heart. Cubism is not a systematic investigation, but a kind of decorum-destroying game: it sends up, rather than blows up, the conventions it inherited, in the way that, say, Gilbert and Sullivan send up the conventions of opera while still paying a kind of smiling homage to them. It is not, as is sometimes said, that the Cubists bravely rejected the perceptual representation that was the legacy of the Renaissance, those systems of modelling and of perspective that had conquered the visible world. There *is* perspective here, at odd angles, and an old, Rembrandtesque enigmatic play of light and shadow on objects in the world. But the neat registry of shapes as they exist in the mind is registered, too: we see with the part of the mind where objects exist alongside words and tunes and headlines.

In the paintings of the Impressionists, it's certainly the case that our eyes already flicker from shape to pattern restlessly; part of the joy of a Monet is to approach the picture and see all the discreet, minute touches of independent colour that combine as we step back into a lily pond shimmering at dawn. But these delights, though far from superficial – their pleasure in nuance becomes a principle of living all its own – are still optical. Cubism is the first self-consciously *cognitive* style. Every time we look at it, it reminds us that we see with our minds.

Picasso and Braque had no manifesto, no plan, and they resisted, indeed hated, any 'explanation' of their purpose. They were, if you like, sublime tinkerers. It is no accident, I think, that their contemporary heroes were not found among the philosophers and scientists; their real heroes were the Wright brothers, who in those years had made their first heavier-than-air flying machine and brought it triumphantly to France. Picasso and Braque liked to call each other Orville and Wilbur, and their collages are filled with references to flight. 'Our Future is in the Air', one famous clipped headline reads in another collage. What fascinated them about the Wright brothers was that they had just made things up, non-systematically, changed this wing-shape and changed that positioning – and suddenly, we flew. Man flew when he tinkered; and pictures escaped the old gravitational pull of the Renaissance, not when they kicked and complained, but when they punned and played

Well, so what? Why does *that* matter in the way so much else of the art and literature of 1913 so obviously matters – as a book like Marcel Proust's first volume of *In Search of Lost Time*, published that same year, still touches our sense of memory and meaning? Part of the answer – I can't avoid it – is indeed historical, and lies in what happened next in art. Cubism was as potent to visual culture as Einstein's equations were to physics. Picasso and Braque, like Orville and Wilbur, made something . . . useful. Cubism, a language without an ideology, appeared at a moment when many artists in Europe had an ideology in need of a language. Cubist style became their common tongue. So much that would happen in modern art is deducible from this modest-looking collage: the abstract art of Mondrian is prophesied in the dissolution of object into geometry; the more mischievous painterly elements of Dada in the intrusion of the principle of chance, the one that puts the guitar hole here and its neck over there; Futurism took from Cubist syncopations a surging pictorial dynamism; even Art Deco design, of the kind I see around every day in New York, with its geometric frills and broken rhythms, begins here – and so, certainly, does the Pop Art that rose fifty years later, with its love of erasing the line between the uncelebrated actual object and the solemn actions of art.

But there is, I think, a deeper, and more broadly humane, reason this art still resonates, other than that it made more art happen. I may lose whatever credit I have left with art historians if I say this, but I think it is true: Cubism is above all a *happy* style, and it partakes of the joy of a largely joyful moment. This not-so-still still life from the Tate still suggests an entirely positive view of modern urban culture, of modern energy, and even of the levelling force of modernity, where you read *Le Figaro* and re-imagine art as part of one morning's experience. A small daily paradise made of the most ephemeral bits and pieces of our daily life, the café table given the dignity once held only for religious icons, a rebus re-imagined as a ritual – that is the spirit that still resonates from this picture. It encourages us to live, and to see in our daily life-urge, the possibility of a humming redemption of the ordinary.

Was 1913 the last happy European year? Our future, all too horribly, *was* in the air: the air of armed combat, and eventually of the bomber and fighter . . . Perhaps it is not nostalgia, but real communication across a century, that makes us relax and smile when we see this exactly a century later. When we look at the collage, we see a small world: coffee is made, the studio gossip over, and the morning papers, seen and cut at a glance, still seem merely to hint at news of distant Balkan wars, worth a shrug and a scissors, to cut them out. The deadpan joke, the visual pun, the play of the mind in the morning, seems like very slight and ludicrous and, yes, absurd ammo to aim against the monuments of official art and the monsters of modern madness. Yet what other ammunition do we have? We look at this collage and think that little morning battle of making is won! The Great War that will erase so many mornings seems far away. The cataract of rushing modern time that provided energy for their own work seems to halt, for once, at the edge of the abyss. Living in time, the Cubist picture stops it.

Sex and the French

17 January 2014

Whenever a French man of state has sex with someone not his wife, people call me up and ask why he did it. When I say people do, I really mean journalists (a sub-species whose personhood is sometimes in doubt), and I suppose I really mean newspaper editors and radio producers (a still more dubious class). But they do call, and they do ask. This is simply because I lived in France for some years and have written a lot about life there, and the false assumption is made that I am intimately expert on all its corners, including those obscure from my view. This is a version of the popular journalist's 'fallacy of omniscience by proximity'. I'm sure that anyone who ever wrote from Korea gets similar calls: 'You lived there, right? You must have often seen out-of-favour relatives being eaten alive by ravenous dogs? Can't you tell our listeners something about it?'

So, though I know nothing, or damn little, of the specific habits and sex acts of French presidents (when a French statesman thinks of having illicit love, his next thought is not 'I must call Gopnik to share my feelings and get his view'), still I do have a view about President Hollande's recent activities, and his supposed tryst with the actor Julie Gayet.

In this instance, of course, this is a case of a man having sex with someone not his wife because he had, in fact, no wife not to be faithful to (if that makes Parisian sense), only a series of apparently increasingly embittered partners and some kids. As I say, I claim no expertise about it, but I do have a view on it, and it is a double one that I shall inexpertly but passionately, if not illicitly, unpack for you now. And that is that the good French principle of a right to privacy against all comers is not quite the same thing as a right to pleasure before all else.

To begin with, I think the French view of sex and life is essentially right and ought to be universally applicable: sex with children or by force is wrong, and the rest is just the human comedy, unfolding as it will. Puritanism is a sin against human nature, and the worst of it is that puritanism is the most leering and prurient of world-views. Far from wanting to keep sex in the private sphere, the puritans can't wait to drag it out in public. Puritans are the least buttoned-up people in the world.

They can't wait to pin a scarlet 'A' for 'Adultery' on someone's clothing, or hold a public humiliation ritual.

Nothing could be more illustrative of this than the tone of outraged indignation directed by British tabloid journalists at their reluctant French press equivalents in the past week. 'What is it with these people?' the Brit journalists keep saying, speaking of the French ones. 'Why do they refuse to invade the privacy of someone they've never met, or hang around all night to grab a few illicit pictures, causing immense pain to some stranger's wife and children, in order to obsess over a sexual affair of a kind they wish they were having themselves? And they call themselves journalists!'

Well, France is not a puritanical society. It accepts that human appetites for sex and food are normal (or '*normale*', to use a word much prized there), and that attempts to suppress either will make men and women nervous wrecks at least. French presidents have love affairs. President Mitterrand had not just a wife and a mistress, but two entire families (which reminds me of the old vaudeville joke: 'What's the penalty for bigamy? Two wives.'). President Sarkozy famously switched first-*dames* in mid-administration, beginning with the ferocious Cecilia and ending with the beaming and beautiful Carla.

But in truth, puritanical societies are less morally alert, because the puritanical societies have the judgements prepackaged, and their hypocrisies, too. In France however, the moral rights and wrongs, I've learned, are adjudicated case-by-case. I recall a Parisian woman whose husband was ill but whose lover had a stroke: which, she wondered, demanded her attention more? The circumstance might have seemed absurd, but the reasoning was anything but amoral. Indeed, the French movie director Éric Rohmer's great films are called 'moral tales' exactly because they are all about the unsettled nature of desire – about whether, say, the sight of a teenage girl's knee on the beach is worth cancelling a wedding over. Morality may be permanent, but sexual ethics among adults are situational: they depend on this knee at this moment on this beach, and on all the other knees nearby. The people so engaged have to think morally, rather than just pantomiming its practice, as we Anglo-Saxons (a term that in French usage includes New York Jews and London Muslims) do.

But – and there was bound to be a 'but' – to be a leader, a man or woman of state, does involve questions of character. And by 'character', I think, we simply mean the power to refrain: to not do the things that we have every right and reason to do because there's some other larger reason not to do them. And by 'character' in leadership, we mean just having the unusual capacity of being able to ask other people to refrain, without looking a prig or hypocrite while doing so. A sane state involves some balance of appetite served and appetite curbed. Right now, in France and elsewhere, ordinary people are being asked to take less from the state than they quite expected, and the rich are being asked to give more to the state than they quite want to. When the leader shows himself unable to control his own appetite, the symbolic message is that the indulgence of appetite is an absolute good – one that trumps prudence, caution, and risks signaling that everyone needs to curb their appetites except for those with power.

No one, of course, is obliged to be a role model. But if you do not wish to be a role model to the public, why become a public man or woman? If you have no desire to inspire, why take up the thankless task of inspiration? Or, to put it at its most cynical, if you do not even put the pursuit of power before pleasure, why pursue it?

Perhaps what's actually being pursued is personal pleasure on the back of power. Perhaps. For how else is a pudgy, balding, middle-aged man to have such a line of beauties in his life? If so, we have a duty to mark down the politician, as we would a bore who insists on talking politics when the occasion calls for gossip. It's the wrong activity for the moment we're in. We have no business in the bedrooms of our politicians, but once the bedroom door opens – as, in our boundless day, it is bound to – there are better things to see.

It is sometimes said that the French attitude towards adultery and politics is elitist. That is, that powerful French people assume an arrogant licence to do what they like, that normal French people aren't allowed. It seems to me that right now the problem is that it is not elitist enough: it does not make sufficient demands on people with power and privilege. It is no accident (it is a rather good joke, actually) that the expression in English *'noblesse oblige'* is – obviously, really – French. *'Noblesse oblige'* does not mean that the elite have special privileges; it means that people with power have an obligation to pay even more scrupulous attention to the symbolic vibrations of their acts than the rest of us do. It is not that we are obliged to genuflect before nobles; it is that nobles are obliged to defer to us. The price of privilege is prudence.

All this talk of appetite reminds me of that other great invention that sits besides the open door of the French bedroom, and that is the French table. It was just a year ago that UNESCO declared French gastronomy one of the world's cultural treasures, like Angkor Wat or the Tower of London. Finally, the behaviour of the French political elite is extremely selfish, and one wonders who takes any interest in raising their children. It would not surprise me if they make extensive use of nannies, since clearly the parents put their own pleasure ahead of a commitment to raise the children. I think that one of the ways the French table civilizes us is that it asks us both to indulge our hungers and to control them, at the same time. We do not gorge. We wait until everyone is seated. We consider the company even as we eye the dishes. The point of great French dining is not that we should simply sit down and celebrate our appetites, but that we have to transform our hungers into civilized desires. Learning which fork to use means learning when not to. Self-righteousness about other people's appetites is uncivilized. But not being able to control your own when the social occasion demands it is very bad manners. And that is one more thing I learned in France.

Self-Drive Manhood

24 January 2014

I do not know how to drive a car.

There: it's out. In Britain, I think this is merely a little unusual; in the US, it is positively shaming. People give you strange looks when you confess this, as though you had confessed to not being able to perform some other, wholly natural function.

Like all people with a guilty secret, I have a perfectly good explanation. I grew up within a couple of blocks of the university where my pedestrian parents both taught, and I eventually went to school there, and then, right out of university, I went to New York, where no one has a car, and have lived here ever since (plus a few years in Paris, where no one in their right mind would try and drive).

My wife, fortunately, grew up in a Canadian suburb and learned to drive there. She is a wonderful driver, and when we go up to Cape Cod in August for our annual three weeks by the beach, she drives the family up, and then around. And the sad truth is that by now no one wants me to drive a car – my reflexes are too aberrant, my tendency to daydream too marked. My fourteen-year-old daughter is firm: 'I'm never getting in a car if you're driving,' she says grimly. 'You would be thinking about something you're writing, and then bang, it's over for us all.'

But the blow to my masculinity is real. I sense that I am, even in this properly post-feminist age, in the wrong seat. Not the one (the right front in your country, the left front in ours) where generations of fathers have sat, pressing down on pedals, and cursing the competition on the road. Instead, I occupy the traditional mother's seat and fill her role – shushing the children when the driver is tired, or changing the music on the radio as the one listenable station fades out into static.

I feel, I'm afraid, the insult to my masculinity so much that when a cop or a garage attendant approaches the car and gives me what I take to be a slightly puzzled, pitying look, I immediately slouch down and scowl resentfully in an impressive impersonation of a veteran driver, whose licence has been taken away after a lifetime of high speed, recklessly entertaining *Dukes of Hazzard*-style driving.

'Cursing the competition?' my wife just said, reading over my shoulder. 'The other cars on the road aren't competitive. And is that why you get the weird look on your face?

I can't believe that your concept of masculinity involves that much petty vanity and pointless displays of competitive ego in some . . . self-invented contest,' she concludes – not seeing that if it were not for petty vanity and pointless displays of competitive ego, mostly in meaningless self-invented contests, we would have no concept of masculinity at all.

So you can easily imagine how excited I was when I first read that Google, the great, good search-engine company out west, is many years and many hundreds of millions of dollars into the process of developing and road-testing, and some day soon selling, the thing in life I most desire: the self-driving car. And Google isn't alone in the pursuit. Many companies are engaged in it. You will programme your destination when you set out, and the car will do the rest, even on the busiest motorway – find the exit, make the turn, maintain the speed, avoid the . . . well, the competition, and turn the fog lights on to penetrate the mist. You can sit behind the wheel, if you like, and pantomime the act of driving, but the car will do all the work itself. Since self-driving cars never get tired, drunk or distracted by their husbands trying to find a decent jazz station on the radio, Google and the other companies promise to bring road fatalities down to near-zero.

There is a problem, though, I've discovered, reading eagerly on. It is that human drivers are engaged every day not just in navigating roads, but also in making ethical decisions as they drive, and these too will have somehow to be programmed into the software of the self-driving car. Each self-driving car will have to have its own ethical engine.

Drivers, for instance, know that it is right to swerve to avoid an animal racing across the road, though not at any risk to their passengers. But they are also prepared to take a little more risk with the passengers to avoid a cat or a dog, which we instantly recognize as pets with human owners, than, say, a squirrel or raccoon. Even graver ethical choices, often studied by philosophers and psychologists, regularly arise. What to do when faced with a choice between, say, mowing down a couple of bystanders and ploughing into a school bus packed with children? We compute these ethical costs and choices in an eye blink, and not just the choices, but the moral reasoning behind them, would have to be programmed into the self-driving car. And should there be a different module that switches on if the bus is packed not with children but with, say, ailing nonagenarians from a nearby hospice? And there are even simpler but still real ethical dilemmas that human drivers understand – say, that a speed limit of 50 mph on a fine day is really 60 mph, while on a wet and foggy day, really 45 mph. How do we programme this kind of flexibility into a machine?

It will not surprise the Eurosceptics among you that the European Union, in its own parallel self-driving car pro-gramme, is trying to solve this dilemma through a system of bureaucratically imposed obedience. What is called, almost unbelievably, the SARTRE project – a joint research mission by

Ricardo UK and Volvo, among others, and the EU – works on the convoy or 'road train' model: a single truck with a human driver leading the way, and up to five computerized self-drive cars following sheep-like behind. 'Because they're all taking the same orders,' the engineer explains, 'the cars can travel just a few metres apart.' SARTRE is an acronym for 'Safe Road Trains for the Environment', but it is a perfect tribute to the great French philosopher who ran his own ethical café-convoy, leading his zombie-like followers from absurdity to absurdity over many decades.

But why only Sartre? It occurs to me that, given the huge market for customized niche products these days, there should be a variety of ethical engines to install in your self-driving car. There would be many ethical apps to develop and download into the software of your self-driving Volvo. You could choose, say, a Nietzschean engine, which would drive right over everything. (Why not? God is dead anyway.) Or the Albert Camus model, which would stall and pause in the middle of the highway while the traffic backs up behind – and then suddenly shoot off, bang, because the existential leap must be made, and some pedal struck.

There would be an Ayn Rand-model ethical engine, named after the Russian-American free market fanatic, which would use chip technology to scan the bank account of each pedestrian, calculating their net worth, swerving to miss the makers, and mowing down a taker or two. (Who needs 'em?) And there would be its technical relation, the Richard Dawkins model, which would use portable MRIs to heat-seek and discover which pedestrians you distantly share genes with, while steering you directly into the ones who are, alas, no relation. There could even be a Woody Allen ethical engine, which would start apologizing as you press on the gas, and continue all the way home. And a Ludwig Wittgenstein model, which would announce wearily that there is no motor in the car anyway: all there is, is the activity of driving.

Yet the one thing that all philosophers and engineers are agreed on is that no one is yet nearly as good, as flexible, as vigilant – not to mention as perpetually self-justifying – at these things as people are. We are our own best ethical engines. And who more expert than those of us, that small persecuted class, the non-drivers, who have been watching the road without the distraction of actual driving for years?

And here, I realize, is where I could really cash in. Instead of developing those ethical apps, I could become one myself. I will hire myself out as a full-time on-call ethical chauffeur, the moral rule-maker within your self-driving car. I will sit behind the wheel, just like a real driver, but making philosophical judgements rather than right turns – 'This raccoon lives', 'This bug dies', 'Miss the school bus', 'Run over these oldsters'. I might even enforce more aesthetic ethical injunctions – say, to stop at every lookout on a scenic road, simply to admire the view.

There I will be at last, front right or front left, depending on the country, for the first time the guy inside, clutching the wheel, promoting the beautiful, saving the vulnerable, dooming the deserving, almost like a god. Almost, for that matter – well, almost – like a man.

WHY SPORTSMANSHIP MATTERS
2 February 2014

Here in the US, this weekend, we are about to celebrate the Super Bowl – the American championship of American football, which of course everyone in the US refers to as the 'World Championship of All Football'. It will be held, very unusually, in New York – well, in what many in the US are referring to as New York. Actually, it will be held in New Jersey, land of *The Sopranos* and marshes and traffic jams.

But what most people have been talking of in the run-up to the game is not sport but sportsmanship, and particularly the case of Richard Sherman, the fine defender for the Seattle Seahawks. At the end of the last round of play-offs, in a post-game interview, Richard Sherman taunted and mocked a wide receiver he had bested on the final big play, announcing: 'Well, I'm the best corner in the game! When you try me with a sorry receiver like Crabtree, that's the result you're gonna get! Don't you ever talk about me!' – implying that Crabtree earlier had. Fox Sports, showing the game, couldn't have cut away from him quicker if he had begun to deliver a thoughtful talk on the superiority of socialized medicine.

What was odd was not the immediate ugliness – what the tabloids would call a tsunami of tweets denouncing Sherman, who is African-American, often in nasty terms, for poor sportsmanship. It was that the push-back in his favour was quickly louder and more indignant. Sherman was being victimized, the consensus seemed to suggest. What was wrong with someone glorifying their own achievements? Sherman's freedom from constraint was more inspiring than the constraints had ever been. And because Richard Sherman, is, on the whole, an admirable character – a poor kid who did well at a good school and writes an entertaining column on sport every week – the push-back had credibility.

I will confess that my stomach clenched a little as I watched him – and then, over the next few days, my mind revolved as I saw the considerable truth in what was being said in his defence. And what is a true moral quandary but exactly the moment when the stomach says, 'Ugh!' and the judgement says, 'Well . . .'?

As I say, the indignant defence of Sherman scores many points. Is it not the height of genteel hypocrisy to demand that someone who is paid above all to compete should suddenly pretend not to be competitive when the cameras go on, in order to conform to a nineteenth-century English gentleman's notion of sportsmanship? Indeed, isn't what we call 'sportsmanship' just the manners of a long-dead colonizing time, imposed on classes and clans who don't want them, and shouldn't be forced to conform to them?

The notion of ostentatious fair play, like its twin, amateurism, which we'll pretend to celebrate very soon in the Olympics, was, after all, designed to exclude working-class people in Britain and ethnic people in the UK. False modesty is a rich man's privilege. Only when it doesn't really matter if you win or lose, can you, in the most literal sense, afford to be a good sport about it. Is sportsmanship not just another word for 'Be like us'?

I throw any stone in this dispute, I should add instantly, from a pure glasshouse. I am the model of a sore loser, and a bad sport. When I am watching my home team, the Montreal Canadiens, play ice hockey, I exult in the agony of the opposing goalkeeper when the Montreal team scores. A middle-aged provider of sapient on-air editorials, I have been banished three times from the despised Boston Bruins chatboards for trolling Bruins fans. Such is the adrenaline of the contest. Fans type trash on their keyboards; why shouldn't the real athletes talk trash on the field?

Sport, it's been said, is what men have instead of emotions; but maybe a better way of saying it is that sports are the emotions men have. The purpose of sport is to remind us that it is possible to have aggressive emotions that end: a robust and violent competition that doesn't end in death. We can try to eliminate our passion for competition every day by detaching ourselves from those passions, and that is why you will see me every day sitting cross-legged for twenty minutes, thinking kind thoughts about the Boston Bruins (or trying to). Or we can try – and this seems to work much better for more people – acting out the aggression in neatly controlled ways that leave us in the end with something other than blood. Sport is the best kind of mimic warfare that we have. And in mimic warfare we limit our victories instead of exploiting them to the max. We exult enough to please our fellows, and not enough to insult our enemies, because we know that they are our enemies only for today.

So the true value of the intricate code of sportsmanship is that it is a way of keeping a sense of proportion on our love of stylized violence. It's significant, I think, that sportsmanship seems to vary inversely to the violence of the game. Rugby, which to the non-initiate looks like a mass mugging interrupted by panting, is the most sporting of all games, as anyone who has seen a post-match rugby party knows. Ice hockey (my sport) is the only one where fighting is actually permitted. But it is also the only one where both teams always line up at the end to shake hands.

If one goes deeper into the historical roots of sportsmanship –

all those sonorous nineteenth-century poems and inspiring maxims and public school exhortations – one may find them absurd, but not uninspiring. There are many ridiculous aspects to the Victorian world-view, its puritanism and its hypocrisies. But there is one good and shining thing about it: its faith in resilience. 'That men may rise on stepping-stones / Of their dead selves to higher things,' as Tennyson said. The point of being a good sport is not simply to show a stoical front. It is that there is always another game, and with it another chance of victory, or defeat, tomorrow. Do not exult too much today and do not anguish too much tonight, for the season starts . . . well, these days, the season starts immediately, but anyway the new season starts soon enough.

We have all rightly been moved by the story of Nelson Mandela's love, in prison, of the Victorian W. E. Henley's poem 'Invictus': 'I am the master of my fate, / I am the captain of my soul.' It made a fitting title for Clint Eastwood's film about Mandela uniting post-apartheid South Africa as the Springboks became champions in the 1995 Rugby World Cup. It was surely no accident that Mandela's inspiration rose from that seemingly remote Victorian age. Victorians are really good on resilience, because they needed to have it. Henley had lost his leg to tuberculosis of the bone, and then lost a child to another form of the disease. He was revered in his time, not for his stoicism but for his resilience of heart and mind.

Sportsmanship is just a way of nodding to the long cycle of

the seasons. No state in life, neither winner's podium nor even prison, is ever permanent. People point to Muhammad Ali as an athlete who taunted his foes and was persecuted unfairly – but we need only look at Ali today to find a different kind of pathos in those taunts. Sportsmanship is triumph's salute to time. It is this day's anxious glance towards the coming week. We will not always be the winner. In fact, next week we may be the loser, and it is best to recognize that truth today – before that truth is on top of us tomorrow.

On YouTube these days, along with so many clips of taunting and exulting and athletes making the choke sign, there is a lovely video showing ten minutes of moments of pure sports-manship – penalties wrongly awarded, and then deliberately missed, wrestlers stopping in mid choke-hold to assist an opponent, bitter old foes embracing at the end of the game. It has a quarter of a million views. May it have a few more soon. Richard Sherman may shine this weekend or he may well be unmanned by Peyton Manning – that happens, too. He needs – we need – an attitude for all occasions.

Why I Don't Tweet

7 February 2014

'I do not tweet, and yet there are thousands who wait for me to tweet.' That sentence, which would have been a spoken symptom of madness, a crazy man's sentence, a few short years ago, is now a simple form of confession. Well, it is a form of insanity, I suppose, but of a different kind. I'm sure you understood what I meant – that, while I have a Twitter account, I almost never use it. I'm not sure why I don't. Partly because there seems something embarrassing, self-advertising about it. Partly because I just don't have the habit. My fourteen-year-old daughter not only sends tweets. She speaks tweets. If I say, for instance, that I never Google myself, she replies: 'Hashtag: Obvyliesdadtells.' Yet I have many Twitter followers – only because everyone even marginally 'public' does. And I leave them unsatisfied, untweeted.

Nonetheless, I'm not convinced that never tweeting is actually very different from tweeting all the time. I am, you see, neither an optimist nor a pessimist about social media, neither an enthusiast nor a Luddite. I am what might be called a steady state technologist. Everyone insists that the technological transformation of the daily shape of our lives by new gadgets is enormous, while allowing that their emotional effect is more dubious, leaving us with emptier, or at best unaltered, souls. I think the truth is closer to the direct reverse. The emotional effect of new devices is overwhelming – they are like having new pets, new children, trailing with them an overwhelming attachment. But the transformational effect they have on our lives is actually, looked at squarely and without sentiment, quite minimal. After the introduction of a new device, or social media, our lives are exactly where they were before, save for the new thing or service, which we now cannot live without.

I couldn't live without my computer, for instance. The idea of going back to a typewriter – a thing with keys that clack and an inky ribbon that jumps – is impossible to imagine. But my professional writing life is neatly divided between the typewriting era and the word-processing era, and I was exactly as productive when I was banging keys and struggling with correcting fluid, as I am now that it's all instant cut-and-paste and spellcheck. The most productive writers who ever lived preceded even the typewriter. Would Dickens or Balzac have written an extra line with it? How could they? They had no time. They made our industry seem like torpor, our era's idea of energy look like stasis. To describe my relationship to my laptop, I use the language of affection: I *need* it, I *depend* on it, I'm *attached* to it, I would be *bereft* without it – more than the language of real necessity. I couldn't do my work without it? Well, I could. I did.

And, while I merely like my computer, I *love* my smartphone. I clutch my phone tight to myself, I hold it in my hand like a talisman; a feeling of panic overcomes me when in a strange city I find I have mislaid it, or that I forgot to bring its charger. But though it has altered the shape of my days and hours, has it really altered the life those days add up to and achieve? No. Less than a decade ago, I had no smartphone at all, and nothing was significantly different in my life . . . except for the possession of my phone. I never felt particularly remote from my family; I seemed to get all the email I needed. The distribution not just of happiness and sadness in my life, but of all the smaller domestic emotions that small domestic devices are presumably there to assist, existed in exactly the same amounts. I talked to my wife as often; I worried about my kids as much; I was in the same amount of contact, or not, with my friends. It is not merely that I got along fine before I had it, but that I got along in exactly the same way, in precisely the same spirit, in days that were shaped along exactly the same lines – save for the fact that I was not, then, consulting my smartphone every five minutes. Like so much modern media technology, it creates a dependency without ever actually addressing a need.

Which has us circling back to Twitter, and its discontents. Twitter, spitting out its brief public messages, is given credit for making revolutions – and certainly, throughout the Arab Spring and the Ukrainian and Iranian near-springs, the instant news shared by its tweets raced around the crowds and helped order its actions. But in truth, every popular social revolution since at least the French one has followed (I think) the same pattern: a government weakened by war, or financial crisis, or both, meets popular resistance, which for the first time takes in members of the elite and the masses. They find a meeting space – it could be Tahrir Square or a French real-tennis court – and occupy it. Then, in the crucial moment, the army, called on to disperse the mob, identifies with the cause and refuses. The government is forced to surrender. Then, time after time, the best organized of the militant minorities takes over – and then, in eighteenth-century France or twenty-first-century Egypt, there is a contest to see if the militant minority can dominate the army or if the army will destroy the militant minority. Whether texted and tweeted or papered and pamphleted, the shape of revolution is about the same.

I have, indeed, a larger theory: that while information technology gets all the glamour (mostly because writers use it), all the really great revolutions in modern times have involved transportation more than information. I happened to be reading a letter by the great nineteenth-century English wit Sydney Smith the other day, where he talks about the transformations of his time. All involve transportation – hansom cabs, steam boats, above all the train: 'It took me nine hours to go from Taunton to Bath before the invention of railroads, and I now go in six hours from Taunton to London!' (The only other technology he mentions is the umbrella.)

It's true. That I can travel from New York to London overnight really has changed my life. In principle, at least, I can go to interview an artist or rescue a stranded teenager in six hours. That I can send an instant message to London should change my life, but when I review the old and new, the amount seems about the same as it has always been. The speed of human bodies travelling changes, but once the secular miracle of speed-of-light communication was achieved more than a century and a half ago by the telegraph, each advance since has been, so to speak, essentially an advance in envelopes.

Why, then, do we love our smartphones and Twitter apps so much?

Because we want to be lovers of our time. The urge to belong to our age is more powerful than the need to use our time efficiently. My kids use text-messaging at every moment. It's painstaking, time-consuming, finger-jamming and ultimately inefficient. 'You'd resolve this in a second if you phoned her,' I say. But they fear something much worse than being inefficient. They fear being traitors to their time, renegades to their generation.

That it is our desire to be in our time that moves us is evidenced by a curious block, a kind of pre-emptive amnesia, that all of us share. The one thing about the future that we know for certain – absolutely for sure – is that whatever seems most thrillingly modern now will look most poignantly comic in the future to come. Hashtags and Twitter feeds will say 2014 as much as the cranks on cars say, maybe, 1906, or fax machines the 1990s. We know that we will laugh nostalgically when someone in a distant movie set in our era tweets, and acts as though it matters, as we laugh now at the microwave ovens in *American Hustle*. Knowing that the future will laugh at us, we still cannot take part now in the laughter without being alienated from our age, and that is a sad thing to be. The people from earlier ages who were alienated from theirs – those Luddites and hold-outs – get our sympathy but rarely our affection. We love the early adopters (the old, late early adopters I mean) because we see our own selves in their enthusiasm: they mirror our necessary naivety.

So, I shall arise now, and tweet for almost the first time. I will enjoy the brief romance of relevance. Thousands, perhaps, will follow. I have in mind to tweet these simple words: 'Nothing is real.'

SHORT AND SUCCESSFUL

5 October 2014

Just a few weeks ago, an interesting and lengthy paper by a pair of sociologists from New York University made a lot of noise in what I suppose would these days be called 'The Community of Short Men' – a community to which, as it happens, I rather inarguably (one might say entirely) belong.

Its subject was what is called 'assortative mating' – the way people divide themselves up, two by two in that ark-like fashion, for life. It was one of those wonderfully solemn sociological papers in which the utterly self-evident is systematically recast as the cautiously empirical. The authors point out, early on in their report, that 'social psychological research suggests that attractive people are favoured in numerous situations' (a thing you would not have guessed without social science), and soon after we learn that attractive and physically fit men report going on more dates and having sex more frequently than others. But the conclusion of the paper, once one has weeded through, is striking and well documented. It is simply that short men make stable marriages. They do this in circumstances of difficulty and against the odds and consistently over ages and income groups, and they do it with the shorter women they often marry, but also with the taller women they sometimes land. Short men marry late but, once they do get married, tend to stay married longer and, by social science measures, at least – I assume this means they ask the short men's wives (I hope so anyway) – they stay happily married, too.

Many assertions about the assortative can be put forward to explain why this is so, but trust me, it is not hard to figure it out. There is a simple reason short men make stable marriages: it is because short men are desperate. Short men live in a world of taller men and know that any advantage seized is better kept. Desperation makes short men good husbands. We know the odds instinctively, and knowing that we have lucked out, intend to continue playing a good thing.

It is not, I should rush to add, that short men are desperate to please. One of the most interesting findings of the study is that short men actually do less housework in a typical marriage than tall men do – though the study points out, delicately, this may be because, with tall men, 'the nature of their housework is different'. In other words, we are too short to reach the tops of closets where the heavy house cleaning equipment is kept.

No, short men do not make stable marriages because they are desperate to please. It is because they are desperate to prevail.

An instinctive sense of the odds, born in schoolyards and playgrounds, tells the short man to redouble his efforts in every area of life – the office, the motorway, (God forbid) the golf course. This is of course called the Napoleonic complex, but in truth it is not so much that short men become Napoleonic as that Napoleon was typically short – in his ambition, his drive, his uxorious devotion to his wife Josephine, whom he left only because he wanted to leave the French with a male heir. Hers was the last name on his lips, in the last sentences that he uttered, dreaming of that old stability.

Contemporary accounts state that Bonaparte's height was five-foot-two, but at that time, the French measured 13 inches to the foot (Napoleon himself oversaw France's conversion to the metric system). Given this discrepancy, Napoleon's height would have been 67 inches, or five-foot-seven in modern measurements – about the same height as the current French president, François Hollande, and taller than his predecessor, Nicolas Sarkozy.

There is, I think, a broader moral here. In every area of life, we underrate the merits of desperation, and persistently overrate the advantages of free choice. We insist that we ought to all be equal, free to make the choices we want and find the partners we need. In fact, people who have this kind of freedom rarely use it well. Fashion models, free to choose, inevitably choose rock stars – and since rock stars, freed by their glamour to choose, invariably choose to take a lot of drugs and go on the road and smash up hotel rooms in preference to being in a stable relationship, the models are always badly disappointed by their choice. You see them crying on the shoulders of the short men – dipping their long swan-like necks way down to do so, perhaps, but there you are, they do. Frequent failure is the true price of free choice.

If we look up – or rather down, even below the knees of the short, to the ground itself – we find this same truth embodied as an economic principle, where it is called 'the curse of resources'. Countries with vast natural resources, such as oil and copper and gold, tend to do less well economically than countries that have none – the short-people countries, in other words. This is because resources, easily found, are easily squandered. Countries and city-states with few or no resources – the short lands, one might call them – must rely on their in- genuity and effort, as Singapore and Switzerland do. They end up being more productive despite – indeed, because – they have so much less to work with. They have made, so to speak, stable marriages with the planet.

Well, what of short rock stars? I have been hearing you asking that question for the past two paragraphs. Don't they make unstable supermodel marriages? Isn't it really a question more of status than simple stature? Well, first of all – are there short rock stars? An online list of short rock stars turns up people like Angus Young of AC/DC, and Flea – but surely these are Second or Third XI rock stars? A rock star nicknamed Sting is a rock star. A rock star nicknamed Flea is not really a rock star. Angus Young, yes, is certainly a star – but a rock star of a very self-consciously short kind, famous, as we all know, for wearing schoolboy outfits on-stage.

In this way, indeed, short men (including short rock stars), in their desperation, shrewdly piggyback on one of the few human predispositions that I think can actually be called hardwired: what we might call the 'neotenic illusion'. By this I mean our readiness to think that anything that has the short stature and plump cheeks and rounded body of a human baby must actually be like a human baby. If we did not think babies were hopelessly cute, after all, we would kill them for being so exhausting. And so panda bears and chipmunks, and short men too, have smuggled their way into our affections through the same cognitive door that was meant to open only for the infants. A typical penguin is as full of rage, violence and dignity as a tiger but they resemble our young, and so are pinned as adorable. They are classified as cute, as short men are, too.

But there is another, more easily overlooked truth that short people know that resource-short countries don't. The concept of shortness, among men at least, is surprisingly elastic. There is a period in the life of a short man – between his early adolescent unhappiness at being short, and his later awakening to the miracle of having achieved so much despite it – when his own shortness becomes invisible to him.

With our suits hemmed and altered, the waist cinched in by a painfully sympathetic tailor, we give the same appearance, in a mirror at least, with no comparison (I almost wrote 'no competition') around, of being about the same as anyone else.

For the prime of a short man's life – Napoleon is the model here again – his shortness is not thematized at all. On horseback in the paintings by David or the Baron Gros, or enthroned by Ingres, Napoleon may look moon-faced, and the little ringlet that dangles above his eye may seem dandyish, but the last thing he looks is short. It is only later on Elba and St Helena that his diminutive stature becomes part of his self-knowledge. The true Napoleonic moment is when age and circumstances conspire to remind the short man of his stature. It was when the emperor had lost the last battle that the truth returned: *I am no longer an emperor. I am merely a short man on a lonely island.*

So, short men learn early this essential truth: that long odds make for good lives. A man's mate should exceed his height, not to mention his little grasp, or what's a heaven for?

It is not an accident, I think, that the great periods of civilization tend to follow on, and then appear, not in moments of abundance alone, but of renewed relief. They come shortly after some disaster that has given an entire community the same sense of having made it by the skin of their teeth that a short man feels, looking gratefully at his wife in the early morning.

Renaissance Florence appeared in the wake of the Black Plague that halved its population. The Paris we love most, that of the Impressionists and the Belle Époque, rose with the smouldering ruins of the Franco-Prussian war still visible in its centre. They were reduced – shortened, one might even say – but they clung to pleasure. Entitlement and its disappointments make wars. Desperation and gratitude build cities.

The Football Fallacy

19 October 2014

I am back in London, a city I love – love more, I think some-
times, than the people who live in it do these days – and where
I've lived at times in my life, and where my football club,
Chelsea, now reigns. When I first supported Chelsea, back
in 1973, the side was made up of pale-faced Englishmen and
ruddy-faced Scots. They all wore tiny, tight shorts and had that
strange shaggy, discouraging Seventies hair – 'mullets', they
were called. You only had to watch them, on a smoky Saturday
morning, to tell at once that they had been raised to a peak of
fitness on diets of beer, bad whisky and boiled potatoes, each
provided extra pace by a pack-a-day cigarette habit. They were
thrilling until, loaned to their national sides, they played other
countries and you found that they weren't, really. It didn't
seem to matter.

Now Chelsea is owned by a billionaire from Russia and made up of several millionaires from Spain and West Africa, with a couple of Englishmen left over to cower on the sidelines, wearing fake suntans and curly black wigs and hoping to be taken for Brazilians. This strikes me as a completely positive change, making them much more exciting to watch – but some of the local flavour is gone, including the peculiar local flavour of not being very good.

My enthusiasm means that I end up talking to my London friends a lot about football, and I am struck to find them still just a bit aggrieved about England's failure in this past summer's World Cup, even though it was indistinguishable from England's failures at the previous twelve World Cups. The reason for this is apparent to me, at least, and I have shared it with my English friends, though for some reason they seem reluctant to embrace it.

It is simple. The English lose at football games because they are not good at playing football. They think they are because they are very good at watching football. That's a skill unto itself. When I follow the *Guardian* live football blogs, the jokes are terrific – far better than they ever are in the parallel French football blogs. But England loses all the same. Simon Gray, in one of his wonderful diaries, describes observing the poet and editor Ian Hamilton's passionate, self-annihilating habits of watching Spurs. A Parisian playwright and a Parisian editor would never do that together – none of them, or very few, live and die with Paris Saint-Germain. The English football lovers convince themselves that their passion for football is so intense that it must express itself on the pitch. It doesn't. The intensity of their attachment to watching makes them naturally assume that their fellow countrymen are equally good at playing. They aren't. But the illusion persists. It will rise again in four years.

This is, I think, a general principle. I am on my way shortly to my previous hometown of Paris. Now, nothing is truer than that the French love writers and admire literature. To be a writer in France is to be blessed with a reverence that no British or American writer can ever hope to attain except in France. Yet, let us be honest, you probably have not actually read a novel by a working French novelist in a long time – though you may well have read in college an obscure bit of French theory about books by a French book theorist. The French talk spellbindingly about great literature more often than they actually make it.

The French, right now, are not very good at writing books. But they are matchlessly good at being literary. This is why, as happened just this week, they keep winning the Nobel Prize for Literature even though the writers who win it are the authors of extremely – and, it must be said, often deservedly – obscure books. The last French Nobel laureate, for instance, was an exceptionally tall man, who spoke six languages, and looked like a cross between Henry Fonda and Max von Sydow.

I was delegated to interview him for PEN, the writers organ-
ization, when he came to New York and I barely came up to
his shoe tops. In my best double-breasted suit, I looked like
a ring boy at a wedding. He was eloquent, gently humorous,
and truly planetary in consciousness. I would have voted for
him in a second as President of World Literature – despite
the truth that I was then and still am struggling to finish any
of his novels, which tend to have all the excitement of the
narration of a UNESCO documentary. I am still not sure how
good a writer he is. But I know that he was a great literary
figure, and that is, after all, one of the things the Nobel Prize
is there to reward.

Call this 'The Constructive Fallacy of the Secondary Activity' –
or perhaps 'The Delusion of Mastery through Proximity'. The
very worst case of this is one I know at home. No one talks
more about democracy, republicanism, self-government and
liberty than Americans. But in truth Americans have no special
skill at self-government – they are only good at dramatizing
their struggle for it. In many respects, the United States is the
least democratic of the big democratic countries. The entire
Constitution, fetishized by Americans to a religious degree, is
designed to keep the country from ever actually becoming a
representative democracy.

The Senate, in which tiny rural states are given as much
power as the large metropolitan ones – so that Wyoming has
as much weight as California – is a permanent barrier to the

majority of Americans ever having their interests fully represented. The system is absurdly tipped against cities, by design, and remains wildly unrepresentative – which is one reason why we have some of the richest farmers, and some of the worst inter-city train travel, in the developed world. The presidency is the site of the most passionate and expensive electoral contests in the world – but then turns out to be an office of almost absurdly limited powers, except in wartime, which may be the simplest explanation of why American presidents so often start wars.

Americans are not very good at practising democracy, but we are very good at advertising democratic ideas – which makes us also imagine, God help us, that we are good at spreading democracy, with the results we know. What Americans are uniquely good at is the rhetoric of republican virtue. British people mostly mumble with embarrassment when you praise their parliamentary traditions – well, the British men I know best mostly mumble in embarrassment if you praise their anything – but they do have the Indian Parliament to point to with post-colonial pride.

One could persist in this line of inquiry. English people, for instance, wrote so many sex farces, for so long, in response to the absence of sex in English life – essentially the same reason, in reverse, that explains why there is so little good literary food writing in France. Our natural gifts are never the subject of our obsessions. No one obsesses over what they do best. Obsession is the subject of what we long for most.

There seem, in other words, to be many kinds of talent at large in the world. Among them is a natural talent for doing things; another, a talent for dramatizing things that we do only with great difficulty. There is a natural talent for performance, of the kind given to the Maradonas and Messis, and there is an acquired talent for the self-conscious presentation of what the talented perform naturally. This need not be a small thing. The self-dramatizing, presentational talent, though it includes lowlifes and small fry like critics and weekly radio commentators, also includes fully equal kinds. Being a great conductor, a Bernstein or a Klemperer, seems no less a talent than being a great composer. The composer makes the music, but it takes the conductor to dramatize it properly.

People always tell you that the path to glory lies through doing what you do best and love most. But for the rest of us, there may be another kind of wisdom. The secret is not to find the thing you do best and then do it more. It may be to find the thing you like most but do least well, and then do something that is almost like it. From this secondary, self-dramatizing activity, you may still make a primary life. You may lose at the World Cup, and yet see your books on football conquer the world. You may write poorly, but represent literature well. Like the Hobbit Bilbo accompanying the dwarves, knowing full well in his heart that he is no burglar, but going on into the dark mountain as if he were, we all make our lives from our longings more often than from our natural talents. But then the longing becomes another kind of talent – and suddenly, there! The dragon is dead.

A Lesson from Love-Locks

24 October 2014

I am back in Paris, a city I love most in the world – I would follow an older wit in saying that New York is my wife and Paris is my mistress, only that seems an insanely self-satisfied masculine thing to say these days – where one of my children was raised and the other one born, and to which I sometimes feel I have an almost too professional amorous relation. I mean by that that people assume, knowing that I lived here and wrote a book about it, that I must return to Paris with the theme of *An American in Paris* playing somewhere in the background and hearty waiters trilling '*Sacré bleu!*' as they pop open bottles of pink champagne. In truth I meander back in a state of advanced melancholia, and clack my heels on the narrow streets in an unsmiling state, wreathed in a raincoat.

Not that Paris is melancholy – well, actually, it is. The grey drizzle and implacable violet skies of Paris in fall and winter remind us that the Impressionists, with their bright dappled light, were first of all fable makers – surrealists. The heroes of Parisian literature all clack their heels, unsmiling, in raincoats on the narrow streets, from Inspector Maigret to Camus. But in my case, at least, something is added – an over-abundance of emotion, a surplus of the heart that has nowhere useful to be delivered or relieved. Even when I am here simply to report a story for a magazine, as I am this week, I feel it.

Paris is a memory-rich place for many – and I am among the many. The girl who became my wife ran away with me to Paris when we were still teenagers, shared a little room in a hotel called, of all things, the 'Welcome', the Hotel Welcome, just like that, and swore to come back some day. We did, and when we did, fifteen years later, two of the most significant things that I think can happen in life (well, after first love in a hotel room) happened to us here.

The first big thing is to watch an infant become a child – to see a tiny consciousness become a distinct, entire human being with a tongue and an articulate imagination and an original point of view. And then, the complement to that big thing occurs when those who were happy as lovers, somehow have to learn to become parents. When once, not long before, you were a boat out on a sea, still watched, perhaps, by a parental eye from a distance, now overnight you become a harbour yourself, with a life-defining responsibility to a new boat, out on its own voyage.

All those perfect, painful things happened to me here, and when I walk the streets, I feel them all again. I still push my son home in his pushchair from the Luxembourg Gardens, see my wife at the corner window nursing our baby and waiting for us to come home – and, belonging as they do to the past, and yet being still so present in my heart, I find that I have nowhere in particular to place the feelings.

There are some emotions in life so strong that there is nothing to do save feel them, over and over again – and that is really no good. It is as if there was a lock of love shackled tight around my heart in Paris. I cannot help but feel it beating, overwhelmingly, and yet there is nowhere for that beat to drive me, save backwards. These are happy memories, of course, but, being past, still make me somehow inexpressibly sad. (I mentioned this emotion once to Marcel Proust, and he said there might be an idea for a book in it.)

I was lucky, of course, to have big things happen in Paris – it makes for pretty pictures of the past. But in a sense it doesn't matter where it happened – I have equally love-locked memories, and a sense of not having anywhere to put them, in Philadelphia, the American city of my birth, where I passed from infant to boy, as my son did in Paris. And Philadelphia is, more or less, the Manchester of America – meaning no ill will to Manchester, just that it, like Philadelphia, presents less pretty pictures than Paris does.

I walk in Paris in the past. All I have left to do now productively, freshly, newly, in Paris is . . . buy socks. There's an unribbed cotton kind here I like that you can't find in America. I think this is a significant fact – I even encourage my fifteen-year-old daughter, who likes to write, to someday begin her autobiography right there. She should begin her memoirs, I tell her, with the sentence, 'My father went to Paris to buy his socks'. Or, more poetically, 'My father bought his socks in Paris', or, still more iambically, 'In Paris, father bought his socks . . .' But she gives me a steady, opaque, slightly sickened look at the suggestion, and clearly already has memoir-opening-sentence plans of her own, probably also involving her father.

In this melancholy mood, I wandered over just yesterday to a favourite bridge of mine, the Pont des Arts, the footbridge that connects the left bank to right – or rather left bank to the Louvre. These days, the bridge is covered, horribly congealed with, groaning under, another kind of love-lock – the small real padlocks people attach to the railings of the bridge, as a sign of their commitment, or at least of their willingness to spend enough on a lock to pretend to be committed. The practice, which I'm sure you've read about, is simple, and by now repeated in the tens of thousands: you buy a padlock, you and your beloved both inscribe your initials on it with a heavy felt pen, you lock it to the bridge – and then fling the key away into the river, indicating that your love will never be unlocked.

The coming of the love-locks post-dates my leaving Paris – they began in the mid-Noughties, I gather. It must have been a touching sight when they first began, and there were only two or three or then five and ten attached to the bridge's grillework. They must have provoked a wry smile from a melancholy walker in a raincoat. Now, they are a ghastly, unsightly nuisance. The bridge groans under their collective egotism, their self-centred marking. Unsightly, ugly, they are a form of three-dimensional graffiti, and dangerous too: part of the parapet of the Pont des Arts collapsed under the weight of the love-locks earlier this year. So much love assembled together – causing so much public ugliness to be locked in place. Even if one guesses that only one in ten symbolizes actual love with any chance of ripening into adulthood – even if they were bought only to buy a night in a welcoming Paris hotel with the other signatory – still, what could be better? And yet how unsightly they make the bridges. The overcharge of love is ruining Paris as a place to be a lover.

The City of Paris, engaged in the inevitable argument with the Prefecture of Police and the Ministry of Culture about exactly whose province love-locks are, has only now begun to do something about them, and that has only made things worse. They have installed sheets of plywood over the thousands of love-locks, which themselves become sites of graffiti. The full irony of this – that the City of Light has to send out the gendarmes to prevent lovers from declaring their love in tangible form – is not lost on anyone. Standing there, appalled by the violence and vulgarity of these affectionate gestures, I recalled Kenneth Clark's famous statement that while one nude is the subject of art, many nudes together are merely naked. The love-locks are raw, naked too, in that sense.

And I felt, suddenly, then, what I am sure the listener has felt before I could say it: that my own love-lock, this tight tangle of memory and longing, is really just as burdensome to the soul as the love-locks are to the bridge and to Paris. For (I thought then) love should never be symbolized by a shackle. Love – real love, good love, love to grow on rather than to be trapped in – is a lock to which the key is always available. Another choice, another day, even perhaps another city, lies out there.

The ugliness of the love-lock lies not in the locks themselves but in the false dramatic gesture that put them there – the key thrown into the water. That kind of love has not really been entrusted to the river. It has merely been abandoned on the bridge.

'I shall buy you a lock,' I vowed silently on the bridge in the rain, 'and you will keep the lock in your pocket while I shall keep the key in mine, and together we would choose, every day, never to need it. Love enchained is what we dream of, but love unlocked is what we need,' I added, trailing into bad blank verse again, as Parisian bridge epiphanies make one do. So I said to myself; or rather, spoke, unheard, to my wife of so many years, at home now, far away from the scene of our first love, caring for our children. And then I resumed my melancholy Parisian walk, feeling, at least momentarily, liberated. And then I went and bought new socks, which I am wearing as I write.

FOUR TYPES OF ANXIETY, AND HOW TO CURE THEM

23 November 2014

I returned home to New York this week, after reporting trips to London and Paris, to find the city in a mild panic about . . . Ebola. Now, Ebola is one of those things that really *are* worth having a panic about – a horrible and highly infectious fatal disease of mysterious vectors; on the list of things to worry about, this is real – unlike whether Chelsea's Diego Costa was fit enough to play, another item on my worry list. But *how* to worry – and how not to; that's the question. I am a professional worrier, anxious by vocation, one thumb always hovering above the panic button: I am so quick on the iPhone keyboard that, in London, riding the rising midnight tide of a toothache, it took me no more than thirty seconds to find an all-night dental clinic on Baker Street – not far, I noted, still a tourist at heart, from Sherlock Holmes's lodgings.

Undue anxiety is the New York affliction, as unearned melancholia is the Parisian one – and over the long years I have discovered various cures, or at least treatments, for galloping anxiety, which I shall now share. Four overlapping but largely distinct types of anxiety afflict modern people, each with its own pathology and palliative. They are: catastrophic anxiety, free-floating anxiety, implanted anxiety, and existential anxiety. Let us take them one by one.

Catastrophic anxiety is the fear of something really horrible happening, right out of the blue: the plane goes down, the virus was left lingering on your plane seat, the terrorist bomb goes off in your bus. By far the best treatment for this fear I've ever found came from a professional guide to cheating at cards. There was a period in my life when I was spending time among great sleight-of-hand men, card magicians, in Las Vegas, and one of them slipped me a guide to card cheating that had been privately printed by a professional card cheat. (Card magic and card cheating are Siamese twins, and no great card magician has not flirted with fiddling his neighbours at cards.)

It was a sour piece of work, but it taught me something vital. Since a card cheat can only cheat effectively on his own deal, unless he has the cards marked – hard to do – the rest of the time he has to just play smart, and this means fully internalizing, as instant reflexes, all the statistical probabilities of card playing. I recall the cheater's insistent formula about these odds, almost his precise words, with indecent clarity. If the odds on whatever it might be – say, drawing to an inside straight – are ten to one, you'll see it this week; if it's a hundred to one, you won't see it this week, but you will see it this year. If it's a thousand to one you won't see it this year, but you will probably see it, once. Anything more than that – ten thousand to one, a hundred thousand to one – you're never going to see at the card table. It's just never going to happen. 'Yeah, but it will happen to someone!' you say. '*Someone* draws an inside straight.' Yeah, he said, but *you* won't.

The great virtue was to think of the odds in terms of things you want to have happen rather than things you fear are going to happen. Turn the fears into desires, and you see how remote they really are. People draw five cards for a royal flush, some-where. You'd be an idiot to think you ever will. Planes do go down. Yours won't. Those are a-hundred-thousand-to-one odds, too – probabilities so remote that you can live your life in the conviction that it will never happen, and you won't be wrong. Even among catastrophic events the odds are often better than you think. The level of casualties among British soldiers in World War One were about 10 per cent – the odds of surviving as a British infantryman were actually very good, considering. This doesn't make World War One any less of a catastrophe; but it reminds us that even catastrophes are rarely as catastrophic as we fear.

Now, free-floating anxiety is the worst kind of worry, because each worry can always be replaced with another: there will be no work tomorrow, the rent or mortgage can't be paid, the school fees, the work overdue, the . . . I have known it to get so bad, even with seemingly serene people, that it can only be treated with medicine, which works, fortunately.

But it can also be sublimated, accepted as inseparable from an aspect of human nature and human ambition; you can learn to use it because it simply means work to be done. Self-renewing worry is a legacy of our predatory nature. Herbivores graze nonchalantly across the pasture of the world; lions and tigers, for all their glory, are anxiety-driven beasts. Watch their eyes and you see, not majesty, but worry, floating free: *Does the impala see me now? Has it seen me yet? Am I close enough? When to pounce? And will there be another impala to feed the cubs tomorrow?* It does make for a driven life. But it is better to be a little bit driven than forever drugged. Zoo-fed lions, they say, become depressed.

Implanted anxiety is like the catastrophic kind but raises less from the fear of big disasters than from the ever-changing tides of long-term public worry – from the headlines. Yesterday, it was ISIS in Iraq, today it's Ebola in West Africa, and always the next thing coming to get us all. It is a natural consequence of living in a news culture: headlines are scary and the larger proportion of good news is not news at all. All over New York, in the early morning light, infections that would have killed in a minute are being cured; women who a mere century ago would have died in childbirth are cuddling their ingeniously delivered babies; hearts are being mended. And one man is isolated for an Ebola infection. But he is all we see.

This asymmetry of implanted anxiety is built, blessedly, into an open society; only totalitarian ones insist on reporting only the good news. But the daily dosage is still often unhealthy. The only remedy is to absent yourself from it, however briefly. Our family learned to do this, at first by accident, by going away for three weeks each summer to a house with no internet, no television, and no cellphone reception and variable electricity. We emerge and find out all the anxiety-causing events we have missed, and are puzzled by them. Hair-raising as they were, our hair was not raised, and by now most everyone else's scalp has flattened out too. (Of course, nothing fixes everything; flee, say to a small West African nation to have no internet, etc., and you may find yourself in the midst of an Ebola epidemic. But one can say of the absence-treatment the most that can be said for any analgesic: it helps, usually.)

Of deliberately implanted anxiety, the kind that cynical politicians have used to control and regiment their people, not enough bad things can be said. After 9/11 in New York, a horrific but specific injury was deliberately levered into an apocalyptic panic. In the annals of courage and utter cowardice, none are more vivid than the contrasting pictures of Churchill on the rooftop of 10 Downing Street, coolly watching the Blitz, and Dick Cheney cowering in a bunker to make his fear contagious.

Of existential anxiety . . . well, this is the inescapable kind. Our mortality is not a long shot; it is, so to speak, a dead cert. And even if we can hold that anxiety at the arm's length that we mostly manage, the existential agony for those we love is too great. One dead twenty-year-old on the Western Front took many other lives – his parents', his fiancée's, his friends' – with him. Grief is absolute. The best that we can do is to take control of the other three kinds of anxiety, so that then there is a possibility that in the time we have left we will have the mental space to seek out pleasures rather than focus on unfixable problems.

I mentioned my London toothache and its Baker-Street-at-2-a.m. cure. As I sat in this strange, single examination chair on the third floor – with, to be sure, the themes, and many scenes, from *Sweeney Todd* playing in my anxiety-prone head as I did – I thought of how lucky we actually are to be alive now. The fix was pricey – about the cost of a meal for two in a good London restaurant. But it was worth it. At 2 a.m. I had my tiny preoccupying tooth fixed, and felt exuberant, the weekend to look forward to.

If humanism has a message it is not the fatuous one of progressivism that says everything will always get better; but the real one of the all-night dentist and his lonely, well-lit chair: many pains can be relieved, for more and more people. And the good feeling after is not an illusion but a weekend's worth of wonder. For millennia, the world has had a toothache – and thanks to use of critical reason applied to human pain, we do better; we have novocaine and electric drills and late-night dentists with well-washed hands.

The thrill of the ameliorative solution is built into our mythology of the modern, right there on Baker Street, by Arthur Conan Doyle. Sherlock Holmes is not a miracle worker. He is a problem solver. The people in the Holmes stories don't become immortal or blessed when the Red-Headed League is exposed or the Hound of the Baskervilles shown to be no more than a big dog covered with luminescent paint. They just get to carry on living. Sometimes, Dr Watson even gets a wife out of it.

The job of modern humanists is to do consciously what Conan Doyle did instinctively: to make that thrill of the ameliorative, the joy of small reliefs, of the case solved and mystery dissipated and the worry ended, for now – to make those things as good to live by as they are to experience. We cannot cure existential anxiety, but we can show that there is no necessity to have big ideas worth dying for in order to find small pleasures worth living for, and that the best use of intelligence is to solve real problems rather than seek imaginary consolations. Some days, or late nights, I think we do this a bit better than we once did. Other days I think that the endless cycle of anxiety, of needless panic and false promises, will win. It is, perhaps, my chief remaining worry.

WRITING AN ORATORIO

25 June 2015

Everyone thinks he can write a song, and now I have. The haunted, wild look you see in the eyes of professional song-writers at cocktail parties rises from the popular idea that any of us, given the chance, can do what they do as well as they do it – while the fur earmuffs you see them wearing even on the hottest summer days are there from a desperate attempt not to have to listen to the songs the rest of us write and insist on playing for them. 'I think I just feel how everyone feels, that I have three or four really great folk albums in me,' Hannah says complacently on *Girls*. Everyone thinks that.

But now I have done what all of us amateurs dream of doing: written words to someone's music and heard it sung. Not a song alone, but an entire work – called when I am in a puffed-up mood an 'oratorio', when I am feeling more modest a mere 'song cycle', and when I am feeling more modest still a 'concept album', as yet unrecorded. It's called *Sentences*, with music by the inspired young composer Nico Muhly, and seeing it premiere, a few weeks ago, at the Barbican goes high on my list of things I did that made life matter – like the birth of a child, only with less sweat and better dressed. (Yes, it *was* nicely received. Writers, as they will be the first to tell you, *never* read reviews but, oddly, they have the good ones forced on them against their will by friends, and then feel obligated to forward them to everyone on their email contacts, out of a reluctant sense of social courtesy.)

The story we told was that of the great computer scientist Alan Turing, and it was sung by the amazing countertenor Iestyn Davies – but I won't detain you with its genesis or my own interpretation of what in it works and what doesn't. I will say that I was working on the libretto for the song cycle even as I was also writing the script – what is oddly called the 'book' – and the words – what are, less oddly, called the 'lyrics' – to a Broadway-style show. Working for the commercial theatre, every syllable – no exaggeration – gets argued over: does it lead with the inevitable pull of emotional logic to the next step in the story? In our Barbican-directed oratorio a great deal of indirection and obliquity was welcome. This has led me to announce that, in our age, the difference between entertainment and art is that in entertainment we expect to do all the work for the audience, while in art we expect the audience to do all the work for us. If they are baffled, they are intrigued, even impressed. In show business, if they are baffled, they leave.

But the deeper relation between words and music – the way they land in the listener's ear, and then her soul – is more complicated than it seems. Music alone is puzzling enough: how it is that the mind makes sound into music and music into meaning is one of the big unanswered questions. Music and words together, no matter how hard we craft them for lucidity and shape and dramatic clarity – and it is the good faith of the art form to do so as elegantly as we can – exist, in the end, in an older realm of magic and enchantment, a place where the nursery rhyme and the church hymn and the pop single all meet. They work as spells do – that is, either entirely or not at all. We sing – and the magic door swings open, or it doesn't, and there's no explaining it. Three boys from Liverpool sing 'She loves you, yeah, yeah, yeah' and the world turns off its axis. Had they sung, as Paul McCartney's father wanted, 'Yes, yes, yes', the old path would not have changed.

The libretto writer, I should add at once, is not merely the junior partner – or not even a partner. More like the man who sweeps out the candy wrappers from the theatre floor after the patrons leave. Who now remembers the name of the man who set the texts for Handel's *Messiah*? The only libretto writer whose name anyone remembers – other than the great lyricists of the American musical theatre, the sacred law firm of Mercer, Loesser and Hart – is Lorenzo da Ponte, who is my hero. He was Jewish and a priest, and a Venetian and a New Yorker. It's a sympathetic package, and he wrote – wrote for, more than with, Mozart – the three operas that may well be the height of all artistic creation: *The Marriage of Figaro*, *Così Fan Tutte* and *Don Giovanni*.

This is a big claim, I know, but think about it: they are witty, universal, marry the art of poetry to the mysteries of music, and touch all hearts. Michelangelo by contrast is enclosed is the sublime exaltation of a single superstition, and Shakespeare belongs, in the end, to our tiny band of English speakers. But no one doesn't get those operas. If the aliens arrived on earth from Neptune and asked us, 'What should we go out to see first that you have made?', I think we would say, '*Così Fan Tutte*.' (Though I also think we would add, 'Oh – and watch Cary Grant in *North by Northwest*.' But then the aliens would say, 'Oh. *North by Northwest*! Yeah, we saw that already on Neptune. Everybody in the galaxy has seen *North by Northwest*.')

I will say to all the amateur songwriters out there – not to mention Sunday opera librettists – that the real challenge in writing words for music lies in the tiny space between convention and contrivance. Musical theatre of all kinds, whether leading to song or aria, from the highest of Mozart to the lowest, or most pop, of One Dimension, er, Direction, is inherently conventional. It has to be. It depends on a completely unreal convention: people singing when they would speak. One embraces the conventions, explores them, and soars with them. Rhymes and English oddities shape one's language as much as one's emotions. For the Turing piece I wrote the lyrics – the libretto – first, and tried, as best I could, to capture in stanzas the *sound* of a man caught between great clarity of mind and confusion of the heart: lucid about ideas, muddled (or repressed) about emotion and desire.

But a single touch of contrivance spoils it all. Any time we feel the composers creating coincidence or engineering emotion, making melodrama rather than musical drama – moving incidents rather than exploring character in collision with itself or another – we rebel inside. In *Così Fan Tutte* we accept the convention of disguised Albanians. But we accept it because Mozart writes his most sublime music for the silliest parts. If it became cute, we would rebel against it. That 'Yeah, yeah, yeah' mattered because it was what such a boy would actually say to a friend about a girl. The smirk, or the hack's weary, knowing devices, are both enemies of enchantment, and without enchantment, music and words mean nothing.

The force of music is mysterious. We know this from experience of the music we love: that it casts a spell before it spells out sense. The second side of The Beatles' *Abbey Road*, with the tacked-together fragments, is a powerful anthem of passage – from the delicate bittersweet feelings of adulthood in 'You Never Give Me Your Money' to the affirmation that you'll 'Carry That Weight'.

That they knew this, or planned it – intended it – seems

impossible. But that they achieved it isn't. None of it makes any sense. None of it needs to. Music is so emotionally overwhelming that it pushes the discursive and explanatory roles of language aside – and it is part of the job of the writer to get out of its way. Even in Handel's *Messiah* we recall lyrical fragments more than whole stanzas: 'Unto us a child is born', 'How beautiful are the feet', 'And we, like sheep'. When we think through our experience of our favourite oratorios, our favourite arias, our most important pop songs, they are almost always the experience of a forceful fragment: three or four words – 'How beautiful are the feet' or 'Shake it up'.

It is a mysterious, semi-physical response, in which the audience does do as much work as the artists. It works or it doesn't. Small fragments of sound and sense strike our hearts as shrapnel our skin; they lodge and wound us, independent of their intended trajectory of the shot. The audiences respond or they don't; they are less like a crew of supercilious analysts and more like a magnet set to one pole or another. If the pole is right, they are drawn irresistibly to the sound on stage. If it isn't, no amount of seduction or intelligence can draw them in, any more than a physical magnet can be made to adhere to metal by goodwill or affection. Sung words belong more fully to the world of ritual and routine, of incantation and mothers' murmurings, than to the fully lucid and well-lit world of argument and dramatic advance. They work, or not.

The one thing I have learned is this: our minds make

meaning out of music by not making *too* much meaning out of lyrics. One learns as a librettist to tiptoe to the edge of argument, and then back off to the limbo-land of implication and indirection. The most memorable lyric of Stephen Sondheim is the most offhand – a rueful farewell, but exactly to whom or exactly why, we never know: I hear the producer or book writer saying, '"Send *in* the clowns"? Shouldn't it be "Call *off* the clowns"?'. But in the clowns must come, for reasons only clowns and composers know.

Honouring the ancient mysteries of the rituals of word and sound is where the simplest song, and the most advanced modern music, begin. I have not learned why music matters most, but I have learned a great deal about the power of voices, the limits of language to explain, and its power to invoke, and about the mysterious unpredictable magnetism that passes between an audience and art. Above all, I have learned that musicians are a superior race. We are lucky to share this planet – or any other – with them.

A Lesson from iPhones
31 July 2015

Not long ago, I got to spend a couple of days in my favourite city of Paris, and while I was there I lost my iPhone. I wasn't sure exactly when, and I wasn't sure exactly how. We were staying at an old-fashioned hotel right across from the Gare du Nord, which is the great train station in Paris where iPhones go to be stolen. It seems to have a kind of magnetic attraction for smartphones of all kinds – meaning, really, just that it's a locale for pickpockets who can, in effect, wangle a smartphone from your pants by sheer force of will from across the station floor.

We had gone to the Gare du Nord to find a taxi to take us out to Saint-Denis – for my work – now a slightly grimy suburb of Paris that in its day was the cathedral seat of the French kings. All I knew was that by the time we got back to the hotel, I no longer had my iPhone. In the strange way of these things, I had no memory of the last time I had held it. One of the oddities of our time is the phenomenon of the phantom iPhone – the certainty that you feel your smartphone vibrating in your pocket when, in fact, it isn't. So I could remember it at various moments, thinking that I had felt it vibrate, but couldn't be sure if it had, or if it was just my nerve endings.

All the odds suggested, though, that it vanished some time and place around the Gare du Nord – that a skilled pickpocket had taken it. I ran my head back through all of our encounters and intersections as we had searched for a cab, but I couldn't pick out the telltale pickpocketing moment. No one had asked me to sign a petition; no one had brushed alongside me or accidentally spilled something on or near me; no child had tugged at me plaintively . . .

I knew the full catalogue of those distractions because only a year before I had come to Paris and the Gare du Nord to write a reporting piece about, as it happens, pickpocketing in Paris, a subject that, in Paris, often unfairly but inexorably, leads to the subject of the Roma in France – to the people we once called gypsies, and sometimes Romany or Roms. It was one of those pieces that well-meaning liberal writers write, thinking that they are exploring prejudice in order to defuse it. I had interviewed Romany activists, and leading Roma thinkers in and out of France – I could even tell you what symbol would have been on the Romany flag if one ever flew over a Romany nation. (A wagon wheel.)

The distinction that I was trying to make when I wrote up what I had seen was that while it might be true that some Roma engaged in pickpocketing, that was not at all the same thing as thinking that the problem of petty theft was ethnic. The horrible stereotype of Jews as grasping and greedy certainly contributes to the hatred of Jews with all its horrible consequences. But, still, when Woody Allen, in his old cabaret act, held up a pocket watch and said, 'You see this watch? On his deathbed, my grandfather sold me this watch,' I not only laughed, but knew that, speaking from within his own culture, there was sufficient truth in the stereotype to earn a laugh. My own great-aunt had asked me, on her deathbed, exactly how much the *New Yorker* magazine actually paid me.

These questions of others and aliens was, as it happened, very much on my mind, as I was also in France to talk at a seminar about one of the great French Jewish philosophers of the twentieth century, Emmanuel Levinas, whose subject was how we deal with the Other – the big, philosophical one, with a capital 'O'. His philosophy, which tends towards obscure articulation and gnomic utterance, at heart is simple: that we discover ourselves by looking at Others. It supplies a different model in place of the classic French inquiry that Descartes began – what can I know, what can I see, how do I know that I am at all? – since everything I see and hear could be a dream, or a delusion imprinted by a demon, or one implanted in your head by a machine. Tolerating other people is not the second thing we learn laboriously; it is the first thing we have to know in order to know that we are alive at all. Look someone in the eye, sense her mind at work, and you will feel alive yourself. 'Know thyself' is actually bad advice. 'Look around' is better. I felt a certain kind of rueful self-mockery and shame, familiar to liberal journalists, when I realized that my iPhone had been sacrificed to the purity of my sentiments and the loftiness of my philosophical allusions. I had waltzed through the Gare du Nord, having persuaded myself to be imprudent, glorying in my encounter with the Other, and while I was glorying, the Other had taken my phone.

Then on our last night in Paris, as we packed and talked to our hosts, Richard and Agnes, an email arrived – an email written in stilted but fluent English.

'Hello,' it read, 'I am actually the daughter of the taxi driver in Paris and we have found your phone between two seats in the taxicab. So how can we give your phone back? Chong Caroline.'

I answered at once, got her phone number, called. The trick of course was that we were leaving in the morning, and so we arranged for M. Chong to meet us outside our friends' apartment just before our taxi came. We should have left it at that, but then it occurred to all of us at once that it seemed rather pointless to arrange for a taxi driver to drop off a phone five minutes before a taxi driver arrives to take you to the airport, so we called back in a fit of inspiration and arranged with Mademoiselle Chong to have her father come round in the morning, pick us up, return the phone, accept his reward, and then conclude the merry occasion by driving us to the airport.

This negotiation took more time than perhaps this description suggests it should have, since it had to be worked out, in tri-lingual form, with Mademoiselle Chong's fluent French and formal English being translated to her father in Mandarin.

It seemed thrilling. But of course it didn't work. We went down to wait for him – and then waited and waited – and when we finally reached him, discovered that he was indeed waiting for us – at the airport, where he had, virtuously, already gone. Tri-lingual negotiation had its limits, and he had thought we wanted a pick-up.

We found an Uber, and raced off. And here is where the story becomes, I think, a bit special. M. Chong, far from driving off in exasperation as he had every right to do – and as indeed he probably should have done to get his rush hour business – M. Chong, we discovered when we got to the airport, had circled the terminal (you're not allowed to stay in place long) – had actually circled the airport, over and over, waiting for us to call so that he could return the iPhone to us. His view of the Other was so courteously humane that he circled the airport for two hours with the Other's iPhone. Searching for his among the lookalike taxis, all the while I felt shamefully that I would not recognize his face – because I had in our perfectly courteous trip out, never really looked him in the eye. It was, exactly, Levinas's looking around. What had begun as a philosophy had now become a practical question of parking. Would I know the Other when I saw him, having failed to see him properly the first time?

We intersected at last, recognized each other – 'Oh, yes, of course, you!' – and with the plane about to leave, the security line beckoning, I grabbed my iPhone and thrust the small reward at him – which he refused to take. Then off he drove, and once again I had my photos and my screensaver and my notes and my music. What I had feared would be a story about the tragedies of immigration in France turned out to be one about its triumphs, albeit in a suitably muted tone – not about ethnicity but about . . . M. Chong and his daughter. Or maybe a better way of putting it is that there are no tragedies, no triumphs, there are only individual cases, which may merge together into muddy patterns – at times, they may even gang up in train stations – but are finally, ineffably singular. The Other comes to us only one by one, with a daughter with elaborate but imperfect high school English. There is no Other with a capital 'O'. There are only others, circling the airport in a moment of dogged and unearned charity.

As soon as we got home from Paris, I told our kids the story and was about to unload some moral lessons on them. My wife cut me off before I could. 'Dad's right. There is a life lesson. Always – *always* – look back at the seat when you leave a taxi.'

I couldn't argue with that.

Long-Form Television

10 August 2015

Many people I know have recently been overtaken by a kind of paralytic illness. It involves hours spent in apathetic torpor, addicted to a mindless, slow-acting and exhausting drug. There is no known cure, and, as addicts will, the addicted like to share details of their addiction, shrug off its bad effects, and beg for more.

I am referring, of course, to the plague of the long-form television series in its deadly DVD form, which you can also catch in the form of on-demand video if your kid has the right wi-fi equipment in his video-game console. The hollow eyes and the exhausted looks – not to mention the insanely tedious conversations – that you hear rise over dinner parties and on commuter trains, all result from binge-watching *Breaking Bad* and *Game of Thrones* and *Mad Men* and the rest. Hour after hour is spent following the intricate plots and, in the case of *Game of Thrones* at least, completely inexplicable plot twists and bottomless interchangeable dramatis personae, of each series.

The business of choosing a long-form television series to become addicted to is eerily like the act of marriage itself. One or two episodes are viewed. They please. They intrigue. They give pleasure. And then, as with marriage, a commitment must be made: if you decide to watch *Homeland* or *Downton Abbey*, you do not really have the option of watching an episode here or there, any more than you can be married for an evening. You are committed to entire programmes – to 'seasons', sometimes six or seven seasons. This means hours – hours and hours and *hours* – of committed viewing. You debate it with your spouse, your friends. 'We're thinking of starting *House of Cards*,' you say nervously. 'You mean the original British one or the American one?' they reply anxiously, in the tone of specialists diagnosing a disease. 'The British one,' you say, and you try to read their ambiguous expressions, as with doctors. (Do they know something they won't tell us?) Soon, everything else in your life – theatregoing, museum visits, eating, breathing – has vanished in your commitment to seven more hours of following the ins and outs of petty crime in Baltimore or the adulterous lives of slow-emoting admen in Sixties New York.

Now, of course, at one level, this is something to celebrate: these series are – well, I except *Game of Thrones* – actually *good*. The miracle in which a true pop-culture form intersects, however briefly, with art – with accomplishment of subtlety and depth and meaning – is so rare that we should sing hosannas any time it takes place. It happened with . . . oh, drama in seventeenth-century London, and opera in eighteenth-century Italy, with the novel in nineteenth-century Europe, and with Hollywood movies in the 1970s. Great work was done and made available to all. And, since we know from history that such golden moments are astonishingly brief – there was a new, great verse tragedy on stage in London every afternoon in 1600, and since then, nothing – we should cherish these moments. We are in the midst of one, and, I know, should not complain.

But we can analyse. For there is that additional oddity about this moment, and that is the appeal of sheer length. We live, after all, in a culture which is famously short of attention span, supposedly quickly amnesiac – a culture so impatient that teenagers no longer have time to talk to each other on the telephone for three minutes, but must text each other in cryptic shorthand, while simultaneously texting some other three teenagers, a practice that, by now, has passed to their parents. (The most eager texter I know is a forty-five-year-old actress.) Political speeches have been reduced to talking points; journalism to money quotes; long-form reporting to mere takeaways.

And yet this same culture now has an appetite for slowly wrung-out storytelling that would have shamed the Greeks, listening to a bard recite in monotone the ancient epics of their race; or, for that matter, would have shamed the Elizabethans, watching the original *Hamlet* wend its way through a mere five or so hours. By comparison with *Breaking Bad*, *Hamlet* at full length is positively epigrammatic. Even the Victorians, with their multi-volume novels, are usually portrayed reading them bit-by-bit in bed, over six months or so. I don't recall the binge-reading of *Middlemarch* or *Our Mutual Friend* consuming many hours of the Victorian evening. They snatched at their stories, as we once did at ours.

I have a theory, therefore, which I shall now present to you: you can call it 'Gopnik's Law of the Conservation of Cultural Capital'. In any cultural period, I believe, a steady, similar amount of information, emotion, narrative – of art and entertainment – is being dispersed throughout the society. But there are invisible laws of compensation at work to be sure that a fixed capital sum remains in place. If the prose of public life is eloquent enough to demand our attention – as it was, say, in the Augustan eighteenth century, when Burke's speeches could go on for days and even wretched condemned men were expected to orate before they died – then the literature of the period will be relatively aphoristic and condensed, offering neat verse couplets and short, mordant allegories. And, from Pope's rhymed poems to Voltaire's *Candide*, that's what the popular literature of the Enlightenment was indeed like. The letters, the poems, the public life of the time are all equally aphoristic, sharing the fixed sum of narrative capital. Ben Franklin's memoirs are concise because the Declaration of Independence was just as well worth reading.

If, on the other hand, public life is especially tedious or unduly pious, and so rife with obvious hypocrisy as to be almost unendurable – as it was with the Victorians, and is with us – then the forms of popular entertainment and art will be spacious and long-winded. They will, so to speak, take up the slack, inject the truth of human affairs into our lives where it's missing. Or, if we live musically with three- and four-minute popular songs, as we mostly have done in the past thirty or so years, then when serious opera does appear, as with the work of John Adams and the like, to get from Act One to Act Two will take what feels like several days. (Yes, there are many exceptions to this rule; write to the BBC, not me.)

And so in this YouTube and Twitter time, the Compensatory Law of Cultural Conservation insists that our larger forms will be . . . large. Really large. Ten hours, twenty hours – stretching out over seasons and years, and compelling their admirers to sit, helpless and enslaved, in front of their televisions. If we did have time to telephone, if we thought that texting was shameful, we would have no time for *The Wire*. Eliminating one forces equilibrium in the other.

Small causes can make great art. One reason for the explosion is that the great cable networks in America don't need ratings or commercials, they need *subscribers*, and the talk these series generate is valuable in and of itself. In Hollywood in the Seventies, for a few brief years, pessimistic endings were suddenly acceptable in popular entertainment – and really, there was, in first impulse, no more to the tragic maturity of *The Godfather* and *Chinatown* than that. Now the new feeling is, that if you have sixteen hours to fill, then the characters must be filled out. This simple thought has inspired this renaissance in popular drama.

And it too will end? Possibly. The other, frightening – or seductive – future that this rule entails is also obvious. As communication, public and political and spiritual, becomes ever more condensed, as newspapers close and are replaced exclusively with Instagram feeds, as texting becomes ever more enciphered, and as the demotic slang of teens (which we all speak sooner or later) becomes more abbreviated, then we can expect, or dread, ever longer compensatory popular narratives. The next great HBO or BBC event will take, not hours, but days, then weeks – until at last we shall, doubtless, arrive at the nirvana of narrative: the moment when the programmes we watch take exactly as long as the lives we lead, with each episode of the story consuming twenty-four hours of our lives, the circuit between life and art finally complete, and no time in our lives at all to do anything but hold our devices on our lap to tweet and text, while our eyes are fixed relentlessly on the series that engrosses us. It may be called *The Singularity*; or merely *Life: A Nostalgic Salute*.

I am getting ready for the day.

Vanilla Happiness

19 February 2016

Men and women have long searched for the fountain of youth, the meaning of life, and the secret of happiness. Well, youth still passes, life still puzzles, but the secret of happiness has, it seems, at last been found. It is vanilla yoghurt.

This is not a facetious conclusion, or at least was not intended to be when it was offered not long ago by a team of Austrian, Finnish and Dutch scientists who have been filling their dark winter days studying the emotional responses of subjects when they eat different kinds of yoghurt.

You may think that people don't actually have emotional responses when they eat yoghurt – that eating yoghurt is a way of *avoiding* any emotional response. It is arguably the least feeling of all the breakfast foods – very far from the emotional excitements and hedonic highs of toast, bacon or marmalade.

I once went to a wedding where the bride and groom actually exchanged marmalades during the ceremony. (Yes, it was in California, but they did.)

No one does that with yoghurt. As it happens, I like Greek yoghurt for breakfast – but it is a way of seeming to be engaged in something while my spouse talks about her dreams, her symptoms and her plans. Then the little dog gets to lick what's left in the plastic cup. It is a ritual, but it is hardly romantic. Nonetheless, the tri-national team persisted. They found that while fruit flavourings in yoghurt made no difference to anyone's happiness, there was, and I quote, a 'highly marked hedonic response to vanilla'. Eating vanilla yoghurt made people happy.

I should add that they used an odd technique to measure the happiness of their subjects. Asking people how they feel when they eat something is, apparently, too easy. It is a principle of psychology that people try to please psychologists by saying what they think the psychologists want to hear. So, instead, the psychologists showed their subjects seemingly unrelated photographs of seemingly unrelated people and asked how happy the subjects thought *those* people were. Apparently, it is also a principle in psychology that we project onto others – or photographs of others, anyway – what we feel ourselves.

Showing a combination of Austrian tenacity, Finnish purposefulness and Dutch flair, the researchers pursued the question more deeply. *Why* did vanilla yoghurt make people happy? And here is where the subject blossoms and blooms and swells and begins to touch on issues larger even, if you can credit it, than happiness and its keys.

For one simple explanation is that vanilla is just inherently pleasing; it has long been known that vanilla scents in hospital waiting rooms make patients calmer and happier. Well, it says that in the study: myself, I've never noticed a vanilla scent in a hospital waiting room. Hospital waiting rooms have hospital waiting room scents. Still, apparently this is so, and it is not an accident that vanilla is, so to speak, the base scent of our lives. It is because it has long been intuited to be the most quietly pleasing of flavours. Vanilla has gotten a bad rap for the same reason that parliamentary democracy does: it works too well to make much noise.

The other theory, though, vibrant and equally persuasive, is that what was making Hans and Jari and Johan (I am assuming that the subjects were divided along the same national lines as the scientists) happy was not simply the scent and flavour of vanilla. It was that they were *not told in advance what they were going to eat*. They looked at the white stuff in the breakfast bowl, and assumed that what they were about to eat was plain yoghurt. Tasting, they discovered that it was instead vanilla – and their pleasure rose with the surprise that it did not taste like yoghurt but like *vanilla* yoghurt. It was the element of unexpected pleasure that was the secret of happiness. The secret of happiness was not eating vanilla yoghurt. It was *not expecting to eat* vanilla yoghurt, and then eating it. You expect plain yoghurt, you get vanilla, and bliss descends and stays.

I'm sure you've sensed, as I did, that no experiment in eating, or in anything else, has ever so neatly laid out the dilemmas and secrets of all aesthetics, erotics and the philosophy of pleasure. All arguments about what gives us pleasure in art, in bed and in life are vanilla yoghurt questions. Are the intrinsic qualities of something more powerful than the context in which we perceive it, or are what we call the intrinsic properties really only the effect of expectations and surprise?

Do we admire famous paintings, for instance, because they are intrinsically beautiful, or because we have been coaxed by our expectations into finding them so? Take, say, the Mona Lisa. You may recall that the aesthetes' view, popular in the nineteenth century with critics like Walter Pater, is that she is intrinsically beautiful and mysterious – those settled hands, those blue mountains, that smile. The other view, argued in our time by the art historian E. H. Gombrich and his disciples, is that countless unsmiling sober Italian ladies had to precede her for Mona to have the effect she does. Against those expectations of sobriety, a minimal smile creates maximal mystery. A small smile delights when none precedes it. Our minds prepare for nothing, and then get vanilla, and we are happy.

Music theorists say similar things – that the overwhelming

emotional effect of music doesn't rise from the sounds themselves, but from the expectations of our ears. We hear the C minor chords in Beethoven's Fifth as extreme only because our minds are accustomed to hear C major as normal. The chord itself is nothing; the preparation all. There are no sad sounds or happy sounds. There are only expectations, manipulated by the composer.

Sex, of course, is the greatest arena of these effects. The truth is that we keep our marriages alive by a skilful coaxing of yoghurt flavours. It may seem odd to insist that we have to try and pretend that what we are about to eat is not vanilla in order to enjoy the fact that it is vanilla – but in truth we do that all the time. We try to create a circumstance where we do not know what the flavour is of something whose flavour we know all too well, or well enough.

The second honeymoon, the weekend getaway, are instances of this power of self-created context. Money is spent on plane tickets, at Agent Provocateur or La Perla, or at the chemist's counter, or for that matter at the men's cologne shop, to create a context of the unknown, of uncertainty. What flavour, so to speak, will this yoghurt be? Well, it's still vanilla, but, having coaxed ourselves into the fantasy of not knowing, the vanilla is enough to make us happy again.

So vanilla yoghurt alone is not the key to happiness – it is not knowing what we are going to get – or pretending not to know – and then getting vanilla. What we ought to spray in hospital waiting rooms is the scent of surprise – or at least we should leave the room unscented day after day, only to delight the patients one morning with vanilla.

Ever since I read this study I have been eating vanilla yoghurt for breakfast, hoping to be happy. And I am now prepared to announce that the truth of the matter is utterly different from what the psychologists suggest. For the hidden truth, shamefully concealed by the Austrians and the Finns and the Dutch, and their photograph-staring subjects, is that vanilla yoghurt never only contains vanilla. Vanilla yoghurt is, above all . . . sweet. It always contains sugar, and it is the incidental sugar as much as the vanilla scent that surprises us so at 8 a.m., and then makes us happy. Vanilla is merely the free rider.

Once, when I was very small, I was so intoxicated by the scent of vanilla extract when my mother used it in baking that I slipped into the kitchen closet secretly, found the bottle, opened it and took what I expected would be a delirious sip. It was revolting – bitter and alcoholic. I can taste it still: it taught me the truth that pleasure is deceptive, and compound. For the scent of vanilla is nothing without the sugar in the cake. The secret to happiness is the honey.

We dream of sweetness all our lives, and so are surprised by joy when it arrives without warning. Poets have known *that* truth for centuries. Our bodies and our souls do not crave novelty alone. They crave nectar, coming at us unawares. Life does have a secret, and happiness a key. But they are not in a scent or even in a scented surprise. The key to happiness is always the same and it is not vanilla, nor surprise alone. The secret of life is unexpected sweetness.

HUMAN HYBRIDS
11 March 2016

You may have heard of the current kerfuffle here in America about the sin of what is being called 'cultural appropriation'. Some students at Bowdoin, a small liberal arts college in chilly Maine, were punished for wearing Mexican sombreros at a Mexican themed party: they had appropriated Mexican culture as a white person's prerogative. Then, at the Boston Museum of Fine Arts, the practice of trying on a kimono for a selfie in front of a Monet picture of a French woman wearing a kimono was declared *verboten* for Boston, so to speak: it was a form of cultural appropriation of what belongs to Japan, while a production of Gilbert and Sullivan's *Mikado* was closed down for the same reason. It showed only a racist stereotype of Japan, as imperially imagined by white Victorians. There have been more incidents, many at liberal arts colleges, involving Chinese food, and the art form we wrongly call 'belly dancing', and even the hugely popular practice of yoga. They belong to others, and we cannot have them, or take them, for ourselves.

Now, I am *not* about to launch into a tirade against the 'politically correct'. I am old enough to recall that 'politically correct' actually began as a term of self-mockery used by the hyper-sensitive, ruefully, against themselves – lightly guying their own good efforts at eliminating the casual sadism of daily interactions. 'I guess I'm just being a little politically correct here, but . . .' someone – almost always a woman – would say in the 1980s, and then point out an instance of unconscious sexism somewhere in the room. And in truth, 'politically correct' is almost always these days synonymous with 'sensitively courteous'. We know this because when someone says, 'I am not going to be politically correct,' what he – and it is always a he – really means is: 'I am not going to be sensitively courteous to anyone's feelings except my own and that of my gang!' We have a demonstration of this principle every night on our screens over here these days, and it is a nightmare.

Nonetheless, I would be lying if I did not say that the practice we call 'PC' has its absurd aspects. It is funny because it puts more weight on the words we use than the actions we take: always a mistake. My son's dormitory, at *his* liberal arts college, has a live-in resident of deliberately indeterminate gender who wants to be referred to neither as 'he' nor 'she' – they are imprisoning patriarchal categories – nor as 'it' (that would be an objectifying put-down) but as 'they' and 'them'. This is at least convivial. When he – no, she – no, *they* are there, it's always a party.

There is something funny about this undue weight given to words, because we can't be endlessly sensitive and attentive and courteous in *every* interaction we have in life; people who try end up seeming insipid and exasperating rather than entirely admirable. My own wife, for instance, who does try to be so in every exchange, is, though much loved, also famous for the length of time it takes her to extricate herself from a social occasion, having first to be certain that she has been nice to everyone. This leads her, perversely, to avoid many social occasions, for fear of wearing herself out from attentiveness – the price of such niceness can be very high. Prolonged punctiliousness is exhausting to all, particularly to husbands – er, mates – er, partners – er, cohabitating life colleagues.

But the idea that cultures – recipes, or poses, or even hats – belong to one group rather than another is something worse than a moment in a comedy of manners; or, rather, it misses the way that a larger comedy of manners has always shaped what we mean by 'culture'. Cultural mixing – the hybridization of hats, if you like – is the rule of civilization, not some new intrusion within our own. Healthy civilizations have always been mongrelized, cosmopolitan, hybrid and corrupted and expropriated and mixed. Healthy societies seek out that kind of corruption, because they know it is the secret of pleasure.

They count their health in the number of imported spices on their shelves.

One of my favourite stories of how healthy cultural hybrids happen involves Japan and the West – though not, in this case, *The Mikado*. You know those beautiful nineteenth-century Japanese prints – by Hiroshige or Hokusai or their friends, poetically depicting everyday events, or favourite places, all in charming comic book colours, with Mount Fuji often delicately if secretively included in every view (as a kind of sublime *Where's Wally?*)? Those delicate black-edged figures and long, almost cartoonish faces, that startling juxtaposition of foreground and distance, that informal and haiku-like lyricism? Japanese prints had, as everybody is taught in class, an enormous influence on French Impressionist art in the middle of the nineteenth century. They were, exactly, an exotic appropriation.

Well, it turns out that they weren't really exotic at all. They were the product of the Japanese infatuation with Western perspective drawing, which had only recently arrived in Japan on ships and boats as part of their opening to the West. The Japanese artists saw them, and saw expressive possibilities in them that the Western artists were too habituated to the system to notice. The Japanese appropriated Western perspective in ways that Westerners would never have conceived of. Then their pictures got sent back to Europe – where they looked wonderfully exotic, and remade the Western art they originally hailed from. It's exactly the same process that happened in our own lifetime when Howlin' Wolf and Big Bill Broonzy records sailed over to Liverpool and the suburbs of London, got listened to by boys who barely understood their context but loved their attitude. Ten years later you get Mick Jagger and John Lennon. Innocent imitation is always the engine of cultural innovation.

Nor is it just that the borrowings can be beautiful. The things we borrow show us the things we are. Having passed through Chuck Berry, The Beatles and the Stones could better claim their own distinctive Englishness. Hearing Chuck Berry be so entirely black and American, they were inspirited to become, in 'Penny Lane' or 'Ruby Tuesday', entirely British. In the same way, distinctly English food – all those real beers and farmhouse cheddars – has only got better because restaurants that served real Italian food helped show how wonderful a coherent seasonal-market-based cuisine could be. If we want to be ourselves, we have to travel – and nowadays, we do much of our travelling internally.

If all you know is your provincial culture, you don't know enough to know if your culture is provincial or not. When it ceases to be, you're not wise enough to recognize it. American writing became major in the nineteenth century with novelists like Herman Melville and a poet like Emily Dickinson, but mostly no one knew it – it was too jumbled up with bad stuff. After you've read Joyce, you see that Melville really is in the same league, and if you know Christina Rossetti, you know that Emily is better still. When American painting got great in the

1940s, it was because American painters now knew enough to know what great painting looked like.

In no area are power relations so fluid as they are in cultural borrowings. The language of the oppressor becomes the language of the oppressed, as English did for the slave and then philosopher, Frederick Douglass. Appropriation is far more often empowering than oppressing. There's no cheaper way to get the drop on a bad guy than to borrow his hymns and habits and make them your own. That's what diaspora Jews have done throughout their history. It's how German became Yiddish, and Yiddish became the great language of Jewish folk tale and protest.

So, cultures cannot be corrupted enough; civilizations cannot be appropriated too often. Nor is this only seen in heroic acts of original innovation: it's a nightly act of healthy practice. Last night, for instance, I made a Burmese curry, which combines Indian spices – cumin and turmeric – with the Chinese technique of stir-frying. The ingredients came from our local Green Market – and I always mix butter in with the cooking oil, a habit picked up in Paris. The recipe also calls for yoghurt, but my wife, of Icelandic extraction, prefers skyr, and it's put together by me, while I amuse no one but myself by doing my very bad international accents. So it's actually a Jewish-Icelandic-Chinese-Indian-Burmese-French émigré-New York state stir-fry. All in one pot, and five minutes.

That's the norm of cooking. That's the norm of life. Blurring the boundaries of culture is what cooking does. When we do the same thing in ways that last longer than dinner, we call it art. Done often enough, it makes what we call civilization.

So: wear sombreros and kimonos and Mormon underwear beneath, if you so like. Eat Chinese food with Indian spices and French butter and celebrate the range of being human. We are mixed in nature, many in our very essence. We can't help it. To be human is to be hybrid. It is as close to a rule of life as you can ever hope to find.

Why Did Shakespeare Want a Shield?

14 March 2016

For various reasons last week I was thinking about Shakespeare and his desire to get a coat of arms and be made a gentleman. I'm sure some of you know the story – how sometime around 1599, someone revived an application to the Garter King of Arms for a heraldic shield and motto for the Shakespeares, and how it's assumed that this was actually done by young William, rather than by his father, John, the old man having by then got into some sort of trouble – religious, political or alcoholic, no one quite knows – back in Stratford. In any case, William did get the coat of arms eventually, complete with a motto, 'Non Sanz Droict' – 'Not Without Right' – which the great Ben Jonson then mocked by having a simple-minded character in a play boast as *his* family motto, 'Not Without Mustard'. The herald who awarded the motto was later made the subject of

224

a proceeding himself, for having passed out status to a 'player' like Shakespeare.

The story is entertaining, and interesting inasmuch as it proves once again what needs no proof: that William Shakespeare of Stratford and William Shakespeare the poet and actor were the same person. But, as I turned the old details over in my mind in light of some new information about it that I happened to be pursuing, one overriding thought did fill my head: why would Shakespeare want a shield? What are there in honours and glittery geegaws and medals and decorations and mottos that can make a man of genius pursue them – and a man of genius, at that, who knew everything there was to know about 'the bubble, reputation', and the general meaningless of all the things of this world?

I should add, immediately, that I throw this stone from a solid glasshouse – or rather, from what would have been a solid glasshouse, had various thrown stones not already broken all the windows. I have one small honour: a French decoration that makes me a make-believe knight in a non-existent empire – a *Chevalier* of Arts and Letters in the French Republic. It entitles me to nothing, empowers me to do nil, and is viewed by all those who see it – to the degree they do – as a touching joke played on a simple-minded American Francophile.

Nonetheless, it means a great deal to me. I wore the medal for the whole evening after the ceremony, to the snickers of my family and the startled looks of the would-be-actor waiters at the restaurant. With French decorations you wear a small ribbon in your lapel afterwards to stand in for the medal even *you* are too embarrassed to wear on your shirtfront – and there I am, on even semi-formal occasions, beribboned. What makes us want honours we know are more like humiliations? Why do we want prizes – whether the Booker, so dearly desired by so many authors, or the prize in the box of the American candy Cracker Jack, whose jingle – 'Candy-coated popcorn, peanuts and a prize' – is the national anthem of American children?

Well, the system of French honours, as they exist now, is a decent case study in the psychology of honours and decorations, since it's mostly traceable to a couple of cynical and shrewd despots: first Louis XIV and then Napoleon himself. Louis had the insight, upon building Versailles, that one of the best ways to keep his quarrelsome and mutinous courtiers from being quarrelsome and mutinous with *him* was to offer them a thousand small honours and courtesies and promotions, and get them quarrelsome and mutinous with each other instead. They were already ennobled, so it didn't pay to ennoble them further – but an invitation to Marly, the King's hunting cottage, or presence at the King's waking up or going to bed, was a keen honour. Fiendishly clever for a rather dull man, Louis made them ask to be invited. They stood by his bedside, saying 'Marly? Marly?' like twelve-year-olds asking to stay up late to watch *Breaking Bad*. It worked. As Saint-Simon, the chronicler of the court, tells us, they were so preoccupied with meaningless little honours that they forgot that all the actual power was in the hands of one man.

Napoleon a century-plus later, refined this system to bring common people into it, creating a range of decorations and medals and honorific orders that kept his low-born generals and newly created nobles in line as well. It worked. It worked twice. People offered the choice between plotting for actual power and pining for a meaningless prize mostly choose the meaningless prize – or enough of them do, often enough, to mostly defuse the plotting. They preferred the prize, wrapped in candied popcorn, to the red protein of power.

There's even a name for this effect in the social sciences. No, it's not the 'Vanilla Yoghurt' effect – this one's called the 'Dodo's Prize' effect. You all know the text from which the name descends. It's in *Alice in Wonderland*, when Alice, after observing the disorganized caucus race of the many animals, turns to the Dodo and asks who has won. 'Everybody has won,' the Dodo tells her gravely, 'and *all* must have prizes.' And, you'll recall, the Dodo then makes Alice pass out comfits (little candies) from her pocket to all the animals as prizes, and finally, since she deserves a prize herself, give her own thimble to the Dodo, who then presents it to her. Alice thinks the whole thing 'very absurd', but Carroll's chief and shrewd satiric insight was that all the animals, and Alice too, are happy with their prizes despite it. The obviously arbitrary – not to mention indiscriminate – nature of who's awarded what, has absolutely no effect on the authority of the prize or the pleasure taken in getting it. We want honours, not earned awards.

The social science term originates, I gather, with the study of psychotherapy. All forms of psychotherapy seem about equally efficient: whether one talks about one's screened sexual memories of Mother for half an hour on a couch, or seeks out Jungian archetypes of Dad, or just does cognitive work in avoiding another quarrel with Sister, all of these therapies, the argument goes, work, or don't work, about as well as the next. What's therapeutic is the idea of therapy. (Obviously, this is much disputed by the therapists.)

But we can generalize the point past psychotherapy. The Dodo Effect is true in every sphere. All must have prizes? All *do* have prizes, or the equivalent. Whatever their bitterness in private, all professions practise mass congratulation in public. There are very, very few pursuits in life where we don't pass out praise and honours all around – the Oscars, just past, are the chief prize in movies, but there are so many subsidiary prizes that everyone gets one eventually. Even the Oscars go around nicely: we are all startled that this cinematographer or that film editor has won her sixth or seventh honour. We assume that all must have prizes, and we pass them out. The human response to feeling powerless is rage; the human response to not having an honour is to . . . invent another. All should have prizes? We all *do*. And every prize is discounted from the outset, except the one we just got. (This can be, of course, enraging when it isn't us or ours. Almost no one has an annoying dog; no one has a dumb kid.)

But there is a very positive side to the Dodo Effect. The competition for meaningless status shows us, secretly, that status is meaningless. If all had honours, you would think no one would value them – but just the opposite is the case. Everybody at Versailles had something, as everyone on a little league soccer team in America gets a prize: 'Mr Inspiration', 'Ms Congeniality' . . . We want honours, not to prevent others from having them but to have them ourselves. People kill each other for power, but they merely ridicule each other for prizes. They envy each other's money and position, but they do not really envy each other's prestige.

No. The real competition is not for prestige. It is for power. The *actual* Booker Prize is being waged among *publishers*, not between authors. The authors are merely the prizes the publishers give each other. A publisher who has a Philip Roth or a Julian Barnes regards him exactly as the author regards his honours: as a kind of meaningless but pretty bauble. If you tried to take Stephen King away, his power would be threatened. Then you would see what happens. A competition for meaningless honours, known to be meaningless from the outset, is therefore just as meaningful when everyone gets one. Let me say that again: if we all know that the prize is worthless, but we want it anyway, then everyone's getting the prize doesn't make it worth any less.

And so to return to our first question. Why did Shakespeare want a shield? Shakespeare wanted an honour, not to feel superior to others, but to feel better about him. He would have been happy had Ben Jonson got a shield and motto of his own. For a moment the hole we all feel of non-recognition and insufficient appreciation is covered over. Knowing that others share the same emptiness, we don't envy the fig leaf they wear. People go to war over power. They make peace with prizes. Why did Shakespeare want a shield? To keep in a box for himself alone. Sometimes, at night, he took it out and looked at it.

I know.

Can We Ever Find Quiet Time?

18 March 2016

For New Year's, I made two resolutions and now, three months into the year, I can report that I have kept neither. One was to meditate for twenty minutes every afternoon, the other was to listen to good music for an hour every night. By 'meditate' I mean to sit for twenty minutes and breathe while reciting a mantra of my own devising. Well, not exactly of my own devising – I read it in one of the meditation books I buy every year in December to remind me what to think in January. By 'good music' I mean not just good music – I listen to the music of my teenage years as I write, the Stones and Eric Clapton and the like, which long ago entered my bones and vibrates with my heart – but the kind of good music I don't listen to enough. Haydn quintets, Mozart quartets, Schubert octets . . . You know. All the tets.

When I meditate, I sit, and breathe and try not to think nor to judge how well I'm not thinking. I take twenty minutes, and then I bow to the four rivers of my life: the Schuylkill, of Philadelphia, where I was a child; the Saint Lawrence, in Montreal, where I came of age; New York's Hudson, where I have passed my adult life; and the Seine in Paris, where I found myself as a writer, and where my children were raised and became conscious. Those children find this ritual, when they observe it, deeply, intractably funny.

The ritual of music listening is in itself, in our culture, another shot at meditation. Simon Gray wrote a whole good, sad play, *Otherwise Engaged*, about a middle-aged Londoner struggling to listen to his Wagner recording while being interrupted by his friends, and families and, Gray being Gray, ex-lovers and current ones. In our house, my twenty-year-old son is a music major, who actually finds the guitar chords for polyphonic chant and regards my Mozart and Schubert chamber music rather as my father regarded *his* father's affection for 'light classical' music of the Hollywood Strings kind: he is indulgent but bemused. For that matter, my Spotifyed son regards the CDs that I listen to – which for me have some of the gleaming excitement of the 1980s lingering in them – as quaint and creaky as the 78s that you could still find in my grandparents' basement when I was small, twenty or thirty of them necessary to hear a single symphony.

The trick about late night – or even early evening – music listening in a New York apartment is that the sound levels have to be balanced for the neighbour's ears as much as for your own. Every New York apartment building is like one of those precariously nested pick-up-sticks constructions: a single loud sound can upset it all, and bring furious neighbours, with no taste for the cannon in Berlioz, buzzing up. So delicate chamber music of the early-nineteenth-century kind is best – though as my musical son reminds me, at proper volume it would be not delicate at all. If we brought three violins and a piano into the apartment they would not be a mid-range murmur but a loud burst of Viennese passion filling the hallways on the sixth floor. There are rules against loud bursts of Viennese passion, and so we turn it down.

The two resolutions have been fitfully achieved. *Very* fitfully achieved – i.e. not achieved at all. Most days, the space between the end of the working day and the first glass of wine I pour for my wife as I get dinner, meant for that meditation, passes in worry and overwork. Most nights, the music hour passes in watching *Game of Cards* or *House of Thrones* or whatever the long form of the moment is.

Brooding over my failure to do what I set out to do – a not infrequent 3 a.m. activity of mine – I realize that res-olutions represent an appetite for detachment, a desire to escape, a need to be elsewhere while being here. We all feel the need for this escape: it is the constant modern dream of the monastic moment in the day. Some of the pressure that produces the need is local and historical. All of us, without exception, feel overwhelmed by our devices and our computers as we never have before. But I am wise enough, or over-read enough, to know that this has always been the case: feeling the overwhelming intrusion of the Other is what it means to be modern. From the beginning of modern times, when life was furnished with steam trains and telegraphs and passenger liners and all the other now unimaginably appealing and mechanical devices, the first emotion men and women have admitted to is that of being overwhelmed. We are always overwhelmed. And the companion growth of small spiritual practices and the retreat into music – imagined not as a shared sacred activity but as a singular withdrawal – is part of being modern too. Recorded music of course makes this potent, but back in the day it was done with music badly played by the listener herself. Sherlock Holmes had his violin to wail on.

Well, I fail. We all mostly fail at our monastic moments, I suspect – but could it be we fail for reasons not in themselves too entirely dishonourable? The path we dream of after Christmas, the path to purity of some kind, seems always clouded over with distraction. Our ears are never entirely clear of distractions and difficulties. But perhaps we are hearing not only the discords of the self: we hear the music of others to whom this self owes something – dinner, or a draft of homework, desires, recipes and forgotten household duties. What gets in the way of our dream of practising detachment, in other words, is our daily practice of attachment, which may, after all, be the only good thing about us.

Meditation's admirable end is to divorce you from the constant stream of desire that is the human curse, the burn and yowl of 'I want' that can never be satisfied and keeps us from happiness. But when you do meditate – even out on the deck, on a summer morning in a rented country place – you suddenly sense that not just your inner life but also everything on the planet is pushed, governed by appetite, by *wanting* something. Or rather by wanting *something*. The seeming serenity and 'peace' of the morning scene by the ocean is a melodrama of desperation and desire: the little hummingbird is fluttering desperately looking for the sweet sugar nectar that will keep her beating heart alive; our little dog is rooting round the deck hoping for a scrap; the birds are calling desperately for sex and searching for food; and our minds' racing in the midst of all of that, so far from being the alien force, is the mirror of all that wanting. Even the beach dune grass and the scrub trees are reaching desperately towards the sun and sky.

If one meditates past the cries of nature, one lands, for peace, on the sounds of the rest of the natural order, the non-wanting bits: the breeze that blows through the ocean grass, the surf in the distance. They seem so reassuring, so kind, and so serene. Yet the serene sounds, at first so lulling, are, one realizes, exclusively the dead ones. The sounds to set one's heart by are the purely mineral: the wind blowing, the ocean turning. These are cosmic sounds in the most frightening sense: they are completely indifferent to life, possible to find on all the dead planets and lifeless stars, where the wind blows, and the water once fell over itself, too.

The spiritually minded – I have a box of books in front of me by Vietnamese and Californian Buddhists – teach us, correctly, that the human habit of wanting is the source of our suffering. But the human habit of wanting is also the source of our knowing what not-suffering feels like. Our wanting may be the essential thing about us. The truth is that we imagine peace by remembering pleasure. I would like to be less selfish, but the rituals to lead me there seem to be the most self-centred I have. The other selves in my life would rather I became less selfish in a less selfish way.

I will try to keep my resolutions better than I have so far, be truer to them than I can be quite yet. But I will not berate my failure too bitterly. The world is too much with us, yes, but we would miss the world if it weren't, for the world that we escape is the world that we have made. To live among other wants is to be wanted. In life as it actually is, we seek detachment – but we practise attachment. We need to. It's the sticky stuff of our existence.

BOB DYLAN AND THE BOBOLATERS

4 December 2016

Amid all else that has happened recently, it's easy to scale down the wonder of smaller but still startling events. I refer here not to the bigger and more obviously shocking events of the last months, but to a smaller but still big and startling one, briefly pushed aside by those others. I mean the news that the singer and songwriter Bob Dylan has won the Nobel Prize for Literature.

Even more, I allude to the equally startling news that he has, apparently, decided to snub the Swedes who gave it to him. After some toing and froing, it appears now certain that he will not show up at the ceremony in Stockholm to collect his prize – even though it is the highest, the ultimate, of all literary prizes, the one that more conventional writers begin to compose their acceptance speeches for, the minute they get their first (and often their only) good review.

Now, the merits of giving or not giving the prize to Dylan is a subject on which I am, truly, agnostic – and I use that word carefully since Dylan is, in precincts I frequent and among many friends I have, very nearly a god. These Dylan idolaters I call 'Bobolaters'. Bobolaters are the kind of Dylan fans who take his genius so for granted that they struggle to find the inspired point of his every gesture, no matter how strange the Master's latest turn may be. For Bobolaters, Dylan can simply do no wrong. For Bobolaters, no bizarre Christmas record Dylan makes can fail to have some deep, hidden audacity; no Victoria's Secret commercial he appears in can fail to offer some deliciously subtle, ironic comment on commercialism – they are those fans for whom his off-key Sinatra covers are a perverse joy, and for whom even his live recordings, where once catchy songs are turned into an unintelligible system of growls and yodels, are revered. I grew up with Dylan, have his songs in my bones, and understand this view, if I don't quite share it.

On the other hand, I have some intimates who think less of him, and of the award. We have a Thanksgiving tradition in our home – doubtless insufferable to hear about but a lot of fun to share – that everyone must bring a short poem to read between turkey and dessert. Keats usually gets a look in for mists and mellow fruitfulness, and those few poets who manage to be charming, clear and gloomy all at once, like Philip Larkin or Billy Collins, often carry the table.

As a bit of bad-tempered mischief, one of the readers this

year – my younger brother, let us name the guilty party, an art historian with austere tastes – read the words of Dylan's 'Like a Rolling Stone'. They did not, as they say about a bad dog at the Westminster Kennel Club, show well: 'How does it feel / How does it feel / To be on your own . . . Like a complete unknown / Like a rolling stone?'

This was funny but unfair. I listened to the song again, for the thousandth time, the next morning and its entire effect – electric organ and raspy voice and sneering tone – is as thrilling as ever. It *isn't* poetry; it's a song, a great song, lifted by arrangement and vocal attack and the repetition that makes it sound silly when read. If it were better written it might be a worse song.

The relationship between literary excellence and the words of songs is a weird one. Not long ago, I happened to read W. H. Auden's verses for the Broadway show that became, in the hands of a much lesser lyricist, the Sixties hit *Man of La Mancha*. Auden's are incomparably better than the near-kitsch of the eventual lyrics, but quite possibly unplayable on stage – or less playable – not because they are too 'obscure' or literary but simply because they can't be easily followed. They are hard to hear. The listeners strain uneasily, wanting not to drop a beat or a syllable of a complex story-song.

So I am agnostic as to whether Dylan 'deserves' the prize. Certainly he deserves it as much as Dario Fo or Pearl Buck. What interests me more is how utterly predictable his lack of gratitude, or even of normal human interest in getting the prize, was. If Philip Roth or Ian McEwan were, surprisingly, inducted into the Rock and Roll Hall of Fame, each would probably respond more graciously than Dylan has done to his literary elevation, treating the Nobel Prize for which authors pine as one more annoyingly unneeded stop on his perpetual tour.

Utterly predictable, and entirely in character. And here I arrive at *my* Dylan problem, and the source of my fascination with him, apart from my lifelong affection for much of his music. Dylan, a man who has known nothing but unimaginable adulation since he was absurdly young, adopts a tone of aggrieved ill will in almost every circumstance and every artistic occasion. From the first day he recorded a song, he has been revered, the Bobolaters have flourished – and he has rewarded them, always, with embittered ingratitude. 'You gotta lot of nerve to say you are my friend,' a famous song begins about an, I would think, mostly unoffending girl. 'She makes love just like a woman / But she breaks like a little girl.' That's no one's idea of gallant. Even on the supposedly heart-breaking break-up album *Blood on the Tracks*, the tone of unalleviated grievance continues. Remorse takes a back seat to resentment. Watch The Beatles in the recent documentary of their Sixties tour and you see four young men straining to be charming and appealing in extremely resistant circumstances; watch Dylan around the same time in the documentary *Don't Look Back* and you see one young man straining to *never* be charming or appealing, no matter how welcoming the circumstance. Praise gets sullen sneers; uncomprehending admirers are pushed aside.

The really interesting thing is that people continued to reward him then, and continue to reward him for it now: those Bobolaters adore him none the less for being ornery – they call it 'authentic' – and Swedish Academies and graduate faculties alike rush to give him prizes, in a way that they would not, or have not, for those who are his more winning equals – to, say, Joni Mitchell, or Stephen Sondheim, or the sadly late Leonard Cohen. Indeed, when Dylan, a full three decades ago, won his first honorary degree from Yale, he immediately wrote a bad-tempered song about it, called 'Day of the Locusts', in which he announced that he alone could hear the sound of locusts singing on the university lawn, while the poor faculty who had had the bad idea of giving him a degree are mocked for their philistinism and insensitivity.

This suggests a deeper and in its way more terrible and intriguing truth, larger than one award or one academy or even one poet-singer. It is that in life, and certainly in art, they flourish most who are best able to dictate the terms on which they are received. A handful of artists in any generation invent not just a taste by which they can be judged – Dylan certainly did that – but also a space in which they can reverse the usual rituals of manners and still be admired for it. The critic Kenneth Tynan once referred to this ability with a French verb, which I think he slightly misused. '*S'imposer*', he called this gift – the ability to impose oneself. If his French was shaky, he was surely right to see the gift of imposition as an artistic ability as great as any more conventional gift for drawing or singing or rhyming. D. H. Lawrence did this, so did Picasso – and Bob does to. They sneered when we praised their singing, and we wanted them to sing all the more.

For the secret truth is this: people like to be rejected. The artist anxious to please his audience, play their favourite songs at length in the style they like to hear, is scoffed at. Dylan, who plays his songs with bored and under-rehearsed bands in barely recognizable forms, is beloved. Put simply, nice people tend to cater to rude people, while rude people, in the presence of nice people, just go on being rude. This means that the nice people cater to them all the more. The obvious answer when someone is being rude is *not* to cater to him or her. But this is easier than it sounds. People are tragically impressed by indifference, pitifully contemptuous of the charming, and utterly disdainful of the needy, even when what the needy need is what we all need as well.

I am vulnerable to this truth, and envious of this gift. I want to be liked – and it is slightly shameful to like the likeable. To like those who don't want to be liked is dignified, and to idolize the indifferent, puts us in touch with the first springs of religion: we idealized the fifteen-year-old boy or girl who won't look at us, and then we turn that emotion to higher objects. God was first made, perhaps, on the Bob Dylan model in the pre-literate world: the fascinating character that doesn't care if we admire him or not. Idolatry came before Bobolatry.

I wonder if this is not what we really mean by that dusty word derived from religion, 'charisma': not the ability to attract and seduce, but the ability not to *need* to attract and seduce, the ability to be so self-defining – and self-enclosed, not to say self-approving – that others are drawn to cede authority to you even before you ask for it. The political application of this truth may be clear. People *like* to give Dylan praise and prizes even though they must know in advance that he will only have contempt for their doing so. 'Will he come to our party?' the Swedes asked each other, and secretly, astonishingly, they were hoping he wouldn't.

The Paul McCartneys of the world – eminently gifted, out to charm and delight – win great success, but also, perhaps, a certain contempt. We see through them. And what we see are people like us. The rarer Dylans of the world, refusing to be minimally gracious, impress us as the true egotists we secretly are – and wish inside we had the nerve to be. People give to self-enclosed politicians, too, a great and fatal grant of complaisance, even though common sense tells you that it can only end badly.

We all want to be loved by the unloveable, admired by he who admires no one, are thrilled to be treated with contempt by the all-conquering, because, secretly, it corresponds to our own dubious self-evaluation. The Swedish Academy wanted to

give Bob Dylan the Nobel because they secretly wanted to see
him not show up. 'How does it *feel*?' they asked themselves.
'How will *that* feel?' they sang in hushed Swedish unison. And
now they know.

HOLES IN CLOTHES

9 December 2016

I work hard so that my teenage daughter can have holes in
all her clothes. I'm not sure how far this fashion imperative,
or this formula, has reached into Great Britain, but in New
York, or those precincts of it I live in, it is de rigueur now
for teenage girls to wear jeans that have been pre-ripped and
pre-shredded before they are sold – made to look, not just like
well-worn jeans, but like jeans that have been tragically caught
in a horrific lawnmower accident. The holes occur mostly at
the knees and the shins, and they come in many kinds: rips
and shreds and pulls. The effort that has to go into achieving
this look is of course as difficult to conceive – there must be
teams of designers presiding over each premeditated rip – as it
is expensive to own. Being amused about the vagaries of kids'
fashions is a set subject for those being amusing about things.

But I come to praise the holes, not really to mock them. The existence of an industry of pre-distressed clothing is, I shall argue to you, one of the few things to find hope in this unusually dark Christmas.

There is, I should say at once, no mystery about these holes or their meaning or their social manufacture. Thorstein Veblen, the nineteenth-century American sociologist who was in his way as original a thinker as Darwin, explained it fully in his succinct and exasperated writings. Veblen is famous for the phrase 'conspicuous consumption', which makes people think he was satirizing the competition among the rich in presenting obvious signs of wealth – gold-plated bathrooms and meretricious penthouse apartments and the like. But in truth he spent his time explaining why these flashy things are largely viewed as vulgar – except, sometimes, in extremely primitive countries – while those who aspire to look truly rich don't want them.

His theory (one that no one has knocked any holes in) was that the very rich have what he called an 'industrial exemption', meaning that their belongings don't bear obvious signs of being bought after drudge work for wages in a capitalist society. Their furniture looks old and worn and that is a sign of its not having had to be recently purchased. The only other people in a buying and selling society who have that 'industrial exemption', whether they want it or not, are the urban underclass. The uppers, therefore, and those aspiring to look like them, will imitate the manners and clothes of the under. They pantomime the manners of the distressed to suggest the values of the detached. Sometimes the aspiring ones choose to display archaic or peasant-like artefacts to show off their exemption from the consumerist norm. That's why upper-middle-class people have linen tablecloths and candles on their tables, even though these things need a lot of upkeep, which, these days, the people who display them have to provide themselves.

More often, those aspiring to the fashionable life choose to 'pantomime' the manners and styles of that urban underclass: this was why you used to find only aristocrats and paupers at the racetrack or boxing matches. The point of being stylish is to look as thug-like as possible. These days, a fashion for hyper-baggy jeans may pass from prisons to fashion runways, as now a parallel fashion for the well holed passes upwards from actual street life among those with holes well earned. To have holes in one's jeans, in the first instance, is to signal that one is free from mere bourgeois tidiness; once they become fashionable, the holes suggest that one is free from every other element of mere bourgeois tidiness, like disapproving bourgeois parents.

The extravagance of the jeans' distress leads directly to the confoundment of one's father, which is the real point. (To add to this comedy, there is now afoot in Paris, I'm told, a parallel fashion for what is called 'Gopnik-ware', elegant variations on the tracksuits of the Russian thugs who share my grace-less name.) The fashion for holed jeans is like the fashion for hip-hop post-*Hamilton*: what began on the street passes into the salons, only after it has first been presented on stage.

It is easy to mock this parade of vanities, and Veblen did. I will not. Obviously, pre-shredded jeans are ridiculous – but no more so than dirndl skirts or zoot suits or powdered wigs or any other outpost in the great empire of fashion. And it is interesting. What fashion does, after all, is to create fertile areas of ambiguity. The classic areas of these ambiguities are sexual. Tight jeans and loose tops, codpieces matched with tunics, high heels to lift and flowing skirts to hide – fashion is the area where we always get at least two messages at once. We see this every day, in another form, in the fashion for walking down the street speaking into a no-hands cellphone, or with one of those strange Bluetooth things around your ear. Is this person crazy or merely conversational – engaged in the kind of monologue that should make you cautious or the kind of easy intimate dialogue that should make you envious? You can never be quite sure: the odds are on conversation, but the chances are that one in ten is actually crazy.

We ask the same question about the pre-holed jeans. Is this person fashionable or derelict? Fashion alone creates these areas of intimate ambiguity. The most fashionable man I have ever known wore only grey suits, on the grounds that they were a brilliant kind of disguise: on the one hand, just like everyone else's grey suit, on the other, properly fitted and detailed, standing out as mysteriously enviable, announcing both anonymity and affectation. It was the near-but-not-quite resemblance to the drab businessman that made it chic.

I tried to join the armies of fashionable ambiguity just this week. I have a white polo shirt that has, in its long lifetime, been torn and scraped and ripped. It is full of holes: charming mid-size holes; holes small enough to fit Mike Pence's conscience; and others large enough to fit a liberal's outrage. I tried wearing it fashionably around the house, but it was seized on by my wife and daughter and dismissed as fraudulent. 'The holes have to be strategically placed,' my daughter explained. 'Yours are, like, all over.' 'The aesthetic of the hole couture is that the holes are not, for example, in the seam area – that would imply faulty tailoring,' my wife enlarged. 'These holes are in the centre of the fabric. That's not what it's supposed to be like. It doesn't look like the aesthetic of holes. It just looks like the dilemma of holes.' I am kept away from the glories of being fashionable by the sincerity of my own dilapidation.

I know what you are asking: how can you be rattling on about torn jeans and unstrategic holes in polo shirts when our world, by your own account, may be coming to an end? With our souls torn apart by the sudden rise of tribal autocracy where liberal democracy once reigned, how can we care to distinguish the chic from the fatuous rip? Well, I take comfort in them. Not the comfort of escapism, but the comfort of humanity insisting on its own prerogatives. The cycles of fashion in consumer societies are absurd, but they are also imaginative, creative. We analyse them afterwards, cynically, but we cannot predict them in advance. That is why they astonish us in their audacity, and spur fathers to write startled satirical pieces.

Large-scale liberty is what we fight for, but the little liberties of life – and the arbitrariness of fashion is one of life's most engaging little liberties – are part of the way we recognize that the larger liberty exists. A society of surprising turns of style is usually a society of essential sanity. It is not an accident (as the Marxists say) that whenever we want to indicate a dystopian society – one of near-absolute conformity and oppression – we erase fashion and sew up its holes. In such visions, either everyone is dressed alike in that one-style-suits-all coverall that is the standard outfit of people who live in movies set in the future; or else we see them dressed in obvious binaries, not subtle or at all surprising – as in the *Hunger Games* films, where the wealthy wear the cold vulgar clothes of ugly excess, while the poor and virtuous Katniss has, well, honest holes in her jeans, pointing to nothing save their own existence. In such benighted worlds, there is no middle ground to cycle manners back and forth, churn the possibilities to create new possibilities, tear open a little piece of our imaginations to new manners.

I think often of the poor women in that little village in *Lark Rise to Candleford* who, getting hand-me-downs from the families of their London relatives in domestic service, watched eagerly for the changes in style in the distant metropolis, and made those changing fashions part of their own rural rhythm.

Now, of course, after the television series, everyone is dressing like the poor and thrifty women in that remote rural town.

That's the wheel, and it won't stop turning – and God forbid it ever should. I work to let my daughter have holes in all her clothes, to let her, and me, elaborate a private realm of intimate ambiguities. It is a sign of people working out their own perverse and luxuriant languages of love. 'I believe it because it is absurd,' a saint said once of his religion. The presence of absurdity is always a sign of continuing creative energy. Public life right now is enough to, well, make a man rend his garments. But there is something holy – well, human – about those holes.

'BABY, IT'S COLD OUTSIDE'

18 December 2016

I am a collector of Christmas music. The only collection I know to rival my own is my younger brother's, and it goes without saying that we are both genetically and culturally, if not devotionally, Jewish. It may sometimes seem that only American Jews really care about Christmas music. At least, we make a lot of it.

I have just come home, in fact, from a wonderful tradition here in New York, a cabaret show organized by the song-scholar Steven Blier, called *A Goyishe Christmas* – '*goyishe*' being the Jewish word for non-Jews. Each year, the show celebrates Christmas music written exclusively by American Jews. It never wants for material, year after year, since to a first approximation *all* modern Christmas songs were written by American Jews. 'White Christmas' by Irving Berlin. 'The Christmas Song' by Mel Tormé – a Russian immigrant, too, born something like

Tomashevsky. 'I'll Be Home for Christmas' was written by Walter Kent, born Walter Kaufman – who also wrote, you'll be interested to know, 'The White Cliffs of Dover'. Even where the strain seems hidden, it isn't. The lovely 'Silver Bells' was written by the WASP-y sounding Jay Livingston – but yes of course, he was really Jacob Levison. We get in everywhere. We recruit Italians and African Americans to sing these songs – who wouldn't? Sinatra and Bennett and Nat Cole and Louis and Ella – but, to put it bluntly, the people who killed your God also celebrated his birth. These things balance out. Indeed, the author of pop songs – 'Rudolph, the Red-Nosed Reindeer' and 'Rockin' Around the Christmas Tree' – was, yes, the Jewish Johnny Marks.

Of all these songs, my favourite – 'Have Yourself a Merry Little Christmas', a beauty, but written by a Seventh-Day Adventist, aside – is the one written by arguably the most gifted of all modern songwriters, Jewish or otherwise, though there really is no otherwise. ('Arguably' in this case as so often is a word meaning 'Absolutely and for certain but I don't want to argue with you about it'.) He was Frank Loesser, who wrote the best of musical shows, *Guys and Dolls*, the best score for a children's film, *Hans Christian Andersen*, and, of course, that Christmas song, 'Baby, It's Cold Outside'.

First written and sung in a bad 1949 movie, I'm sure you know it well, and in its many versions – my own favourite being a recent bossa nova take by the great, sly James Taylor and the sadly sweet and late Natalie Cole. Play it if you can find it.

You know the song: 'I really can't stay / But baby, it's cold outside. I ought to go away / But baby, it's cold outside . . .' He, the male singer, is trying to convince her to stay by the fire for a canoodle; she knows that she ought to get home or else scandalize her maiden aunt. He is all virtuous protection; she is all uncertainty. The song ends ambiguously but positively: she's staying, it seems.

It is hard to believe that such a fine and funny song could be the cause of intense controversy, but so it is has become. The song, we are now told, is a hymn to rape or assault – 'What's in this drink?' she asks at one point, and we are asked to recoil at her uncertainty. The intended answer from Loesser, of course, is that what's in the drink is, simply, a drink – alcohol – but in the age of roofies that simple sweet formula isn't clear.

Of course, the song is not about, or not intended to be about, coercion. It is about seduction. It is a song of seduction, and like all songs of benign seduction it is about persuading someone to do something – or buy something, or go somewhere: seduction isn't only sexual – that they really want to do but lack the courage to say they desire. The girl in the song seems to *want* to stay – that's the whole joke. She is an erotic being, unsure if she can claim it for herself. Her shyness is imposed by the maiden aunts; and the charm of the seduction lies in the suitor's tone of injured innocence, which James Taylor captures better than anyone.

Now, I am not so innocent of the world as to imagine that the line between seduction and assault is easy to draw or steadfast in description. I am indeed now about to assault *you* with a flurry of immunizing 'of courses'. Of course, we all know that one risk with seduction is that the seducer imagines consent where none is offered – or imagines enthusiasm where none exists. Of course, 'seduction' is often what an assailant chooses to calls his assault. This problem is neither trivial nor to be dismissed – as the father of a twenty-something son and a teenage daughter I wrestle with both all the time. I want my daughter protected from predators, though I want my son protected from false accusation – and the other way round.

Grant all that, quickly and without impediment. But we also know that relations between the sexes (or *within* the sexes for that matter, boy to boy and girl to girl) involve elements of flirtation, persuasion, charm, that frequently includes one party being at first more eager for the connection than the other. All erotic relations should end in equality of means and motive. But truth tells us that they don't all begin there.

I was, as it happens – and I will now somewhat shamefacedly admit – at the other end of a classic 'Baby, It's Cold Outside' connection many decades ago in Canada (where there is no outside colder), where a very beautiful girl plied me with a bottle of champagne by her fireside one Christmas Eve for her own surprising erotic ends. It all worked out – many decades and two children later – but I remember her more than slight exasperation at my denseness, which Loesser captured perfectly, though in more conventional reverse. Her annoyance persists to this day. Lest you think that I am alone in this stupidity, I'm delighted to add that Jimmy Buffet, the charming American singer of calypso-country songs, has a new version out on *his* Christmas album where he sings the baffled, cautious part – the traditional woman's part – and the charming Nadirah Shakoor sings the traditional 'man's'.

To say that we struggle with a problem says only that the right thing to do is to . . . go on struggling with it. We all know instinctively that relations between men and women – and men and men, and women and women – are complicated in pursuit and passage. We also know that, on the whole, the difference between offering yourself to someone and forcing yourself on someone is not really that hard to distinguish, whatever taboos might reign at any moment.

There's a very funny and apt cartoon from your own National Health Service, now widely disseminated among American teenagers, that makes the point by comparing sex to tea. You wouldn't force tea on someone who doesn't want it, or pour it down the throat of an unconscious friend. The same goes for sex. It is actually easy to tell if someone wants a cup of tea or doesn't. They tell you.

But it is also the case that it is possible to want a cup of tea and be too shy to ask – and offering a cup of tea is not the same as compelling someone to drink it. Asking sweetly for what you want is not the same as demanding brutally what you haven't been offered. I will stand down to no one, as the father of a daughter, in the fight against sexual assault of all kinds, direct and implicit. But I will also insist that the worst thing liberal-minded people can do is allow their liberalism to become infected with puritanism. When progressivism becomes puritanism it ceases to be progressivism, because it then becomes unreal, and unreal politics are always impossible politics. Prohibition in this country, or the drive against exploitative pornography that turns into a crusade against all erotic literature – liberalism thrives on small but vital distinctions. Erase them and we erase the possibility of private life. The use of physical force is not a subtle thing: it is a clear thing. If we fail to police sexuality at all, then we end with brutality. If we police it too narrowly, we end with paranoia. Once pleasure is submerged in policing, the intricacies of human relations become impossible and private life itself becomes a sin and, baby, then it really *is* cold outside.

By the way, I wrote a mildly erotic Christmas song myself this year. It's called 'I'm Spending Christmas at the South Pole' and it is about a man who had an illicit affair with Mrs Santa Claus – she put the 'X' in Xmas Eve, he tells us – and is now the only man on earth trying to avoid Santa. It's a good song. I hope they'll put it in the show . . . I also came up – unimaginable thing – with an actual improved rhyme for a Frank Loesser lyric. The song, searching for a rhyme with 'cold out', now ends awkwardly with 'Get over that hold-out'. It ought to be, more encouragingly, 'This sofa can fold out' – they couldn't write *that* in 1949. It's a good line, and rhyme, and I offer it freely, without a hint of coercion, to anyone, of any faith or orientation, who might want it for the holidays.

A Staircase in Sunlight

9 July 2017

I have just come back from a week of hard work and desperate labour at a literary festival in Capri. I will now pause for a full two seconds to allow you to throw things at the radio. But it is true – or true enough. The literary festival is to the current generation of writers what debtors' prisons and consumption were to earlier ones: the professional complaint, the thing you caught by being a writer. You can go from Hay-on-Wye to Melbourne to Jaipur to, well, Capri, reading choice sections from your latest, dining off the organizers, swapping publishing gossip with new-found writer friends – and when the sober local journalists ask, you say you write only to preserve your language from corruption and to bear witness to the crushing of man's hopes under capitalism.

Of course, I am still baffled by why anyone wants to attend

a literary festival except for the writers themselves. A festival of song means hearing singers; a festival of dance, and you look at dancers. If you are enthusiastic about a writer's' work, you . . . read her book. *That's* the festival. Yet I, too, have done my time at literary festivals, and more than my time at literary festivals. At Hay-on-Wye, for instance, back in the Nineties, I once debated the question of the dominance of American pop culture, good or bad. The American team consisted of the now oft-villainized Sidney Blumenthal, Salman Rushdie, attended by two security guards who looked like Pierce Brosnan's brothers, only handsomer – and me. We worked hard. We got up early and reviewed our logic; we mercilessly exposed weak links in our own argument. The opposing British team included the late and charming A. A. Gill – and they spent the prep time getting sozzled at the Welsh pubs. Barely able to stand up straight, they delighted the audience, and wiped us out, by throwing arguments over the parapets as the British generals once threw soldiers, one after another, without care for the consequences – rebarbative wit reinforced with ridiculous analogy, re-teaching the lesson that in the battle between American earnestness and British irony – or between American sobriety and British sozzle – always bet on the drunken Brits. (Unless there are drunk Australians around, in which case all bets are off.)

I was in Capri this time on a mission, however, as well as for the festival – and that was to find the place where my favourite painting in the world had been painted. This painting is by John Singer Sargent, the patron saint of all wandering Americans. He painted it in Capri in 1878, where he also fell in love with a beautiful local girl named Rosina Ferrara, who eventually, improbably, married another American painter and then lived and died in Westchester County, a suburb of New York that I often pass through on the commuter train. Though the Sargent was once owned by Pamela Harriman, it is very little known now. I saw it before it was auctioned in New York a few years ago; it is now back in a private collection again. It shows a single, high white staircase somewhere in Capri.

I am going to talk about a picture you can't see. Still, let me try. It is a narrow white picture that shows a narrow white staircase – the picture's format and its subject are the same. It is a shaft-like staircase – narrow, impossibly steep and high, asymmetrical as it turns just a bit to the left as though made by an eccentric mason. This narrowest and steepest of staircases – itself white-stuccoed or made of white marble – is neatly wedged between two high and also white walls. The sheer whiteness of the whole is so thematic that when one looks, one notices that Sargent has highlighted the left, or sunstruck, side of the stairs, with pure enamel white taken direct from the palette, applied in causal constructive rectangles, while the right side of the stairs, out of the sun's glare, become blue and mauve. It is truly a study in white, of the kind that Whistler imagined but only Sargent achieved.

The white stairs, one side in that glaring light, one in relative blue shadow, climb up high, high, *high* . . . but to nowhere in particular. It is a picture about stopping to look at something for the pleasure of having stopped to look at it. In New York, the picture sold for just over four million dollars – a lot of money for you or me, but for the sellers a sign of how depressed the market is in nineteenth-century masters, compared to that for contemporary art, which has a much larger demand, emanating as it does from Japanese industrialists and Russian oligarchs and Chinese entrepreneurs. You need merely be a multi-millionaire, rather than a billionaire, to own a Sargent.

Why did I, why do I, love it so? Its virtuosic abstract whiteness, perhaps, which is both minimalist and . . . chatty. And perhaps still more, because it represented the most ancient symbol of spiritual aspiration – the climbing stair – but showed it sweetly, as a form of luxury, something to look at in dappled sun, as a small wonder, a folly, a pleasure, a café table – and luxury and leisure posing as spiritual aspiration is, or was, an American preoccupation. Americans always treat Mediterranean necessities with wonder: making poetry of hotel rooms and fishing boats and even bidets. I cannot find a French or British painting quite like it, because a French painter would regard it as too embarrassingly obvious a subject, a Brit as merely a virtuosic one. But Americans love minimalist luxury and aspiration without ascent – or to put it another way, we want spiritual rewards without working for them. We think that looking at something is the reward. Aestheticism is not the American form of protest at too much solemn piety; it is the American form of piety. Watching white stairs that go nowhere and dapple in the sunlight is not merely our idea of a good time, but of an altar.

The paradox of course is that, loving a picture that represented for me the easy presence of dappled leisure, I was now, like a good American, virtuously pursuing it. And here this becomes a story with a simple punchline: the joke is that *every* stair in Capri looks like the Sargent stair. Because of the rocky mountain that Capri is built on – and yes, how odd it is that a landscape so essentially vertiginous and mineral would inspire a reputation so sybaritic and even erotically dark – the staircase ascending narrowly is more necessity than lovely folly on the island. The only way to get from place to place in Capri is to build and climb a high narrow staircase. What I took to be a symbol, something specially celebrated, is a feature of Caprese life. The island's vertiginous ascent demands steep stairs, and the sun shines on them: Sargent's is simply an illustration of a set architectural feature.

The picture was, I discovered on my walks, reportage more than poetry – the poetry resided in the reportage. Narrow stairs leading up white alleys abound everywhere you look. And so, in homage, I decided to picture them all. With my iPhone camera, the sketchbook of the twenty-first century, in hand, I became a fetishist of the vertiginous, a dry-mouthed searcher and snapper of narrow stairs, a lover too easily dazzled by every turn. No Capri tourist of the nineteenth century searching for local beauties, of either sex, was more obsessive in his search. The stairs, I saw, were not a vision. They were merely a functional feature that became for Sargent a fetishized focus – which, come to think of it, is true about the attractive bits we stare at in beautiful human beings, too, whose fetishized parts first exist, independent of our gaze, as functional features as well – made to nurse and birth and touch, born as stairs to become our stars.

So, while our hosts were pointing out ruins and my poor becitified wife was ostentatiously gasping at bougainvillea – condemned to city life by her marriage to a city pigeon like myself, she has never entirely reconciled to it and thinks that a judicious gasp or two at natural beauty might bring me round yet – I was photographing stairs and then bringing them home. When the customs men of the Trump era go through my phone, as they surely will, I will look suspiciously like a man with a staircase fetish, one who grows sexually excited at the sight of steps.

I have not found it. But I have found something. And that is a truth that we all know but cannot retell too often: art draws far more often on things seen than things imagined for its poetry. Monet's water lilies really do look like that. They are figures of his imagination – and they are what grew in the back garden. If we had only Carpaccio's images of the piazza of St Mark's in Venice to look at, we would think, 'Oh, see, how stylized!' Well, it isn't: that's the way it looks. Because the piazza has survived the centuries intact, we know that the art is the perfect mirror. Yet the companion truth is that we can only see when we first have an image to draw on to help us see selectively. Art and life are one, as a search for a staircase in sunlight reminds us. The staircase in sunlight is just an ordinary staircase scene; without Sargent's having seen it, we would not search for it as a symbol of our own aspiration. He was painting what he saw and what we see is what he painted.

This perpetual, strange paradox of the imagination is also, after all, the best apology for literary festivals: they celebrate the truth that life and art are forever entangled, sometimes comically, sometimes beautifully, sometimes even drunkenly. The staircase is there, somewhere, in lovely and temperate Capri, to remind us of that truth, oft-told but still too true: most of what we think of as art is really life; much of what we know as life began as art.

On Musical Theatre

6 August 2017

As I think I may have mentioned, not long ago I returned from eight weeks in the small American city of New Haven trying out a musical comedy – I had written its 'book', or script, and the lyrics to all the songs – and I now wish to report on what happened. The show, which is about a little restaurant in New York, had a fine run of four weeks. It went well. Audiences sat down at the right time, mostly took the seats which had been assigned to them on their tickets, left for the intermission and then, mostly, came back, and clapped their hands when it was over. Some of them clapped their hands while standing up. I don't know that you can say more than that about a theatrical event.

I will add that we got through it – the creative team, that is – with our friendships and mutual respect more or less intact, give or take a few heated moments and a few extended silences. I think we would all work together again – and that is a kind of miracle. For the long and distinguished history of musical theatre shows that there is nothing like trying to make two hours of amiable middlebrow entertainment for a large popular audience to create permanent, bitter, undying enmity among the creative people who are doing it.

The history of the musical theatre is, as a wise theatre historian once wrote, simply one of Jewish men yelling at each other. Richard Rodgers first resented Hart, then came to despise Hammerstein, while when Rodgers and Stephen Sondheim worked together they came to hate each other so much that only their mutual hatred of the book writer, Arthur Laurents, allowed them a moment's respite from their quarrels. Everybody, meanwhile, always hated Jerome Robbins. The legends are legend. Once, the incomparable composer and lyricist Frank Loesser told a director to tell an actor not to sing a song the wrong way, and after the director obligingly did it, Loesser screamed at him anyway, 'But you didn't hit the son of a bitch!' The producer Cy Feuer tells of how Carolyn Leigh, the wonderful lyricist, actually called the cops on him once in Philadelphia during an out-of-town tryout: actually went outside and got a police officer to arrest him for having cut one of her songs.

I am certain that his story is perfectly true, and the only surprise is that the cop didn't get into the spirit of the thing, once inside the theatre, and club somebody himself after offering his notes. Not long ago, the book writer for Broadway's *Spider-Man* musical (an amiable and harmless entertainment if there ever was one) wrote a frightened memoir about how everyone who worked on it came to hate everyone else who was working on it – that is, all of those who had not actually died first from the stress. That really happened. The great Lerner and Loewe musical *Camelot*, in an out-of-town tryout, got stalled when the author was hospitalized with a heart attack from arguing with the director, a problem only made worse when the director joined him in the hospital with another after arguing with the composer, two days after. By then, of course, the composer and lyricist had long since stopped speaking to each other. The director of my own musical says that he will call his memoir 'I Didn't Know Grown-Ups Could Talk That Way to Each Other', after what his frightened eight-year-old daughter remarked once, upon seeing a normal rehearsal session for a nascent musical comedy.

Having seen this process – having participated in it – I am trying to understand it. Why do musical comedies make men and women miserable? I have arrived at a theory I believe is true – and that is that there is no natural author of a musical show. By 'natural author' I mean the one who takes authority more or less inevitably, owing to the nature of the form. The director, for instance, is the natural author of a movie: there are many producer's movies and more screenwriter's movies than any director likes to admit, but the director is the natural source of authority. He is there from six in the morning to ten at night; he coaxes out the performances, allows the improvs and makes the cuts in the editing room. It is the director who, in every sense, calls the shots. Even if you tried to take authority away from him, it would be hard. If you started movie making over from scratch, the guy or girl who played the director's role would still mostly be its author. That's why the French movie critics of *Cahiers du Cinéma* were not wrong to see even the old studio system Hollywood movies as the product of authors, *auteurs*; those Hollywood directors Hawks and Fleming were, even when no one expected them to be. A choreographer, in the same way, is the natural author of the dance – they get the credit whether they entirely deserve it or not. A dancer may deserve most of the credit for a dance, and the editor, once in a blue moon, most of the credit for a book. No matter: the vast preponderance of times, the natural author is the actual author, and the exceptions leave us grumbling, off to the side.

But a musical has no natural author. It has five or six or seven. The composer is the actual author of the most powerful emotional beats in the piece – we remember Richard Rodgers's music in *Carousel* far more than any other element – but composers tend to be inarticulate and are often out-talked or out-argued by their script-smart fellows in the rehearsal room. The book writer, as he is archaically still called (elsewhere, simply, the playwright) is by far the most important maker, but though he provides the structure in which the songs may take place, no one recalls the structure, only the songs. Some of the best book writers are obscure to the point of anonymity even though their contribution – as in *Fiddler on the Roof* – was the essential one. They live in frustration. The director is often powerful to the point of omnipotence – but no one except special groups of insiders will ever think of it as his show. The lyricist, meanwhile, has a reasonable claim to be the actual author of the show – the music's emotional force *only* takes specific meaning through the words it accompanies – but he or she will often end as the most invisible of all. It is not at all unusual for even a wise singer to announce a 'Burt Bacharach song' instead of a 'Bacharach–David' one. Meanwhile, the choreographer believes himself to be the natural author of all the things the director is doing badly, but is also sure that the director will get the credit even if the choreographer fixes it. And while the actors play a crucial role in creating the piece – one bad actor, or miscast or merely out-of-tune actor, can ruin the work of eight years – actors, as one of the best of them said to me, have to show passion and accept powerlessness: they know that they have no real authority at all. This makes them mutter. Add to this the truth that songs that delighted salons of backers bore audiences silly, and that the things that worked perfectly in rehearsal die a dog's death on stage and you have a natural abyss of authority.

And when there is no natural author, there is a natural

vacuum, and into that vacuum rush all the resentments of a lifetime. Seven creative people collaborating where each thinks their contribution is key is not possible. A seven-person creative team of equals is called a 'war'. Add to this another factor: musical theatre almost always begins with a six- or eight-week experiment out of town. This means that, while the authors are feuding with each other, they are also, well, fondling the company, which is already fondling itself. Life out of town has all the proximity and propinquity of life on an ocean liner, with shipboard feuds and shipboard romances. In his autobiography, Arthur Laurents, that much-disliked book writer, in his case of the classics *Gypsy* and *West Side Story*, talks about the dissipated and far from sublimated sexual acting out that went on in the old Taft Hotel in New Haven which, in his account, makes the place seem like Versailles with bad décor. Well, that's where I was – that's where we were! – albeit in a new condo-ized form that they call the Taft Apartments. Sexual energy is everywhere – not in *my* room, to be sure, where the only bedside ornament was *The Diaries of Kenneth Tynan*, but I'm told, and think I heard, its presence in many of the others.

So, the material for misery is built into the machinery of the musical. Too many authors struggling for too little control; too many actors and authors struggling for too much intimacy in too few rooms. Between the vacuum of authority, and the erotic unease, and the perpetual power struggles, it is like *Game of Thrones*, played mostly by middle-aged Jewish men. It is . . . impossible.

Why then does it go on – and why does it remain the goal of writers, who have after all known success elsewhere, to take part in it? That has a simple, not a complicated explanation. There is nothing – truly nothing in the arts – that can equal the feeling of satisfaction when the musical theatre works. When a singer and a song and an emotional moment all strike the audience together it has the thrill of . . . the Brazilian team at its height moving together in the World Cup to score a goal, of teamwork and epiphany combined, and the rush that hits the audience, and the authors, is unequalled. Of course, if you're lucky there's money in it too. But that's one more thing to fight about.

Factional Measures

DON'T MENTION THE WAR?

29 June 2012

Over the past few weeks, I have been talking about bees, and The Beatles, and babies (at least ones who are babies no longer), and also about books and bad reviews. I am as deep in the B's as the crew that went hunting for the Snark in Lewis Carroll.

I hope you will forgive me if I turn this week to something, if not more serious, then more obviously sombre, and that is the question of what the memory of World War Two ought to mean to people now. It recedes, its soldiers die, its battles become the occasion for camp fantasy, or Quentin Tarantino movies – the same thing. Recently, the *Economist* published a long book review asking just that: what World War Two ought to mean to people now.

We know already what it means to publishers and television networks. The publishers love new books about the war's battles, and the cable shows can never get enough Nazis. A German friend once complained to me that educated Westerners often know far more about the German government during those five years of war than they do about all German governments in the sixty years of subsequent peace.

But then, as the *Economist* wrote: 'The sheer magnitude of the human tragedy of [World War Two] puts it in a class of its own, and its relative closeness to the present day makes claims on the collective memory that more remote horrors cannot.' Does it, should it, make such claims? Of course, there is a band of American neo-conservatives who insist on seeing every new year as another 1938, with whomever is the monster of the week cast as a Hitler figure. On the other extreme, there are those who insist that there is, in a sense, nothing to learn from what happened then, because it was so uniquely, horribly evil. There is even a principle, frequently repeated during internet squabbles, and half-jokingly called Godwin's Law (after Mike Godwin, an expert in internet law of the unjoking kind, who first invoked it). It states simply that as an online discussion grows longer, the probability of a comparison involving Nazis or Hitler gets greater. The stupider the argument becomes, the more likely someone is to use the 'reductio ad Hitlerum'. Therefore, Godwin's law implies (and this is the law-like bit), one should try never to compare anything or anyone current to Nazis, Nazism – or, for that matter, to mention 1938, Munich, appeasement or any of the rest of the arsenal of exhausted exemplars. It's a bit like Basil Fawlty's old rule when the German guests come to the hotel: 'Whatever you do, don't mention the war!' And, to an extent, this caution is sane and sound.

The people on the right who invoke 'liberal fascism' should be bundled off – with those on the left who morph Thatcher's or Blair's picture into Himmler's – shut up in a library, and made to read some history. But I'm always haunted by the simple words of the historian Richard Evans towards the end of his good book, *The Third Reich at War*, where he said that we should always remember that what happened was not some act of Satan – though satanic acts took place – but the result of the unleashed power of long-latent traditions of militarism, nationalism and the hatred of difference. It was the force of three ever-living things, braided together like hissing, poisonous snakes around a healthy tree. The danger is that each of these things is not necessarily evil on first appearance, and each seeks a new name in new times.

The old distinction between patriotism and nationalism, made many times by many people, has never been more vital to our mental health than it is now – as vital for the health of the country as the distinction between sexual fantasy and pornography is for the health of a marriage. Patriotism, like fantasy, is a kind of sauce, a pleasing irrationalism that is part of what makes us human – and saucy. Nationalism, like pornography, is a kind of narcissistic addiction that devours our humanity. Patriotism is a love of a place and of the people in a place. As G. K. Chesterton understood, it becomes more intense the smaller the unit gets, so that it was possible for him to feel more patriotism for Notting Hill than for Britain. Nationalism is the opposite belief: that your place is better than everyone else's and that people who don't feel this way about it are somehow victimizing you.

Recently, in America, 'exceptionalism' has become the new name for this illness. All nations are exceptional, but some are more exceptional than others, and America is the most exceptional of all. This sounds like a mordant joke, but it is actually what many people in the US believe, and want everyone else to believe, and routinely arraign President Obama for not believing in enough. (As it happens, for good or ill, he does.) To believe this, it is necessary first of all to be exceptional in never having lived in any other place that thinks itself exceptional. Canada, where I grew up, rightly believes itself to be exceptional among the world's nations in its ability to cover an entire continent in common values without the government's ever having once resorted to internal violence. France, where I was lucky enough to live for many years, believes itself to be exceptional among the countries of the world because . . . well, I haven't time to enumerate all those reasons, though they were nicely summed up in Noël Coward's remark, just after the death of General de Gaulle. Asked what De Gaulle might say to God, Coward said that that depended entirely on how good God's French was.

Exceptionalism, it seems, is the least exceptional thing on earth. Just as nationalism is the opposite of patriotism, not its extension, so militarism is an emotion opposed to the universal urge to honour soldiers for their courage. Militarism is the belief that the military's mission is moral, or moralistic. That the army can be used to restore the honour of the nation, or to improve our morals, and that a failure to use it to right every imagined affront, is a failure of nerve, rather than a counsel of good sense. After 9/11, in the US we suffered from a plague of militarism of this kind, again mostly from sagging middle-aged writers who wanted to send someone else's kids to war so that the middle-aged men could feel more manly in the face of a national insult. Militarism is not the soldier's faith that war can be conducted honourably, but the polemicist's belief that war confers honour.

Thirdly, hatred of difference: notice I carefully did not say 'racial hatred', or 'religious hatred'. Hitler hated Jews because of their religion, and because of their race, but he hated them above all because of their otherness. When I read well-intentioned people talking about the impossibility of assimilating Muslims in my adopted country of France, for instance, I become frightened when I see that they are usually entirely unaware that they are repeating – often idea for idea and sometimes word for word – the themes of the anti-Semitic polemics that set off the Dreyfus affair a century ago. For those writers, too, believed, not that Jews were eternally evil, but that Judaism was just too different, too foreign to France, and tied to violence against the nation and its heritage. And indeed there were Jewish anarchists in Europe, as there are Muslim extremists now. But there was never a Jewish problem in France, any more than there is a Muslim problem now. This is a question in which, after a half-millennium of religious warfare, the results are really all in. If we accept the Enlightenment values of tolerance, coexistence and mutual pursuit of material happiness, things in the long run work out. If we don't, they won't.

So, from now, when we evoke Godwin's Law, as we ought to, I would like to propose Gopnik's Amendment to it: We should never believe that people who differ from us about how we ought to spend public money want to commit genocide or end democracy, and we should stop ourselves from saying so, even in the pixellated heat of internet argument. But when we see the three serpents of militarism, nationalism and hatred of difference we should never be afraid to call them out, loudly, by name, and remind ourselves and other people, even more loudly still, of exactly what they have made happen in the past.

We should never, in this sense, be afraid to mention the war. We should say: 'Listen, you've heard all this before – but let me tell you again just what happened in the garden the last time someone let the snakes out.'

It is exactly the kind of lesson that history is supposed to be there to teach us.

THE IRRATIONALITY OF NATIONS

5 April 2013

Not long ago, thinking in despair about the American inability to stop shooting its own children, I wrote that every nation has a core irrationality, some belief about itself that no amount of evidence or experience can alter – and a blindness about the need for gun control was ours. I began to wonder if I could identify the true hard core of irrationality in each of the four countries that I know best and have lived in longest. Yes, I'm about to engage in national stereotyping – but without apologies, because it is the thrum of our normal talk about our experience of the world. The thing we learn when we travel, or ought to, is that each country is a different world, and so to describe the differences is to respect them even when they seem to us more than a little mad.

Let me start with my own country – don't worry, your turn

is coming. The core irrationality of American life is its insularity, which can be captured in three words: The World Series. This is, of course, the annual championship of the American-invented game of baseball, a championship played almost exclusively in American cities and, until recently, entirely by American players – yet still referred to, without a hint of irony, as the global championship. In all my years in the US, not once have I ever heard any American who found this name mildly ironic, or even strange. It is not even a rueful national joke. It's just a fact of life, and when you point out its absurdity, you get a puzzled look.

It isn't just baseball. The winners of the Superbowl in our US version of football cry out, 'We're world champs!' as the gun sounds – and they do the same at the end of the American championship of the 'world sport' of basketball. When Americans play other Americans in American cities for an American audience, the world championship of whatever sport they are playing is thereby decided. The real irony is that there *is* an actual world championship in baseball – and Americans do very badly at it. No one cares. It is broadcast on an obscure cable channel and no one pays any attention as the Dominicans or the Japanese triumph. This irrationality infuses those other, darker domains.

Americans can't solve their child-killing problem in part because Americans refuse to believe that other rich countries have gun laws that work. Americans refuse to believe that other rich countries have laws at all. The accumulated wisdom of the world on the question of health insurance is completely unknown to most Americans, and enters the debate only to be scoffed at. Not only does everything happen for the best in America – everything happens in America alone.

Now, about France. I feel about France a little the way the Hobbits in Tolkien felt about elvish Rivendell: I love it; I lived there for many years of wonder. One of my children was born there, the other raised there. In France the core irrationality is not its insularity. The French are unduly aware of what others think and say. In France, the core irrationality is the national sense of insecurity – every move has to be evaluated for the potential insult it might contain. This truth may shock visitors to Paris, who see arrogance, not any inferiority complex. But that's very misleading. The French are infinitely sensitive, and much touchier about other people's opinions than they appear. I think of it as the 'Asterix Syndrome', after the wonderful comic book about the permanently besieged yet truly civilized Gaulish village, surrounded by Romans. When someone tries to criticize the Gaullist village, they are not really trying to improve it, they are trying to infiltrate or besiege it or Romanize – that is, anglicize – it.

This galloping touchiness makes even sane and modest reformist projects in France almost impossible. Everything is at stake when anything is at stake. Every suggestion box is really a Trojan horse, and whichever group is most recently offended can shut down the country, since the other unoffended groups want to preserve their right to shut it down, too. The insecurity comes less from the vagaries of history, which no one remembers, than from the brutalities of primary school, which no one forgets. The French educational system is one in which a negative take is pounded into each French child, so that they emerge swearing that no one will ever give them lessons again. The disasters of recent presidents begin here. Sarkozy's Napoleonic energy dissipated in the face of his own galloping insecurity. People will forgive a short man with a beautiful wife if he seems sufficiently surprised; Sarkozy seemed too anxiously, too insecurely, showy with his.

American insularity, French insecurity. Of Canada, the country where I grew up, where my family still lives, where my wife and children are citizens – well, the Canadian core irrationality is an absence of irrationality. Canadians make a fetish of non-violent unexcitability to the point of making their country seem less vivid than it really is. Apologetics are Canada's national form. When Britain made a wonderful show of its new self in its summer Olympic ceremonies – all those pop stars and NHS beds – Canada offered, when we did the winter ones, a sort of charming, apologetic anti-ceremony. Don't ask for magic when you can have more moose and more Mounties. 'Same old Canada, and we know it,' they said. The comic genius of Canada – and it is an almost safe bet that if an American is funny, he is Canadian – lies in the ability to play off this national habit of self-deprecation against the grandiosity of what we still call 'The States'. This is also what makes Toronto the greyest of all the world's great cities. I am reminded of the beautiful Canadian model whom I heard once commenting on the opening of a La Perla lingerie store there: 'That place is a real budget-buster.' Canada is the most excellent of countries – and it must be an erotic country inasmuch as there are always more Canadians – but it usually finds amazingly resourceful ways to dampen the Dionysian side of human experience.

About Britain, and to conclude alliteratively, as I suppose I must, I think there the core irrationality is inwardness. I think of this as the 'Greenwich Mean Time syndrome' – the belief that the time in the UK is the true time in the world, that British values and manners are the obvious norm for values and manners everywhere, just the way the world should be. The British alone speak without an accent, their view is obvious common sense, their grammar correct, and everything else is a variant. This inwardness is not always self-congratulatory, as in America, or tetchy and defensive, as in France. It is often highly self-critical: 'It is the fate of mankind to be like us, and what a fate that is!' It goes hand in hand, too, with a perpetual capacity for embarrassment: embarrassment you feel yourself on behalf of others who are soon going to feel embarrassed. Anyone, a visiting American, for instance, who violates the British norms is likely to make himself seem foolish – and condescension, in theory, wards off the approaching embarrassment of the other guy. To be sure, manners in Britain have changed more in the last three decades than those of any of the other nations I know. But this unconscious sense of centrality hasn't. The lout urinating in public on a Saturday night – you might convince him that there are other louts elsewhere who act otherwise, but he will still believe that his is the right, the only way, to be a lout.

Having now doubtless gotten myself banished from the four places I've called home – thankfully, I'm told that the Faroe Islands are a very welcoming place – I shall add at the end what I'm sure has been self-evident to you from the start. The irrationalities of nations are inextricably linked to the permanent national virtues: the insularity of America is linked to its openness; the insecurity of France to its love of ceremony and courtesy; the absence of obvious passion in Canada to its informality and decency; and the condescension of the British to the beautiful continuity of their institutions. Our core irrationalities are who we are. All we can do is hope to see them with a slightly clearer eye. When they work against us, we should work against them. That's very bland and banal wisdom, I know, but then true universal wisdom almost always is. It may be why we prefer it with a national flavour.

For myself, I am proud to share in the core irrationalities of all four of my adopted cultures. I am, I'll think you'd all agree, insular, insecure, dull and condescending. Surely that marks me as a man of the world.

POWER, PERSECUTION AND PLURALISM

10 June 2015

One of the strangest consequences of the recent Supreme Court decision here in America – the one that made marriage between people of the same sex legal in all fifty states – is the amazing persecution mania it has engendered among religious people who don't agree with it. They don't just disagree with the decision, as of course they would: they feel threatened by it. They feel that the reality that men in San Francisco are now fighting over who should be first in line to rent formal wear has thrown them, the faithful, back into the catacombs, where they tremble at the tread of the legions and hear the distant roar of lions. They feel victims of a form of secular martyrdom that could easily bleed over into the real thing.

It's hard to know why. No church has been closed, no temple shuttered, no sermon suspended; no one who thinks that gay marriage is an abomination has been kidnapped and thrust, chained and dressed in leather, into the depths of a bar on Christopher Street. If you run a business that is open to the public, like a wedding caterer, then it does seem that you may have to cater gay marriages along with straight – but that was a civil rights battle fought and won at the lunch counters of the South fifty years ago. If you are open to the public, then you are open to the public, and have to take the public as it is: multicoloured and many-sided and oddly angled.

Now, it has always been my view that gay marriage is the religious conservative's best friend. If it is your aim to remove potentially subversive sex from the American scene, then marriage is always the answer. Indeed, if your goal was to stop gays from ever having sex again, then you ought to want to make gay marriage compulsory. But this essentially conservative decision creates an odd panic. 'What will come next?' they cry. 'Polygamy? Or legalized bestiality?'

Well, all such 'slippery slope' arguments are silly, because *all* social life takes place on a slippery slope. Once we have banned walking across the street when the red light is on, what is there to prevent us from imprisoning all pedestrians? When once we have a speed limit for cars, what is to prevent us from enforcing a rule of absolute stasis on every Volvo? Well, nothing, except all that protects us in any case, which is common sense and the experience of mankind. A law lowering the drinking age does not mean that some day soon all babies will have bourbon in their bottles, and gay marriage no more implies polygamy and bestiality and incest than a law against breaking and entering implies the abolition of windows and doors. The courts bless gay marriage now, in any case, because it was already blessed by our entertainments and its own peaceful existence. Manners make laws, and manners alone can repeal them.

No, what the opponents of gay marriage really cannot stand, I realize as I read them, is being criticized in the same spirit as they choose to criticize their opponents – not as holding a morality that might be too stringent to be obeyed, but as holding a morality that was never really moral at all. Their complaint is, in its way, one that seems fixed in the political choices of the late Roman Empire: the only alternatives they can recognize as real are either persecution or power. Either you are the magistrate making rules, or else you are the martyr being sacrificed to them. This love of authority, and panic at its absence, is perhaps their central shaping conviction. This is why fundamentalist theologians tend not to mind hysterical atheists, who run around miserable at the loss of a super-deity, but do mind complacent atheists, who cannot see what the fuss was ever all about. They do not mind people who long for a lost order they cannot recover; they do mind people who find nothing to mourn over in what's lost.

I have, I will confess, a certain intellectual sympathy with the believer's position. There is a built-in contradiction between the claims of religion properly so called, and those of a tolerant society. A religion, in its nature, if it isn't an ethic or world-view or philosophy – notice I didn't say 'merely' an ethic, since there's nothing 'merely' about those – makes astonishing cosmic claims about the nature and destiny of life itself, and usually about some supernatural incident in history. If you truly believe these claims with any degree of seriousness, then you are bound to believe that everything else retreats into insignificance before them. If I truly believed, say, as countless wiser people than I once did, that the rulers of the world lived on a mountain in Greece and divided the realms and oceans among them and could be pleased and placated only by sacri-ficing heifers and rams and pigeons – well, I would be racing to Whole Foods to find a heifer to take out. No pigeon on the Manhattan street would be safe

We've learned, though, by painful experience over the mil-lennia, that ceding control of human life to those beliefs is catastrophic – as we see every day in the Middle East, where the true believers of ISIS give us an indelible picture of what rule by pure, unrestrained, urgent belief actually looks like. Those who slaughter heifers to the benefit of their gods are soon slaughtering people to the same good cause. So, as much by clandestine cooperation as by any declaration, we have learned how to move absolute belief from a seat of secular power.

But it has been done, and must be done, gently; the dispos-session of faith from power is a long and slow one. The best studies of how religious toleration came to the Western world rightly emphasize that they did *not* come in the spirit of religious conversions, in wild waves of enthusiasm and ideological conviction. Tolerance came slowly, often clandestinely, and more in the form of uneasy working truces than open sieges and surrenders. A painful practice of grudging coexistence created time for reflection – and the peace provided provoked the possibility that maybe the cosmic truths were neither quite so cosmic nor quite so true as they might have seemed.

What people forget now, I think, is that in the middle of the terrible twentieth century there was a kind of religious revival among the most humane poets and philosophers – I think of W. H. Auden, of T. S. Eliot, of Simone Weil and Dietrich Bonhoeffer. The reason was simple. They wanted to reaffirm the sanctity of individual conscience in a time of genuine totalitarian coercion – the real thing, with camps and gulags, not a fantasy of it, with mean things being said on Twitter. Some of them longed for authority to be re-established, and pined for old popes and Byzantine emperors. But the best – I think particularly of Auden, a gay man twice married, in effect, whom my own son is named after – turned to an idea of divinity because he thought it the best way of doubting the dictators. To keep a conscience, he thought, one must at least imagine a soul. He turned to faith because, by making the individual's inner life paramount, it seemed a form of dissent from a mass society devoted to warping all those outer selves. Mass society wanted to take the soul out of the self, and faith could pop it back in.

But these people of faith were too busy doubting themselves to be furious at those who doubted them. Auden knew how little we know by observing the consequences of people in power who thought they knew it all. 'There can be no "We" which is not the result of the voluntary union of separate "I's",' he wrote once. The separate I's are the subjects of belief. Taking things on faith meant taking them on for yourself, not your neighbour, who had to make the leap alone, too.

A crucial third term intervenes between power and persecution – and that is, simply, pluralism. Pluralism is a not a weak doctrine, but a radical one. It accepts the truth of all those I's. Though science has given us genuine certainty about a great deal of celestial and human conduct – we know that men and women sprang from apes, as we know that gun laws limit gun violence – it cannot give us any certainty at all about ends, about what we ought to feel and how we ought to live. We know for certain that men and women sprang from apes, but each of us must choose how to land that leap. At least, pluralistic societies that accept many ways of seeing the world have tended to let us see inside our plural selves. Cults of certainty can only persecute or be persecuted. Communities of common doubt can always coexist.

Will Future Generations Condemn Us?

26 February 2016

Like many of you, I suspect, I've been following the fight over that statue of Cecil Rhodes at Oxford. Since Rhodes, once seen as a hero of Empire, now looks like a racist and an imperialist – both bad things – the notion is that he should not be honoured in an institution of knowledge. Should we tear his statue down? The French have a nice all-purpose idiom to cover the destruction of things of the past in pursuit of the values of the present: '*Il faut brûler,*' they say – it must burn. But must we burn down Sartre or Louis XIV or Victor Hugo over a big thing they got wrong?

I row no boat for Rhodes – though I do think this kind of inquiry can easily become an inquisition. We can rummage through the past of *any* historical figure and find something obnoxious by the standards of 2016. Even so saintly a character and prescient a man as the philosopher John Stuart Mill – who with Harriet Taylor invented modern feminism – can be shown to have been insufficiently attentive to the very real sufferings of the Irish in Ireland or the Indians in India. My own standard is simple: what were the moral positions broadly articulated at the time, and where does the historical figure stand within them? Not too many, but some, saw just how wrong slavery in the American South was in 1860, and Mill was one of them; not too many people thought imperialism evil in and of itself, and Mill was one of those, too.

But more to the point, we should use these inquiries not as a moment of moral arraignment of others but as moral instruction to ourselves: what attitudes and practices that *we* accept blithely now as just part of the necessary arrangement of the world will seem horrific to the future? What will we be morally arraigned for tolerating by our more pristine descendants? I've arrived at a tentative list of four such horrors. I don't say that this is the right list – or even that we ought actually '*brûler*' these things. Just that these are the things that morally curious people with an eye to the future ought to be curious about.

The first is mass cruelty to animals in the pursuit of food: the industrial farm, the industrialized slaughterhouse – for all that we have been told of these things, we still effectively hide away this truth from ourselves and from our sight. The conditions of animals in industrial farms – chickens forced to spend their lives motionless, pigs, such sentient and feeling beings, crowded in pens and slaughtered indifferently – may seem to our descendants as unspeakable as that of the slaves in the Middle Passage seem to us. That we blithely sit down to eat veal chops at conferences on ethics – I did, once – may well seem to them as brutally hypocritical as American slaveholders praising liberty. My own view, articulated at numbing length in my book about eating, *The Table Comes First*, is that, since we would always eat scavenged beasts, the real issues involve the treatment of animals, not just their consumption. An animal raised kindly and slaughtered painlessly seems to me fairly harvested – though I am in the minority in my own pescatarian family, and may, some day soon, convert.

The next moral outrage the future may condemn is cruelty to children in schooling. This may seem like much the lesser sin – certainly, not getting any schooling at all, like so many girls in Islamic countries, is far worse. But the Western school day and school regimen we accept uncritically, are, on the whole, remnants of an earlier time, living symptoms of the regimentation of life in the nineteenth century that also brought us mass conscription and military drill. We've outgrown mass conscription, but we still too often teach our children to a military timetable. We take it for granted that long school days, and much homework, will benefit them, though there is not a scrap of evidence that this is true, and a large body of evidence that it is false. We take it for granted that waking teenagers in the early morning, then having them sit still and listen to lectures for eight hours, and then doing three or four more hours of homework at home, is essential and profitable. All the evidence suggests that this is the worst possible way of educating anybody, much less a fifteen-year-old in need of much sleep, freedom of mind, and abundant creative escape-time – of the kind that John and Paul found by skipping school to play guitars in the front parlour, or that Steve Jobs found when, in a California high school, he tells us he discovered Shakespeare and got stoned, at the same time and presumably in equal measure.

We are taught that the over-regimented Asian societies will overtake us – but it is Apple, invented by that stoned Shakespearean high schooler, that sends its phones to be made in China, not the other way round. Genuine entrepreneurial advance comes from strange places. In the future, when kids arrive at school in the late morning, and we teach maths, the way we now teach sport, as an open-ended, self-regulating group activity, we may well recognize that each mind bends its own peculiar way, and our current method of teaching, I think, will seem quite mad. The future will know that true 'focus' arrives late because focus *should* arrive late.

The third moral outrage I imagine the future espying is our cruelty to the ill and aged in our fetish for surgical intervention. Modern scientific medicine is a mostly unmixed blessing, and anyone who longs for the metaphysical certainties of medieval times should be compelled to have medieval medicine for his family. But no blessing is entirely unmixed, and I suspect that our insistence on massive interventions for late-arriving ills – our appetite for heart valves and knee replacements, artificial hips and endlessly retuned pacemakers – will seem to our descendants as fetishistic and bewildering as the ancient appetite for bleeding and cupping and leeching looks to us now.

Yes, of course, we all know people whose lives have been extended and improved by artificial joints and by those wi-fi pacemakers. But we've also all known people for whom one operation follows the next, and the gains in quality of life hardly seem compensated by the loss of real time for living. Our health system is designed to make doctors see the benefits of intervention far more clearly than their costs. I suspect that the future will shake their heads in wonder at our readiness to put our elderly through so much for so little, and will see it as more ritualized than helpful – an authorized form of official torture – just as we see the emetics and blood-lettings and leech-applications of the past. Not long ago I was reading these words from a doctor about the seemingly benign practice of angioplasty procedures for heart patients: 'It has not been shown to extend life expectancy by a day, let alone ten years – and it's done a million times a year in this country,' the doctor is quoted as saying, adding that, 'If anyone *does* come up with a treatment that can extend anyone's life expectancy by ten years, let me know where I can invest.' Every age puts up a fight with mortality – and every subsequent age looks back and shudders at the weapons the past ones used.

Finally, I suspect the future will frown on any form of sexual rule-making aside from ones based entirely on the abuse of power. Gay and straight or bi or trans – numbers and kinds and actions – all that really matters is the empowered consent of two people capable of being empowered and informed. When Oscar Wilde was condemned more than a century ago in London for having sex with underage prostitutes, he became a figure of utter evil, his life and career destroyed. Within half a century this persecution seemed to us intolerably evil – and for most of the second half of the twentieth century Oscar was seen as a saint of gay liberation. Yet a scant twenty years later, the table has turned again – exactly because it is not homo-sexuality but rather the exploitation of younger teenagers for sexual purposes that seems to us rightly among the blackest of all possible sins. I suspect that the future will be infinitely tol-erant of sexual variety, infinitely censorious of the exploitation of the powerless.

And that perhaps is the central point. Morality does clarify over time – only not to the wrong willing partner or wrong way of eating, or even the wrong way of thinking, but into what's fair, and isn't, in a relationship of power. Not everyone who's been oppressed is right: we know that oppression can blind people to decency, and that cruelty can make its victims, Caliban-like, enraged and morally limited or blind. But if we want a simple moral rule to take through the centuries it might be: 'See who's helpless, and help them.' That always looks good in retrospect. Meanwhile, moral curiosity needs to separate itself from moral hysteria; we need to remind ourselves that moralism and morality are two very different things, and that, even as we condemn our moral ancestors, we need to hold our ears to the wind, and listen for the faint sounds of our descendants telling their melancholy truths about us.

Why Donald Trump and Bernie Sanders Aren't as Revolutionary as They Appear

12 February 2016

I am without exception the worst prognosticator ever to have even briefly attempted the craft of political punditry. I peer into my crystal ball and the clouds part and the beckoning finger of Fate calls me on – but what she shows me coming is never actually on its way.

In the early Noughties I explained to listeners that Nicolas Sarkozy, the French presidential candidate, was putty in the hands of his more regal opponent, Dominique de Villepin – a prediction so wrong (Sarkozy became president once and is running again) that the other day I could not even recall the name of the candidate I wrongly chose. I explained to my readers not long after that Michael Ignatieff was an irresistible force in Canadian politics – but he wasn't – and I thought Al Gore was just as irresistible in 2000.

What is lovely about the life of a pundit is that there is no penalty ever paid by anyone for being wrong about everything. Wrong as I am, there are those still wronger, and at least I am not loud. In 2012, every single right-wing political pundit in America was busy explaining to every other one why Barack Obama was doomed. They really believed it, too. When I need cheering up, I simply go to YouTube and watch their faces alter on election night. My own political sympathies apart, it is a study in the vanity of human wishes, and of the beautiful fragility of human pomposity. But there they all are, without exception, back at the job, and all as sapient and complacent as they were the time before. If horse-racing tipsters were as wrong as often, they would soon be expelled from the track.

So my attempt to crystal-ball the current US political primaries should be bracketed by a complete disclosure that I will be wrong. My theory, though, is that there is somewhat less than meets the eye in the double triumph this week of Bernie Sanders and Donald Trump in the tiny (and unrepresentative) northern state of New Hampshire – but this theory should itself be taken with the right tablespoon of salt. Being wrong all the time at least gives you one advantage: you remember the landscape on which you stumbled before. Failure sharpens the eye.

A consensus has emerged around the week's news. It is that the American electorate is 'angry' or 'alienated' and that 'outsiders' with extreme programmes are suddenly potent in a way they have never been before. I think this is misleading. Journalists, it should first be said, will say such things. Since news is reported once a month or a week or, these days, every other minute, the seismograph of daily occurrences looks hyper-important: there must be a neat causal connection between something new that can be shown to be happening and the way that people choose to vote. This seems so obvious that to state it seems to be stating the inarguable. Of course, the way people vote today depends on the things that happened the month or day before.

But against this, I sometimes wonder if there is not more truth in a kind of devil's advocate theory of social change. That would be a theory that proposes that in modern democracies, ideologies remain remarkably constant from decade to decade and even from year to year. The bearers of those ideas alter, and circumstances can sometimes alter enough to give those bearers access to the power that they lacked before. But contingency and chance work their way across a field of more or less fixed choices with less alteration in real numbers than the over-eager daily reporting will be inclined to suggest. The field on which modern politics takes place is more like a series of fixed magnetic poles of varying strengths, pulling people towards them and then repelling them.

Change does happen, of course, but the play of possibilities remains remarkably stable from decade to decade. This is not because the world is impervious to change, but because the political poles represent permanent features of modern life. The continuities and the contingencies – and, often, the stubborn resistance of voters to what would seem to be their own self-interest – are really more striking than the neat flow of economic cause and political effect. We see, for instance, Reagan and Thatcher as irresistible forces, propelled by a renaissance of right-wing thought and votes. But both were immeasurably assisted by local oddities – Margaret Thatcher by the triangular politics of Britain, and the Falklands War, and Ronald Reagan by the over-hyped American–Iranian hostage crisis. A successful hostage rescue – and it was a very near thing – would have seen Jimmy Carter re-elected, and eventually credited with the economic recovery.

So, Donald Trump's message resonates with the voters, we are told. But in truth Trump has a smaller percentage of the Republican vote in New Hampshire than the right-wing populist nationalist Pat Buchanan had in 1992 – running with exactly the same ideology against an incumbent president. Trump's message *resonates*? Well, yes, but it resonates with exactly the same minority of the smaller of our two political parties that it always has. Trump is not just saying exactly what Pat Buchanan and, in another way, Ross Perot was saying in 1992; he is saying exactly what Sarah Palin was saying in 2008 and close to exactly what George Wallace was saying in 1968. He is saying it in the tones of an oafish real estate developer from Queens instead of those of a dim-witted part-time politician from Alaska or those of a mean-spirited southern sheriff or, in Buchanan's case, an enraged Poujadiste-style Roman Catholic – but the message is almost entirely identical: Our country is under assault from without and within – from without by a force of insidious and omnipresent evil (Communism! Terrorism!) and from within by an educated elite that is either in league with the evil or blind to it.

There is, in truth, no particular evidence from polls or surveys that the American public is particularly angry or alienated. In fact, the voters in the largest political grouping in the country, the Democratic Party, are extremely happy with their two-term leader, and, indeed, no one seriously doubts that if Barack Obama could run again, he would win again. He won last time, after, all with a much weaker economy against a much more plausible opponent.

Republicans are angry, but they are Republicans because they are angry. Anger is a constant, and being more or less comfortable doesn't alter it as much as you think it might. An ideology is not the words wrapped around a falling income. Beliefs are not butter on a thinner slice of actual toast. They are, for good or ill, beliefs. People believe them stubbornly, no matter what the circumstances are that they find.

This does not mean that the current 'crisis' is not real. It means that in a sense the crisis is too real. It is permanent. It is a function of the uncertainty that overwhelms us all. At any moment, in 1968 or 1992, or for that matter in 1917 or 1933, the world will be altering in ways that create anxiety and strain for everyone – particularly for those who feel the most vulnerable. The ideas that are offered in response are almost always either populist nationalism, or else some form of benevolent welfare state providentialism. Bernie Sanders, after all, represents the 'extremist' ideology that has governed all of Western Europe, mostly successfully, for the past seventy or so years. It takes less anger and alienation than a mild reshuffling of the ideological deck in a peculiarly shaped contest to produce results that look, on first glance, revolutionary.

Donald Trump may yet win the Republican Party nomination – but if he does, it will owe far more to the peculiar constellation of events and the feebleness of his opposition that have allowed this consistent strain in right-wing ideology to, well, trump all others, than to some peasants' revolt – much less a single common swell of feeling among all Americans. My own best guess is that he will never be elected president – that the loony side will retreat and that the more usual organized forms of politics, less touched by panic and paranoia, will win out. But then, I am always wrong.

There's an American saying: 'Anyone can become President.' And in the 2016 election we've been trying to prove it. The list of people running for President seemed to include everybody except Beyoncé. And there actually was a rumour last October that Beyoncé's husband, rapper Jay-Z, might run. The US presidential field has begun to narrow at last. Although, to judge by who's left, this is not because of quality control.

ON TRUMP

1 November 2016

Right now, the most significant exhibition in New York is at the Metropolitan Museum of Art, and it is devoted to medieval Jerusalem. Called 'Every People Under Heaven', it emphasizes the coexistence, the entanglement, the often grudging but still real tolerance for each other of the many faiths and peoples who intersected there. A kind of forced practice of pluralism distinguished the city on the eve of the Crusades. People mistrusted each other, but they mostly, astonishingly, rubbed along.

It didn't last, of course. It couldn't. The exhibition is climaxed by two brilliant, scary, shining swords, Crusader-ware captured by the Muslims, proudly engraved in Arabic to mark an exchange of owners in the apocalypse of massacre and counter-massacre that closed the era and bloodied the city. The daily practice of pluralism proved utterly impotent in the face of tribal and credal fanaticism.

It is impossible to walk through the exhibition without thinking of the state of American politics on the eve of the presidential election. To be blunt, we can't understand the phenomenon of Donald Trump without facing sad facts about what, for lack of a better phrase, I will call the perpetual human turn towards hatred and tribalism, which raises its fiendish head at every historical moment, from 1110 to 1914 to, well, now, and reminds us in an instant how fragile even a seemingly well-entrenched principle of pluralism can be. In America this week we are in the midst of a national emergency in which a democratic country – flawed in many respects and unjust in some and certainly inequitable in many, but nonetheless pluralist and prosperous and, by any sane historical standard, successful – is an accident or unexpected vote away from electing to office a man who promises to put an end to all its traditions and norms and practices.

It is bad form, I know, to break things down quite so simply, so tendentiously. Surely there is something to be said on both sides of this election; surely there must be a broader, more broadly 'contextualizing' way to see it, some pious hand-wringing to offer about polarized electorates and the dispossessions of globalization and the rest.

Not a bit of it – or not from me anyway. The American presidential election between Hillary Clinton and Donald Trump posits a simple eternal human confrontation between sensible and crazy, and anyone who tells you that something more than that is going on is not looking deeper into a complicated truth – he or she is just looking right past a simple and self-evident reality because the self-evident reality is too painful to look at.

There have been, it's true, characters like Trump before in this world, and in this country. Some try to comfort themselves with the idea that Trump is like, say, Berlusconi in Italy, a half-witted tycoon who can disgrace his country without endangering it. Don't believe them. Berlusconi was corrupt and shallow and incompetent. We should only be so lucky. His was the politics of empty populism. Trump speaks instead for the darker forces of blind nationalism and vengeful ethnic hatred. Donald Trump runs on vanity and hate, and vanity and hate alone, and anyone who pretends otherwise is in a state of wilful self-delusion.

He is a man without a single redeeming feature. An inveterate liar, without beliefs of any kind other than a desperate narcissistic need for uncritical approval, surrounded and empowered by the most appalling crew of racists and pitiful yes-men and -women that the country has ever seen. Trump's behaviour is not just unlike that of any previous presidential candidate. It is unlike that of any normal human being. In plain English, Trump is nuts. We are warned to keep away from amateur psychiatric diagnosis – but when we change cars on the subway or tube to stay away from the guy who is muttering vague threats and playing with a kitchen knife we are not engaging in tendentious medical diagnosis. We are engaged in common-sense perception. We say, 'That guy looks crazy and dangerous,' and we are right.

Trump has all these traits. Ask yourself if you can recall a single friend who would have represented himself as another person, not even troubling to disguise his voice, in order to lie to a reporter about his imaginary sexual exploits. Well, Trump did that. He boasted about being a sexual predator, then insisted that he was merely a liar; sent his wife out to insist that he was simply so immature that he impersonated a sexual predator in order to impress a D-list celebrity; and then, when at least twelve women came forward to say, 'No, on this one issue he is telling the truth,' he insisted, snarling, that their accusations had all been debunked when in fact not one had even been challenged and many reinforced.

I mention this – much of which you have doubtless heard already – because the terrifying thing is the speed and acceptance with which his daily displays of crazy and evil have been and continue to be 'normalized' every day in America, even as the election approaches. Every week, it seems, he violates some universally accepted norm and standard of liberal democratic debate – does so largely out of rage and pique as much as ideology – and then that standard or norm is nonchalantly dismissed and accepted as we await the rape of the next. His refusal to disclose his income taxes; then the revelation that he pays no taxes; then the embrace of Vladimir Putin; then the refusal to recognize the now-accepted truth that Putin's spies have stolen his Democratic oppositions' correspondence in order to aid his campaign; then his boasts of sexual predation; then his threats to the women brave enough to confirm his boasts . . . Each of these things is regarded with momentary horror, then with doubt, then with a kind of rueful, 'Well, he got away with it again!' and suddenly the latest horror is last week's news.

His own party, despite some early bleats of distress, has, shamefully, gathered around him, partly from self-interest, and partly from a tribal habit of hatred of the opposition, and of Hillary Clinton in particular, that defies all reason. Not that Trump and Trumpism spares his own kind. In the right-wing journal *National Review*, the writer David French detailed how his principled opposition to Trump led to an avalanche of threats and hate directed to his wife and family. And yet the readers of *National Review* – if not its frightened writers – have largely made their peace with Trump, their irrational hatred of Hillary Clinton turning out to be keener than their fear of constitutional death of their country.

The liberal form of the refusal to look the reality of Trump in the eye takes another, more perverse form. It has become a matter of liberal obligation – almost a liberal piety – to look away from the actual content of his campaign and the appeal of his hatreds, and find another cause to explain his rise. It is a journalistic obligation, an interpretive necessity, to go on pre-tending that beneath the rise of Trump some other, essentially sympathetic 'people's revolt' or movement of the dispossessed is at play, however misguided this apparition of it may be.

The trouble with this view is that there is absolutely no evi-dence to support it. There are no correlations between support for Trump and economic distress or the effects of globalization or of economic inequality. Just the opposite – for if this were so, then we would expect to see at least some support for him among the Hispanics and African Americans who have suffered disproportionately in the great recession, and there is none. There is zero correlation between support for Trump and the experience of economic dislocation – and a robust, permanent, demonstrable correlation between support for Trump and over-whelming feelings of racial resentment. His supporters do not crowd his rallies to jeer 'Free trade!' or 'Chinese made iPhones!' They crowd to chant hatred for the media and cry 'Jew-S-A' and to shout 'Lock her up!' about the first ever woman candidate.

Such emotions need no economic explanation. Hatred is its own ground, nationalism its own fanatic religion. It is the oldest and most pitiful liberal self-delusion to imagine that ethnic hatred (or now, misogyny) is merely a masked form of economic distress, the bad way that an authentic emotion expresses itself. This turned out to be folly in the twentieth century and it will turn out to be folly now. The anti-Semitism of the Hitler regime was not a masked emotion for some other, more material one; it was the dominant and self-supporting faith of the regime, easily spread as a pathogen throughout Europe even in the face of economic logic. Nationalism is its own faith, not a form some other feeling takes.

No, we must not delude ourselves. Trump's rise is due to the reawakening of deep atavistic passions of nationalism and ethnic hatred among millions of Americans, and it was capable of being reawakened for the tragic but not very complicated reason that such emotions are *always* capable of being reawakened, everywhere in the world and at any time.

And so we return to Jerusalem. For the deeper truth is that it is not the disease of tribalism that is the thing in need of explanation. It is the truces against tribalism that can sometimes take place that needs explaining, for they are so rare. We have lived in one such pocket in our time. Indeed, here in America we have lived, since the Civil War, within one of the longest historical truces against tribalism that mankind has known. Imperfect, flawed, unjust and inequitable as America has been, the basic rules of liberal democracy have applied: governments change peacefully at the will of the people. Opponents are not imprisoned; the free press continues unobstructed; dissent, though oppressed at moments, is allowed its voice. Donald Trump has made it plain that he believes in none of these principles, and will end as many of them as he can. If he is, God forbid, ushered into power, it will be by what the philosopher Karl Popper rightly called the 'strain of civilization', the permanent difficulty of accepting pluralism as a practice and principle, once again making itself felt. Then a modern apocalypse will be upon us. I fervently wish that this was not all there was to be said of this election, and that I did not believe this to be true. But it is. And I do.

THE WEEK AFTER

15 November 2016

'Well . . . at least pronouns are over,' the young liberal arts college student said, in the midst of his leafy campus, the morning after the unimaginable election. He meant of course that the punctilio of appropriate address – which was right to use towards people for various states of gender shading: 'she' or 'he' or 'them' or 'it', or even 'se' or 'zir'? – though it had been obsessing his little college for the past three years, suddenly seemed terribly trivial. Trivial in the face of more important questions about voting rights, the intimidation of dissent, the survival of immigrant families and the perpetuation of democracy itself. The fine points of identity politics seemed trivial when politics seemed about to crush our identities. When basic principles are suddenly at stake, we have to distinguish between basic principles and best practices. It's not that the best practices don't count. They do. But the best practices can wait while we defend the basic principles.

Well, perhaps pronouns – or obsessing about them – won't end. Irony was supposed to have ended on 9/11, and then ushered in a time so rich in them that a one-man irony operation, Stephen Colbert's, became the best thing on American television. But the idea is right. Decent people must now learn to distinguish, for the next four years and perhaps far longer, rigorously and at times ruthlessly, between, well, the deplorable and the diabolical, between the unwanted and the unacceptable, between the ugly and the evil, between our pronouns and our principles.

A right-wing Republican government – and all American Republican governments are by European standards far right – was, given the natural oscillations of power, and after eight years of a liberal President, bound to come sooner or later. If it had not been Trump it would have been Ted Cruz, and if not in 2016 then in 2020. Liberals may deplore its goals. Overturning Roe v. Wade, abolishing Obamacare: we may find these terrible things. But they are legitimate goals of political action achieved through elections and remediable through elections.

Suppressing dissent, arresting journalists, imprisoning opponents, institutionalizing bigotry: these things, all threatened in the Trump campaign, are not. The difference between deplorable and demonic is the crucial one. Preventing women from controlling their own bodies is evil; making abortion law subsidiary to the state's is merely, in our view, wrong. Making sure that immigrants are not abused, gays not discriminated against, torture never used, swastikas not accepted: these are of a different level of concern than political ones. Some are ground worth fighting for; they are our pronouns. The others are hills worth dying on; they are our principles.

Well, the dragon tail of history has twisted and turned and thrown us all. But let it be said clearly: in any other kind of American election, for governor or senator or congressman or mayor, Hillary Clinton won, with a more than two-million-vote majority, a clear mandate and a clear victory. If this was the Brexit vote, Remain won. Because we are constitutional liberals, we accept the outcome of our unamended consti-tution. But we recall our numbers. Orwell wrote, 'Sanity is not statistical.' It isn't. But it is numerical. We can count. Two million is a number that will not change. It is important to know what happened, to say what happens next. Certainly, if the result were reversed – if Trump had won the popular vote by two million votes – we would be in the midst of a created constitutional crisis. Perhaps history will judge Hillary Clinton too timid in her concession. But the truth is the truth: Obama's 'coalition of the ascendant' is still in place, if and when it is allowed to vote.

What made Trump's ascendancy potentially demonic was not its policies alone but its autocratic effect: the threatened suppres-sion of free speech, the return to torture, the mad belligerency, the intimidation of the free media. It is the Putin programme, not the Spence or Ryan programme, that is not legitimate. It may be – we can only pray it is – part of the bluster and sound and noise of the time, and so not entirely real, and simply the natural opportunism of a natural opportunist eager above all for approval and appreciation. If narrow self-interest and normal political calculation re-emerge, well, not-yet-actually-an-apocalypse seems like a narrow political achievement to pray for each day. But it is now ours.

There is a deeper and more bitter political lesson, and historic agony, for those of us who build our lives as citizens around the values of liberal humanism – the liberalism of J. S. Mill and Isaiah Berlin and Harriet Taylor and Karl Popper. Twenty-five years ago, when Communism fell with the Berlin Wall, for all the fatuous triumphalism that the occasion generated, it *did* seem that the notion that liberal democracy – the consensus on governing norms that extends from libertarians and constitutional conservatives and Christian democrats to social democrats and democratic socialists – was the sane way for nations to conduct their affairs, had won out. It may not have been 'the end of history'. But it was, surely, a lesson from history.

Now all that seems to lie in ruins. Russia is a brutal autocracy, and – in a turn that no one save perhaps a writing team of Aristophanes and Philip K. Dick and Gore Vidal could have imagined – the United States seems set to remodel itself on

Russian autocratic lines. Though Eastern Europe is free, it is far from liberal, and meanwhile the consensus has collapsed in the continent, with Brexit accomplished and now Marine Le Pen grinning piously as she waits to be the third in the trifecta.

Many explanations for this exist, all to be explored. The left believes that neo-liberalism – the undue faith in free market reforms and global trade that may help us all as consumers but strands many as producers – is responsible. Our pockets are filled with smartphones, but our hearts are filled with insecurity. Some other, nameless time feels better, even if it vanishes upon description – and so we vote for those who promise to take us back.

The crisis floats free from obvious signs of severe economic distress, and takes place, indeed, at a time of economic recovery, with a hugely popular incumbent President helplessly turning over power to a man so exactly his opposite in bearing and ideology that he might have been created in Superman's Bizarro world, where everything is reversed. It is the great wonder and question of our time. We each have that computer in our pockets far more powerful than any that filled rooms a scant forty years ago. Now all of us have them, and no one feels privileged – well, almost no one, except the insanely privileged.

The right believes that liberalism itself was always to blame – that a creed based on abstract principles rather than felt identities, on universalist abstractions rather than national particulars, would never survive that thrashing dragon of history. Our forlorn monument is the euro: all those meaningless unnamed bridges and floating architectural nowheres, indicating nothing, suggesting no one's home, showing us nothing except the blank implacable face of Davos man in his blank implacable void.

How can we have hope for a liberal, open society at a moment like this? Only, perhaps, in the faith that liberal politics really do rise from the ground up. Enlightenment liberalism was a philosophical project, a social project and a scientific project, even a poetic project, before it became a political project. It came from people turning telescopes towards the stars and meeting to argue at cafés and building libraries of once-forbidden books, often under brutal regimes, and later the values learned there began to be applied to society.

A false choice has risen in the week since the election between private withdrawal and political action. 'All we can do is go and cultivate our garden,' some say. 'All we can do is begin to defy,' say others. Not only can we do both, our history tells us that one depends on the other. Building communities of like-minded people who refuse to accede to the belief that politics is power enforced by the police – the core authoritarian principle – is the first step in intelligent dissent. Voltaire told us to cultivate our garden, because he knew that self-reliance is the first foundation of social resistance.

By the end of the week, that liberal arts music student was in a grey suit headed downtown to volunteer for the American Civil Liberties Union. That is how democracies defend themselves:

by community, and common action and a refusal to be easily intimidated. We are already engaged in a great struggle (non-violent, let us pray) to see if a constitutional republic has enough residual agency, and enough subsidiary strength, to accept a democratic rotation of power while resisting any impulse to ethnic tyranny or autocratic rule. 'It is what it is' has been, for the past few years, the formula of passive acceptance used for whatever we must passively accept. 'All we can do is all we can do' is our new slogan; it suggests realism, but no passivity at all.

A LIBERAL CREDO

25 November 2016

I am a liberal. There; it's out. I don't mean this in a party-political sense, though in my native Canada, there is still a newly renascent Liberal Party – which I may shortly be in place to vote for again, given what's happening here in America, with our Home Shopping Network crypto-fascism. The liberalism I have in mind takes in everyone from constitutional con-servatives to social democrats, from Disraeli to Denis Healey. I would call myself a liberal humanist (though that is even worse), or a semi-secular Unitarian-style liberal humanist (still worse). Liberalism as a set of ideas, rather than a thing to kick, had a brief bright moment in the 1990s, a favourite decade of mine, but now is once again everybody's favourite target. Radicals hate 'neo-liberalism' even worse than the old kind, as a handmaiden to Capitalism, while true conservatives hate liberalism as they always have, as an assault on the unity of culture and tradition. Liberals are back to being kicked around, or at, by everybody, which they more or less accept. You can't complain: wherever you plant your flag, a wise man once said, there will always be somebody to your left and somebody to your right. Nonetheless I shall, as the sun sets on our creed, act as King Midas's barber did, and go down and whisper in the reeds what I still believe are the essential truths. Not, in this case, that the King has donkey ears. The slow process of the years has wisdom still.

What even wishy-washy liberals object to is the idea that liberalism is merely wishy-washy, a sort of mixed bag of other people's notions, with those notions merely moderated or moved to the middle: some traditionalism, some progressivism, some borrowed Christian values, some transplanted spiritual notions – a mere muddle, rather than a distinct and, in its way, radical philosophy. So at a moment when it seems likely to be drowned out, in America at least, by its opposites on either side, I shall make a small forlorn effort to speak its truths, as I understand them, and sometimes try to live them.

Liberals believe in reason and reform. They believe first of all in reform – that the world has many ills, that tradition is a very mixed bag of nice things and nasty things, and that we can work together to fix the nasty ones while making the nice ones available to more people. They believe in reform rather than revolution, because the results are in: it works better.

Liberalism recognizes how essential mass movements are, for freedom and progress. But it has a deep mistrust of violence, or of burning down and starting over, because violence, in its nature, is exclusive and because starting over means losing too much. Revolutions do devour their own – and other people's own too. Having broken decisively with the past, revolutionaries are incapable of learning from it, and have to demonize its inhabitants and the past's patriots. Liberalism tends to believe that free markets produce prosperity, because they have, but it also recognizes – with Adam Smith, who saw this first and clearly, to this day catching his admirers with their pants down – that without public instruction and oversight, they can become mere clubs of bullies. Liberalism, as I intend it, has an instrumental relationship to the free market, neither a slavish nor a slavishly opposed one.

Reform and reason: liberals actually believe that the processes of scientific reasoning, argument and evidence, can be applied to the problems of human existence. They are not naive. It's clear that the process of reasoning happens generationally rather than generatively. Individuals are rarely reasoned out of their fixations (though that happens), but the children, under the table while the argument is going on, hear. Adults may not alter – but children *will* listen.

Those two values are rooted in a simple moral idea about the source of meaning in the individual imagination. This just means that people make up their values – they aren't handed down from the past or on high. This is the foundation of the humanist ideal, which intersects and animates liberalism with moral energy. And it is a new kind of moral energy. The claim that the good values of liberal humanism are merely a relic of theism seems to me ridiculously false; so obviously false that it is almost embarrassing to have to correct it.

We often hear sneering that the fruits of the Age of Reason are no better than, or no different from, those of the Age of Faith. Well, at the simplest level, I will claim for my family all the fruits of scientific reasoning in medicine – which is exactly the application of organized, self-scrutinizing, critical reason to the problems of human bodies. The sneerers can claim all those of the pre-scientific doctor. We will have vaccines, antibiotics and anaesthetics in surgery, public health measures; they can have leeches, bleeding, the theory of the four humours, and all surgery performed by a barber with a saw who hasn't washed his hands.

For these things aren't mere technology achieved in the absence of spiritual feeling: they are the fruits of a movement made in conscious defiance of many of the claims of organized religion and in rebellion against its dark millennia of cruelty and narrowness. When the greatest of British philosophers, David Hume said tranquilly on his deathbed to that greatest of British economists, Adam Smith, that he hoped to have the pleasure of seeing the churches shut up, he meant exactly that mankind would advance in the face of their ignorance. Pluralism, principled tolerance (as opposed to grudging truce between religious wars), a faith in liberty, a belief in free inquiry, a confidence that the extension of material pleasures to the deprived is a high end in itself, the absolute rejection of any imaginary afterlife of eternal torture – above all, a refusal to believe in essences and pre-fixed destinations for anyone, and a desire to extend its reach to the oppressed and those traditionally denied it . . . No, these things are not the product of a humdrum march of technological improvement; they are the fruits of one the greatest spiritual journeys mankind has ever embarked on: the path towards self-reliance and the unfrightened discovery of the real truths about the world. A faith in not taking things on faith is not the same as a faith, any more than a hot bath is like a cold bath because they both consist of water. One is a dogma. The other is a plan to go on living happily while having merely a best guess.

The moral and metaphysical ideas of humanism are not only different from those of theism but also richer, and far more audacious. The proof lies in its consequences: the emancipation of women, the spread of universal democracy, the extension of civil rights to homosexuals, the end of torture and censorship, a faith in free inquiry about man's origins, and with the discovery of earth's true place in the universe and of human beings' true history on earth; above all, in the redirection of life from worry about the reward and punishment of the heavens or of history, to the ever-increasing well-being of our children and grandchildren. These are the peculiar triumphs of liberal humanism. The central humanist tradition is one not made in the ruins of metaphysics, but in conscious and joyful defiance of them, in which freedom from authority, and the need to make all our meanings for ourselves, is liberating – literally life-giving, inasmuch as it gives purpose and meaning to our lives, and to the wisdom about the world we pass on.

Liberals are also criticized for being fatuous, and complacent in the face of the existential anxieties life presents. And now let me admit at once that this is true – or is true inasmuch as liberalism holds no answer to, or cure for, the persistent riddles of existence, or offers any ways to ease the atavistic emotions it provokes. Every day on television we see that anger, rage, a cheated sense of identity, fear of what the future might bring – this powerful dread seems, again and again, too intense for any smaller sanities to cure.

The liberal imagination reasons and reforms. It models human will and individual imagination. But it is unequal to the cosmic questions. Liberals have no answer to ease the intractability of our mortality, the alienation of ourselves from our surroundings, the basic riddle of why we are here to suffer and be sad. It only tries to make the suffering suffer a little less, and the sad a little happier. For those who dream of ecstasy and transcendence, the credo will never be enough. A better politician than I can hope to be would say that the task of twenty-first-century liberalism is to find a way to make the search for common identity compatible with the assertion of the free individual.

But in truth, it won't work. The only rational response liberalism gives to the cosmic questions remains *domestic*, making men and women happier now, seeming like a large enough ambition for a life on earth – big enough to carry us through from Friday evening to Sunday morning, and a few days beyond. It may not be enough. It may never be enough. It's what we have.

Patriotism and Nationalism

30 December 2016

The shape of our time reveals itself obliquely, and even when we seem to see it, we are not sure if we are seeing the whole shape or some misleading part of it – a curve that will bend into a biting knife-edged ridge, a gentle slope that turns into an abyss.

But we can see some of the shape of our time, and see that some part of it is, at a minimum, frightening: over the past twenty-five years, our confidence that totalitarianism had ended and that the world had – however imperfectly, however spasmodically, with all the deep and dark exceptions – turned towards the values of liberal democracy, has gone. We now seem to sit on the brink – or is it in the midst? – of a new era of autocracy, where the rising wave, engineered by his dark intentions, or just because he was first, is what we can call

'Putinism': a form of simple gangsterism in government, coupled with militarism abroad.

It is different from totalitarianism inasmuch as it seems to give you the choice to escape by acceding. It is the position of the Sicilian peasant, or of the small shopkeeper in lower Manhattan under the five New York mafia families: don't complain, don't raise your voice, and you can survive. Putin isn't Stalin: cross him or cross his goons and you won't be sent to Siberia. Cross him, loudly, and you will be assaulted or killed – or, sometimes, his intelligence services will conspire to disgrace you.

The degree to which this pattern is now passing from Russia to France to America and beyond is obvious. 'But how can it have happened?' we ask. Inequality, economic panic – all these things play a part. But at heart the rise of autocracy re-teaches, surely, the great lesson of the twentieth century, which is not that totalitarian states are strong, but that the politics of nationalism are irresistible. Once evoke our tribe against some other, once make the crucial confrontation not one between opposing theories but opposing bloods, and identity trumps all else.

It seems a reasonable time, then, to revisit the old subject anew, and that is the difference, often mentioned but not often grasped, between patriotism and nationalism. George Orwell, and many others, have talked of it, though the most incisive account is owed I think to the right-wing Hungarian-American historian John Lukacs. Patriotism, we might say, is the love of a place, a consuming love of an area of the world and its traditions and eccentricities, its values and peculiar heritage. It is defiantly irrational: it insists that the inefficiencies of a British hedgerow, or the over-proliferation of French cheeses, or the cheesy abundance of doo-wop motels and drive-in restaurants on the American highway, with their frozen custards and quick-fried burgers, are worth preserving not because they are objectively superior but because they are entirely *ours* (or yours) – part of a fabric of particulars grown over years, or centuries, and in no need of defence before the world's tribunal of rational good.

Patriotism is an insistence that collapse in front of a foreign power, no matter how potent or prosperous the power may be, is wrong because it involves submission of one set of particularities to some other set, even if the other, invading set poses its particularities as universal values. Patriotism can be thought of large and small. Patriotism is De Gaulle defying the Nazis on the strength of his voice alone, declaring a defeated France undefeated because he had not surrendered. It is also Alan Bennett, who I was reading on the plane on a recent trip to London, preferring Leeds and Camden Town as they were, with all of their oddness, to Camden Town and Leeds as they might yet be, with the wrinkles and creases ironed right out.

Nationalism is not love for a place; it is a story about having lost one's place, about having been uprooted. Nationalism is the vengeful certainty that our tribe, or *Volk*, is the victim of some other alien group, who wish to dislodge us from our rightful home and make it theirs instead. It begins with, and thrives on, a consuming sense of victimization. Its slogan is never 'How nice this place is!' Rather, 'How horrible these others are!' Patriotism needs no enemy, but nationalism demands one.

Now, as I said not long ago, the great flaw and failure of liberalism, even in its most cautiously benevolent guises, is to fail to grasp the necessity of shared identity for human beings – particularly for human beings caught in a changing and often alienating world. Liberal democracy holds no answer or cure for the persistent riddles of existence, or ways to ease the atavistic emotions it provokes. Liberals have no answer to ease the intractability of the basic riddle of why we are here to suffer and be sad. It is most often patriotism that fills that gap, that answers – or seems to – that riddle: 'Why are we here?' Why, to extend our connection with a place our parents knew, and our children will inherit! It may not be the most logical of answers, or the most 'inclusive' – but it is at least an answer, one that most people in one form or another resonate to.

I will confess that even as something of what the nationalists call a 'rootless cosmopolite', I feel this emotion, frequently. I am patriotic for Montreal, for Paris, for Manhattan, for London, and in truth only for select parts and even select seasons of all of those. I would fight to keep Montreal winters as they are, and Paris neighbourhoods as they are, long before I would fight for Canada or France.

Liberalism, in its rejection of nationalism, too often has

condescended to patriotism, even of this limited and smaller kind. And liberalism, by ignoring or underrating such emotions, has found itself unable to cope, too often, with their emphatic reassertion as nationalism. And I wonder if that is not, in truth, the great and painful lesson of the past quarter-century. For Orwell and Lukacs, the dividing line between nationalism and patriotism was, in every sense, a battle line. It placed Hitler and the Stalin of World War Two on one side; Churchill and Attlee and De Gaulle on the other. But I wonder if we cannot now see that patriotism and nationalism have a more fluid, a more organic, a more connected relationship than we quite want to imagine. Someone said once that every time one of the offices of the church is rejected, a heresy springs up in its place: if you fail to have a place for confession, as in the Protestant churches, you produce psychoanalysis, which is, on this view, merely a different form of the confessional booth. We must expiate our secret sins with *someone*.

Nationalism, it now seems, is not patriotism's evil twin; it is the heretical form of patriotism, the thing that rises when normal feelings of belonging are slighted or made too little of. When patriotism finds no outlet, cosmopolitanism does not take its place: nationalism rises instead – with all its ills and demons trailing behind.

How we reconcile ourselves to the necessity of patriotism without succumbing to the traps of nationalism – how we continue to embrace the planetary future that is coming in any case, while still ceding to the local and particular its right to be respected – is one of the big questions that we will have to face. We won't solve it. Big questions we're facing never exactly get 'solved'. But they do get *lived* and, sometimes, they create new manners of existence that, when we're lucky, allow our ideal of the good life to go on.

At moments of peril I turn always to the man I think of as the greatest Englishman, John Stuart Mill, who, despite his reputation as an arch-rationalist, spent much of his thinking life trying to reconcile the rational with the irrational, and particularly the cosmopolitanism he practised with the patriotism he admired. He took many writhing turns, trying to define a cosmopolitanism that would still be patriotic, a patriotism that would still be cosmopolitan. From our later and more pained perspective, we might decide that patriotic cosmopolitanism is a contradiction in terms, like trying to love forty spouses at once. But cosmopolitan patriotism . . . Ah, there might be a sort of wisdom in that idea, like loving one spouse over time, and change, and growth, 'cosmopolitan patriotism' meaning a love of place that accepts the evolution of places. We can believe in universal principles, and still like the games we play at home, eat exotically and still cultivate our backyard gardens.

On that recent visit to London, I got to hear for the first time my favourite work of music, Handel's *Messiah* (embarrassing in its obviousness, but there it is: we go to hear it every year at Carnegie Hall), sung in its national home. I couldn't help but think, as I saw lips move and familiarity register all around me in the church, that here was a work written by a German, adapting melodies written for Italian voices to texts translated from Hebrew and Greek – and first tried out in Dublin – and then turned into a patriotic rite of a nation.

Cosmopolitan patriotism may be harder to enunciate as a political principle than it is to practise as a way of life. We share it – we sing it – each Christmas.

What to Call Him?
16 July 2017

You can't call him crazy, because it isn't fair to crazy people. Crazy people suffer and agonize with their illness, are actually often insightful about their own condition, and generally struggle against their limitations and fixations, rather than succumbing to them. If you call him crazy you are diminishing the sufferings and pains of truly mentally ill people, who should not be stigmatized with the comparison. Crazy people, after all, are rarely cruel, at least not on purpose; crazy people – if we include such bipolar sufferers as Robert Lowell and Vincent van Gogh or even a frequent depressive like Winston Churchill – rise from their black dog moments to higher things. They are rarely mired for good in their own madness.

And then you can't compare him to a four-year-old child, because four-year-old children are not in fact tyrannical or egotistical. On the contrary, the experts in child development tell us – my sister Alison prominently among them in the *New York Times* – that four-year-old children are curious about the world, always pursuing new hypotheses to explain events, and eager, almost too eager, to push the boundaries of the familiar to find new things. Four-year-old children want to learn more about the world; they are the last creatures on earth who you can accuse of being locked in an unbreakable shell of narcissism.

You can't call him a conservative – not without offending every true conservative. Conservatism as a creed – the creed of Edmund Burke and Michael Oakeshott and Benjamin Disraeli – rests on a reverence, at times perhaps an undue reverence, for tradition and the wisdom that tradition keeps within it. Conservatives don't insult women, or assault them – and a lie for a conservative is the worst offence, since political conduct is merely a reflection outward of personal conduct: statecraft is soul-craft. The core reverence of conservatism for the small platoons of community means that the true conservative is known by the civility that surrounds him. An isolated man of brutal manners can't be that.

You can't really identify him as a capitalist – certainly not in a sense that Adam Smith, or even Margaret Thatcher, would recognize. Adam Smith believed that free markets depend above all on mutual clarity and mutual confidence radiating through a marketplace where value was arrived at by self-organizing means – on clarity of means, and men, and methods.

Capitalism, on this view, depends on a society of trust, where contracts are met and promises kept and debtors paid. Capitalism of that kind hates cronyism worse than any other kind of thing there is. Money gathered by family connection and kept in bad faith is the feudal opposite of the free market. You make a lot of money by swindling your creditors, but you can't point to the free market as your principal inspiration.

So, then, could you call him a capo or a chieftain – of the kind that typically runs a mafia family or a Third World dictatorship? Perhaps – but this seems unfair to mafia capos and third-world dictators. True, they often use their family as the means of self-enrichment, appoint unqualified dependants to positions of power, and make clan and blood loyalty substitute for all other values – so that the lines, essential to a functioning democracy, between merit and expertise is lost. But most capos don't like chaos: they prefer clear lines of authority and efficient means of enforcement. A permanent cloud of chaos in which the capo is lost watching television and tweeting while his lieutenants stab each other in the back, and his children make up one implausible story after another, would have a short life in any Third World, or for that matter imaginary, country – let alone any Sicilian neighbourhood in New York. Calling him a 'capo' is an insult to capos.

You're certainly not allowed to call him a collaborator with a brutal autocrat who hates civil liberties and kills journalists. After all, the evidence of collaboration is still, supposedly, circumstantial. That everyone around you was doing it doesn't mean that you knew that it was being done. He certainly is an admirer of a brutal autocrat, but you cannot fairly turn obsequious adoration into actual collaboration. So you don't dare call him that.

A 'crazy king'? That's what my friend and debating opponent Niall Ferguson thinks – that you can compare him to, say, King George III at the height of his madness, not least because the mad autocrat could never quite become a real tyrant. The civil society around him – not to mention the court that sought to insulate him – was sufficiently strong that even a mad king could not ruin a thriving country. Life went on. The courtiers knew the King was mad, but the country and its markets and its pamphleteers persisted anyway. It isn't exactly a comforting description but at least it's better than thinking of him as a mad tyrant capable of bringing everything down around him. The trick, though, is that mad kings, back when royalty was still a thing, did not, at a minimum, possess the codes to nuclear weapons. And being kings, their authority was assumed to be in part irrational. Being mad was just another variant of the theme. In a democracy, we demand more.

So what can you call him, then? We are, in truth, at a loss to find a category to fit Donald Trump – President though he is, vertiginous though those words still make one feel. We can't even find a metaphor for him. When a phenomenon of the Trump kind happens, we are constrained to try and assimilate it to something familiar, and the familiar categories always let us down. We want him to be like something else – something familiar, something traditional – because the something elses are things we have learned in the past to handle: 'Oh, come now, you can't really be serious in calling him a fascist or a threat to civilization – why, we've seen just his kind before. King George, for instance, when he went mad. Or, um, Richard Nixon at his worst. There must be something, or someone . . .'

But the truth is that new evils escape our old names. It is the nature of history to throw up new things that are not like any of the old bad things. What's more, it is possible to be all of these things – *crazy* at moments and *childish* most of the time, and *conservative* in the most narrowly nostalgic sense of the term, and a *capitalist* in the most cut-throat fashion, and a *collaborator* with authoritarian regimes, whether or not the collaboration crosses the line to treason – all of it – and still be something new and frightening in the world.

Donald Trump, then, is oddly insulated both by the liberal habit of oversensitivity and by the conservative habit of complacency. Liberals need to remember that words only make sense in contexts as specific acts. We can use words like 'crazy' without implying that all mentally ill people are like Trump, or 'like a child' without libelling children. At the same time, conservatives who have suddenly been inflicted by a desire to keep their favourite terms from being besmirched – 'Don't call *him* a conservative or a good capitalist' – should recall that if there is a signal conservative virtue, it is a love of plain speech about obvious matters.

You *can* call him a 'catastrophe' – a catastrophe for liberal values and democratic principles, of a kind that we will be digging out from for years, whatever happens next. A 'catastrophe', in its original meaning, is the moment in a drama when many ties left lingering in the story suddenly come together with disastrous results – in our case an inability to manage or settle the crises of identity felt by a fierce minority as open societies expand, and the larger forgotten truth that irrational resentment and tribal hatred is a virus far more virulent than we may think when it is in remission.

Call him a catastrophe. And no one can argue, or complain.

Napoleons and Normalcy

30 July 2017

I have been thinking a lot lately about Louis Napoleon, Emperor
of the French. The proximate cause of my reflection was that
insane interview Donald Trump gave the other day to the *New
York Times*, about the state of the world and his insatiable vanity,
with the two neatly enfolded together. It was an interview,
you may recall, that combined both the things there are to
fear about Trump and the things there are that make our fears
sometimes seem overblown: he says loony and reckless and
anti-democratic things, but says them to the institutions of the
free press, like *The Times*, in ways that make it plain that he is
desperate for the approval of the very people he is busy pre-
tending to despise. *The Times* reporters egg him on; you could
almost see them winking slyly at each other as they flattered
him. 'Would that be a red line for you, Mr President?' 'Boy,

that French President sure admires you!' And he responds as mad narcissists do: madly and narcissistically.

One part of his response, you may recall, was that when reporting on his visit to France – in which President Macron played the part of the *Times* reporters, egging the simple king on while winking at his confederate – Trump managed to badly confuse his Napoleons. He mixed up Napoleon Bonaparte (the one who got beat at Waterloo, and thus supplied ABBA with the material for the world's worst song) with Louis Napoleon, his nephew, who ruled France, sort of, from 1852 to 1870, and wore the world's worst moustache. Someone had told him that Napoleon had made the street plan of Paris, complete with boulevards, which is true, but Trump misunderstood and thought it was the first, rather than the second one, who had done it. This is one of the few cases where Trump's idiocy was more or less normal, rather than dangerously normalized. I don't suppose one American in a hundred knows the difference between them – or more to the point, knows much of anything about the second Napoleon, who ruled France as Emperor from 1852 until the misbegotten war with the Prussians drove him into exile in 1870.

I have always had a weakness for him, though I know I shouldn't. He was an opportunist and an adventurer – it was his coup d'état in 1851, compared to that of his uncle, that led Karl Marx to his famous *mot* that history repeats itself, the first time as tragedy the second as farce. And there were many farcical elements to his rule, and some much worse than that. Every decent liberal republican in France hated and feared him – despised him as the authoritarian dictator he was. Victor Hugo, the spirit of French republicanism, and the greatest humanist of his age, chose exile rather than submit to a France under his rule. The leftists in France hated him with even more venom than the liberals did, as the enemy of all social solidarity, while the royalists in France – who thought of the Bonapartes as arrivistes and thoroughly second-rate absolutists – despised him too. And the thing was in many respects a mess that ended with a massacre – the Commune.

Yet though the Second Empire was a flub and a foolishness in many ways, it was also a time of widespread and positive social change, and certainly of aesthetic wonder – a time when prosperity was increasingly widespread and the instruments of modern pleasure were increasingly available. The most famous of these innovations was the street plan of Paris: all those broad, beautiful Right Bank boulevards and parks designed for Napoleon III (as he was known) by Baron Haussmann. The myth has it that they broadened the streets in order to make them harder to blockade in mass insurrections – but a myth is what this mostly is. Broad boulevards spread from Paris to Philadelphia and Bucharest and beyond, and though there may have been a security reason for them at first – as there was said to have been for the national superhighways in 1950s America – they soon transcended that purpose with the beauty of their borders.

(In any case, it didn't help: the Communards who ended the Empire barricaded the streets just fine.)

Perhaps the greatest of these inventions of shared popular pleasure is the department store. Bon Marché began in those years, and the idea of what Zola called the 'paradise of women': the great mixed and open-to-all domed pleasure gardens of material goods under stained-glass skylights. The stores, and the stained-glass skylights, are still there. One need not think that Louis Napoleon was essentially benevolent or good to realize that his ability to alter and direct the flow of national life was extremely limited, and that the civil society of France – the combination of the will and motives of its entrepreneurs, its shoppers, its artists and above all its poets, was far more potent than the government could imagine.

In Second-Empire France, I would have been loudly on the side of the resisters, writing indignant editorials and doubtless getting my paper shut down as I did. But I would also have been one of those resisters who would have missed much in their own society that was already resistant to power. It all ended in tears, and worse than tears, with the Franco-Prussian war of 1870 and what happened after – but the institutions that civil society built within the Empire remained to construct the same world that we still look at, in Impressionist paintings, for images of a common city life nearly paradisiacal. It wasn't; the injustices were real. But the good stuff wasn't an illusion either.

Having lived long enough to see several political epochs,

I sense that something of the same is always true. The space between political history and actual experience, which all journalism conspires to make identical, is always more complicated to articulate than journalism permits us to say. Keeping us from articulating it is what journalism exists to do. Louis Napoleon was the enemy of all I admire – but it takes only a little historical perspective to see that the real life of France went on around him, through him, despite him, and without him. To have obsessed single-mindedly about the evils of the Second Empire, real though they were, was to have missed as much as one saw.

I have lived long enough now to see several absolutely horrific epochs come and go – looking much less absolutely horrific once they're gone. The truth is that the Nixon years of the 1970s are famous for their paranoia, and we engage in a lot of self-congratulation about having survived them. But as one who lived through them as a teenager (but an attentive one, and no one is more attentive than an attentive teenager), the secret truth is that they were exhilarating, because all of the cultural power and currents of the country were running in the opposite direction, right away from Nixon and his silent majority. The Clinton years passed in storm, but it was the invention of Google, the birth of the internet age, all of that, that was far more significant for history and human life, both than the impeachment scandals and the madness that surrounded them.

To put the ball in your court: I lived in London for a while during the Labour period of the Seventies (Winter of Discontent and all that), when my Conservative friends spoke as though the whole country had gone dark (well, it did, spasmodically), and then came back to life during the Thatcher reaction; when, to listen to my Labour friends talk about it, one might have thought that the White Witch of Narnia had taken over the country, frozen the ground and eaten all the talking animals. In truth, neither Labour's nor Thatcher's horrors were ever so horrific, and the life of the country went flowing around politics as much as through them. Not that these governmental things were not grave, and severe, and sure to affect the life of every citizen. But those who gave their minds and heart to national politics too exclusively were not the ones who were paying the closest attention to reality. One might even say that they were the ones escaping the deeper complexities of actual experience for the false sugar highs and easy outrages of merely headlined history.

Yet of course the counter-instances are just as real: those moments when history suddenly collapses like a falling house in an earthquake on the heads of everyone in it. And, at such moments, those who kept insisting on ignoring the headlines and paying attention to the department stores look like the fools they were. The Thirties in Germany were full of people saying that things really weren't so bad, when they were – that all the noise was just a show for the base. We are coming up to the hundredth anniversary of the Russian Revolution (or, as Nabokov insisted, the 'Bolshevik *coup d'état*'), and there the destruction of normal life was soon complete.

The truth to take away is this: as long as the core central civic capital of the country – its commonplace civilization – remains intact, very little can be done from on high to alter its essential course. It is the end of tyranny to destroy that life. Normal life is the tyrant's beachhead. Stalin was very good at eradicating the last traces of normal life; Hitler, a more fiendish fellow, allowed it to go on for those he favoured while turning life into hell on earth for the rest. The relevance of this question to our American time now scarcely needs italicizing: are we every day normalizing behaviour that will bring an end to normalcy itself? Or is the life of the country scarcely touched by the crazy, suggesting that we should not make the mistake of confusing political life – or historical life itself – with actual experience? Every day we check the vital signs of civilization to ask if they are still self-propelled. It is a sign, perhaps, of how much danger we are in that we must even ask the question, and count our Napoleons before they hatch.